Here's what people are saying about
The Call to Brilliance:

"As soon as I read the first thirty pages, I was not only surprised, I was slightly overwhelmed. I could not put it down."
— William Glasser, M.D., President, the William Glasser Institute, Author of *Choice Theory*

"...nothing less than a blueprint to bring life back to our increasingly moribund educational system and to our society which has lost its way."
— John Taylor Gatto, Author of *The Underground History of American Education* and *Dumbing Us Down*.

"A moving, passionate portrayal of what limits us as children and how we can help our own children move past those limits to find their innate passion and brilliance. An empowering solution!"
— Jack Canfield, Co-author, *Chicken Soup for the Parent's Soul*® and Co-author, *Chicken Soup for the Teacher's Soul*®

"As we legislate for stricter learning standards, we find that it does not solve our problems; it deepens them. Most people cannot envision education any other way. Resa came up with a better way. She has not only envisioned it, she has built it, lived it, and now she shares it with us all."
— Joseph Chilton Pearce, Author of *Magical Child*

"...Brilliance, genius and creativity are our children's birthright. Resa shows how these natural capacities can be welcomed and wooed from the inside out."
— Tobin Hart, Ph.D., Professor of Psychology, University of West Georgia, and President, ChildSpirit Institute

"If I was the head of UNESCO, I would insist that *The Call to Brilliance* be translated into all the major world languages and issued to every new mother in maternity wards across the globe. For if these mothers heeded the guidance and wisdom in this amazing story – we could change the course of civilization in a single generation."
　　　　　– Laurel Airica, Creator of WordMagic: An Enchanted
　　　　　　　　　　　　　　　　　　Literary Entertainment

"As we learn to both understand individual difference and accept that all difference is privileged, Resa reminds us that brilliance, and genius, are commonplace…A child's passion and profound interest must author curriculum, not political standards. *The Call to Brilliance* is a must read for parents, teachers, legislators, and others struggling to understand how to prepare children for an uncertain future."
　　　　　– Paul Epstein, Ph.D., Co-author of *The Montessori Way*

"You will laugh, cry, ponder and wonder along with this amazing mother and educator. Resa Steindel Brown will take you on a journey that will give you unflagging courage to believe in and advocate for the brilliance that is unique to your child, and will remind you of your own."
　　　　　– Victoria Kindle Hodson, Co-author of *Respectful Parents,*
　　　　　　Respectful Kids and *Discover Your Child's Learning Style*

"I was so excited about this book that I immediately purchased two books for the mothers of my grandchildren. Then, as Head of School, I decided to give all of my teachers a copy to read over the holidays. Resa Steindel Brown has captured the 'missing piece' in almost all educational methodologies. Without passion, life is a humdrum existence. I deeply believe our destiny as a global village depends on each individual's passion being kindled and allowed to flourish."
　　　　　– Karen Holt, Montessori School of Anderson, Administrator

The Call to Brilliance

The Call to Brilliance

A true story to inspire parents and educators...

Resa Steindel Brown

Foreword by WILLIAM GLASSER, M.D.
Introduction by JOSEPH CHILTON PEARCE

fredric press
California

This is a true-life story. All events have been recounted to the author's best ability. The names of some individuals in this book have been changed.

Visit the author's website at www.thecalltobrilliance.com
Visit the publisher's website at www.fredricpress.com

Published by:
fredric press
1336 Moorpark Road, #332
Thousand Oaks, CA 91360

Edited by:
Nancy A. Tohl

Cover Design by:
Matthew Brown

Library of Congress Control Number: 2006921619
International Standard Book Number (ISBN): 0-9778369-0-8

Printed in Canada

ATTENTION SCHOOLS AND CORPORATIONS:
Books published by fredric press are available at quantity discounts with bulk purchase for educational, business, or sales promotional use. For more information please write to: special sales department, fredric press, 1336 Moorpark Road, #332, Thousand Oaks, CA 91360.

In loving memory of
Colonel Leon J. de Penne Rouge,
my second father,
whose vision steered the course of all our lives.

⋙ Table of Contents ⋘

PART III   School at Home

PART IV   Catch the Wind and Soar!

ꕥ Acknowledgments ꕧ

~To my husband, Dennis, without whose support, encouragement and love there would be no book, and without whom there would be no story. Thank you for the million hours of editing and helping me find my voice.

~To my mother, Beatrice Steindel, who never told me I couldn't do something, never criticized me, always trusted and supported me, and who above all, taught me unconditional love.

~To my father, Sam Steindel, whose short stay on Earth was powerful enough to remind us all who we are and to call us to our highest being—the place from which all things are possible. I love you, Daddy.

~To my children, Stephen, Erin and Matthew, my greatest teachers in all things important.

~To Dr. William Glasser, for believing in the project and taking the time, concern and energy to set this book a-sail.

~To Joseph Chilton Pearce, for lending a stranger your ear and your compassion, for focusing your time and energy on this book.

~To my sister, Cheryl, whose 5:30 a.m. support calls make all the difference, whose unconditional love touches my heart and keeps us together as family, who never grows sick of reading rewrites.

~To my editor, partner and eternal sidekick, Nancy Tohl, who nurtures me while I nurture others, who teaches me unconditional patience, trust and faith on an hourly, day-to-day basis, who reminds me to laugh!

~To my spiritual sister, Heather Beck, without whom I would not be able to find myself, whose continued support keeps my spirit soaring and my feet on the ground. Thank you for helping me translate my earthly experience.

~To my spiritual sister, Judy Crescenzo, for guiding me through my wake-up call, helping me remember who I am and reconnecting me to my spiritual family. Thank you eternally for being my gatekeeper.

~To Christabel Thib, aka 'mom.' Thank heaven you walk this earth. What can I say? I think you did it for me.

~To Darielle Richards, my sister forever through time, for helping me sort things out in the very beginning and for reintroducing me to the wonders of Earth and the capacities that truly lie within and without.

~To Dave and Debbie Chrisman, for holding the vision close to your hearts and demonstrating how true friendship goes beyond any ideology…kindred souls.

~To Claire Heartsong, for your early support and intervention.

~To Kris George, poet and friend, for reading and re-reading the manuscripts and convincing me publication was possible.

~To Roni Keller, for supporting the manuscript, putting the vision into form and connecting an entire community to the writer within. We need more teachers like you.

~To Carole Wilson, for joining us in the trenches and working the vision.

~To Laurel Airica, whose unfailing love and devotion just keeps finding connections.

~To Chuck Bubar, the world's greatest bridge. Thank you for your faith, time and energy.

~To Dr. Salar Farahmand and family, for your love and support for the project.

~To Dr. Valentine Ratushney for being my best teacher and my dear friend.

~To George and Debra Tash, for the G.T. Water School and many years of bliss raising our children together. Our children are blessed and so are we.

~To Jenny and Adam, who started it all.

~To Brian Kearsey, for being both the core and the ballast of the G.T. Water School. Without your gentle nature and love, no one would have blossomed.

~To Uncle Michael and Davut, for giving Matthew the opportunity of a lifetime; you have changed his life forever!

~To Marika Besobrasova, Patrick Frantz, Dennon and Sayhber Rawles and Lisa Lock for training Matthew not only to dance on stage, but dance in life; you will all be in his heart forever. Thank you Lisa for starting it all.

~To Jim and Jan Frazier, for your love in educating not only our horses, but also our children.

~To Master Tom Bloom, Sensei Cecil Peoples, and Master Michael Richey, thank you for helping our children find internal discipline and drive.

~To Guy Campbell, for enriching the lives of my children and everyone else in that computer lab.

~To Frank Sardisco, for helping Erin and Matthew find the artist within.

~To Moorpark College and Dr. Judith Gerhart, for facilitating the growth of so many young children.

~To Steve Sanchez, for introducing Stephen to a bigger world.

~To Dr. Bill Maggione-Smith, for being Stephen's educational advisor, mentor and friend.

~To Alan Brown and Roger Wilson, for bringing Stephen into the business world.

~To Lou Birdt, Steve Henson, Gordy Brown and Chris Brown, for being great role models and trusting in Matthew's capabilities.

~To Joe Nardo, for seeing, supporting and empowering me, for picking me up when I fall, and for having the courage and stamina to put the vision into practice against all odds.

~To Kristy Adams, whose unfailing love and hard work keeps us up and running. We would not have made it without you.

~To Linda Davis, who talked me into walking where light was needed. Thank you.

~To Anita Long, for being the first to read the manuscript and for trusting me as an educator and a friend.

~To Tracy Kelley, Tom and the boys, for seeing the greater picture and sticking with me all these years. I have learned so much from working with you.

~To Fredric Steindel, whose hard work and patience published this book. I hope you're as good at marketing!

~To all the parents who have touched my heart and put their faith in the vision and to all the children who are our greatest teachers, thank you for allowing me to share what I have learned and put it into practice.

To all of you, my most profound and eternal gratitude and love.

Resa

If you are a parent, you may already be aware there is a lot more to the job of teaching than what your child or children are experiencing in school. You may be interested to know that I have been working to improve schools for fifty years. I have had some success but I am still learning.

I started college during WWII, studied chemical engineering and worked for a year as an engineer until I realized that I didn't like what I was doing. I wanted to work with people. I began by studying psychology and then was persuaded by one of my psychology professors to go to medical school and become a psychiatrist.

The medical school I went to, Western Reserve University in Cleveland, Ohio, had already embarked on a different kind of teaching program. It was all about learning. There was no pressure, few tests and a great deal of personal attention from the faculty. We were encouraged both to ask questions and feel free to question what we were taught.

I was very impressed by that program. When I became a psychiatrist and started to work in a juvenile prison with girls ages fifteen to twenty, I was amazed at how similar that program was to what I had experienced in medical school, and I had a chance to add some of what I had learned to it. The girls loved it because there was no punishment, no failure and a girl could even stay in the cottage if she didn't want to go to school.

Contrary to what I'd been taught about delinquency before I went there, the girls told me over and over that it was not their home life that led them into trouble, it was what happened in school. With a lot of attention and no chance to fail, they attended our classes and did very well.

Based on that start, I have written five books on education and have finally developed the Glasser Quality School that has attracted almost thirty very effective public and public charter schools. But then as often happens to me, Resa Steindel Brown, whom I did not know, asked me to read her book. I was skeptical. Reading books from strangers has not always been a happy experience for me.

As soon as I read the first thirty pages, I was not only surprised, I was slightly overwhelmed. I could not put it down. I started in the morning and finished it before a late dinner. Here was a book that went considerably beyond what I'd ever learned especially in the area of home schooling. To make sure, I asked my wife Carleen, who works with me, to read it, and she had the same amazing experience. It is a very personal odyssey by a woman who describes her life as a student, wife, mother, teacher and is still very active in all these roles.

In this odyssey you will meet Resa, her husband Dennis, her daughter Erin and her sons, Stephen and Matthew. This book is a beautiful memoir of a great family. Either as an expert or as a parent struggling with a child in school, you cannot read it without learning a great deal. They say it takes a village to raise a child, but here is a whole family working separately and together who raised three remarkable children. Every one of them contributed to this book.

After we finished it, we called Resa and agreed to not only write an endorsement but the foreword as well. This is a true memoir about the struggles and successes of a very happy family. We are proud to have become involved with them.

I have only one caution to the reader. If you are looking for an author who claims to have overcome unbelievable misery to get where he or she is, this is not the book for you. But I will also make a prediction: you will hear more about this happy family. Their journey has just begun.

William Glasser, M.D.,
President, the William Glasser Institute,
Author of *Choice Theory*

✍ **Introduction** ✍

At fourteen as a result of profound personal experiences, I began to see the vast capacity available to every human being. Since then, my consuming passion has been to understand who I am as a human being and why most of humanity is unware of the limitless potential that is our birthright. My life-long search has been to find the answers to these questions:

1. What does it mean to be fully human?

2. Why are most members of the human race so completely unaware of their own potential and that of their children for brilliant intelligence, extraordinary human effectiveness and deep inner peace?

3. What can humanity do to incorporate this awareness into the way we raise and teach our children; how can we can support them in unfolding the infinite intelligence inherent within the human soul and attaining the quality of life that is our ultimate destiny?

The widespread lack of models for this innate greatness is one of our most pervasive problems. It creates a humanity that is less than what it should be. It gives birth to an educational model for our children that is pedestrian in concept, relegated to processing our children rather than finding their true brilliance. It creates adolescents who feel lost and even abandoned by life. Their natural instincts lead them to the awareness that something great is intended to unfold within them, but it hasn't happened.

The almost universal failure of our human development process has brought us to a monstrous misunderstanding of who we are and who we are destined to become. We have largely lost our capacities to nurture our children in ways that support the unfolding of their unlimited intelligence and capacity for inner peace. Because of our own failure to develop, we as adults cannot provide models for this mode of living, and it can never be a didactic or intellectual process.

For this reason, it is essential that we reform our early childhood development approach and our lifelong educational processes in line with nature's intended plan for all of us.

Our culture has a great impact on our perceptions of reality. The distortions that exist in our culturally-conditioned thinking limit our ability to deal with reality as it is. The structure of our knowledge of the world is built into the neural connections of our brain during infancy and childhood. That structure becomes the underlying and unconscious process through which all future learning and interaction will be defined. Cultural assumptions can either facilitate or inhibit the development of our unlimited capacities and the extent to which we create our world in accordance with those images.

As I became clearer about the details of this biological plan, my concern for children intensified. Everywhere, I saw the symptoms of a serious breakdown in the human development process. The symptoms of this breakdown—epidemic increases in child and adolescent suicide, child abuse, infantile autism, and declining educational performance—led me to the monumental tragedy that has befallen our children.

I began to see that in Western civilization we are living out an enormous misconception of what it means to be human, what an infant is, and what a child is. As my writing and my worldwide lecturing continued, I collected vast quantities of information about how we develop. I began to deepen my understanding of the intense importance of the maternal/ infant bond, of play, of the imperative that, as children, we become our parents, our teachers, our cultural idols and other human models.

I saw clearly that spirit is an integral dimension of human intelligence and not an afterthought. Spirit must be foremost in our awareness in order to see development in its full scope and possibility. I expanded my understanding of the stages of development and of the types of learning that are, and are not, appropriate for those stages.

My concern for our schools increased as I understood that most of learning is state-specific. By that I mean that the state of emotion and consciousness while we are learning is more important to the application of knowledge than is the academic component of what is taught. I recognized that it is the intelligence of the heart rather than the intelligence of the intellect that forms the foundation for the survival of civilization. I learned that our optimal development from infancy to adulthood depends on having a safe and nurturing environment for learning, a clear sense of our source of power at each age, and an intuitive sense of the possibilities which are to become manifest at that stage of our lives.

Successful parents and teachers see that an environment of love and safety is fundamental to effective learning and growth. They know that children are multidimensional, possessing physical, emotional, mental, and spiritual aspects that must develop in an integrated way and as an evolving whole. They understand that life is a dynamic flow and that much of what happens in our relationships with children is unexpected and surprising.

These parents and teachers deeply understand that each of us—adult and child—has a unique purpose and destiny. Thus, they learn to take their cues from the child regarding the stages of the child's development and the kind of experiences that will nurture the child's unique gifts and talents. They understand that nurturing the child's uniqueness requires a depth of emotional and spiritual bonding with the child in which child and parent/teacher become available to each other at increasingly deep levels. They encourage the child's imagination and intuition. They recognize and acknowledge the child's deep capacities for wisdom that can emerge in a safe and bonded relationship. Such parents and teachers seek to embody the sense of wonder, excitement, and trust that weaves parent/ teacher and child into the same state of consciousness.

As I have seen what is needed and what is possible, I have been in despair about the condition of most of our traditional schools. It is for this reason that I felt so very fortunate to receive Resa Steindel Brown's book <u>The Call to Brilliance</u>. This important new book documents the immeasurable benefits available to children, and to society, when we trust life itself and open our children to the extraordinary possibilities inherent in life: when we guide and support their process of learning and full development consistent with nature's design.

By following the passion of the child rather than forcing the child to adapt to the consensus reality of the culture, Resa's approach allows the child to begin to learn from life as it is rather than life as the culture believes it to be. In this process, the higher mind or universal spirit can guide the unfolding of intelligence both within the child and the teacher/ parent—and in such a way that both child and mentor are engaged in an ongoing dance of continuous transformation and transcendence.

I became totally engrossed in this engaging, inspiring, enlightening and unusual work that is the biography not only of a remarkable person but also of a remarkable educational approach. We could say, in fact, that each, the author and her school, gave birth to each other. Here is that author's fascinating account of the unfolding and development of a new paradigm of learning that meets the actual biological, psychological, intellectual and social needs of young people.

In this book, Resa's biographical account of her own childhood experience graphically displays what I had called the 'tragedy of schooling' back in the 1950's. Her keen adult perspective on how things stand today is, again, from the inside out as a teacher and not just another abstract analysis of a critical outsider.

The Call to Brilliance, as she explains, illustrates "a paradigm shift from processing children through a curriculum of predetermined classes and requirements, to an educational system designed to discover the intrinsic talents, passions and brilliance of every child."

Her account of rising to meet the occasion by actively taking the initiative, daring to innovate and explore, taking her cues from the children, and responding to their individual needs instead of taking the easy way of mechanical formulae, is an admirable and remarkable story. In this book, Resa offers us a tangible, living model exemplar of what can be done against all odds in any situation, given sufficient time, energy and attention. She describes the experiences of children who had the opportunity to follow their interests and discover the passion that led to their brilliance. She shows us how the same could be done anywhere and in any situation.

Throughout Resa's writing, appropriate comments and observations from great thinkers old and new illustrate her insights—all of which add up to a unique, informative, optimistic and hope-filled account we can only praise.

As we legislate for stricter learning standards, we find that it does not solve our problems; it deepens them. Most people cannot envision education any other way. Resa came up with a better way. She has not only envisioned it, she has built it, lived it, and now she shares it with us all. This is a book that must be read by every parent, teacher and adult who senses there is a better life possible for their children and all children.

Thank you, Resa.

Joseph Chilton Pearce,
Author of *Crack in the Cosmic Egg* and *Magical Child*

❧ PART I ❧

In the Beginning

O.K. Who Are You Really?

She was determined not to cry. All around her, children were sobbing as though their hearts would break. Each clutched at the hem or pant leg of the parent who brought them. Each parent struggled to free a child's frantic grip and propel that child to the first day of separation. But this little girl was too proud to hold on. She had visions of the beautiful sculptures she would make. She saw in her mind the paintings she would bring home. She saw before her a line of exciting lessons and learnings, of songs and poems and numbers and letters and yes, indeed, worlds she would master. When the tears welled in her eyes, she bravely, proudly, blinked them away. She was ready for kindergarten.

Years later, through the maze of dashed hopes and forgotten dreams, she would recall the brave little girl she had been and wonder what had happened to her. Through the miasma of the struggle for survival and a child of her own whose father she no longer knew, she wondered how a life so bright with hope and pride could have deteriorated to this. "Who was she?" she asked. Where was the courage she had at five? When had the hope evaporated? How had this brave little girl so completely disappeared?

The little boy next to her wouldn't sit still. He was full of life and vigor. The explorer, the mountain climber, he opened his eyes in the morning and leaped out of bed with an excitement that rang through the neighborhood. Already the teacher was warning his father about the possibility of drugging him listless so he would conform to the docility of the other children. She called it 'focus.' It wouldn't be long before he would bend—they would just have to work a while to adjust the medication.

By the time he caught his breath, he would be well past eighteen and wonder how his childhood had passed in a dream. Who was he? What had happened?

The group of children in the corner needed special services. By the third week of school, the teacher could tell. Full of eccentricities not visible in the other students, they listened to the rhythm of their own truths.

One was drawn to music. He could follow any drumbeat, remember any lyric, knew the names and songs of all the current musicians. His entire body pulsated to the tune of the radio. There would be no avenue for him. His talent was not on the curriculum. Instead, he would be dragged through histories that had no relevance to his melodic nature. He would be filled with calculations that would have been understood had they been linked to the beat of the songs in his heart. He could have composed anything, but he never had a chance.

Thwarted from discovering the calling intended for him, his life grew gray. A wife and some kids, the nine-to-five job he fell into because he didn't know what else to do, would feed his obesity, his ulcer and his sense that there should have been more, but he just couldn't remember what. What now? Is that all there is? Who was he then?

Stories like these play out in our schools every year. They create a society of adults who spend the rest of their lives looking for the identity and integrity stolen from them when they were small. According to psychologist Dr. Carl Rogers, the search for a more authentic self underlies all our interactions and strivings. Everything we do, want, crave or try is driven by our need to find the answers to these questions, "Who am I? Why am I here? What is my relationship to others?" Rogers writes:

> As I watch person after person struggle in his therapy hours to find a way of life for himself, there seems to be a general pattern emerging, which is not quite captured by any…description…to be that self which one truly is. (<u>On Becoming A Person</u>, 166)

To which he adds:

> I am quite aware that this may sound so simple as to be absurd... (<u>On Becoming A Person</u>, 166)

But what we most often miss is the obvious. It's the old adage, "I have gone out to find myself. Should I come back before I return, please ask me to wait."

We don't really know who we are. We have lost the connection to a greater self that holds within it the true identity, integrity and purpose of soul—the passion and brilliance with which we were born. A youthful perception finds wonder. A magical moment, without condition, expectation, fear or judgment, engenders faith, revisits connection and fuels passion. The child can lead us back to our innate brilliance with authenticity, integrity and passion, if we allow it. But we forget.

We forget our own childhoods when all things were possible. We stop imagining lands of trust where fantasies merge and dreams materialize. We stop feeling love in its unconditional radiance. We forget thoughts without words and fields without end. We stop dancing on clouds. We keep the grass and the breeze waiting. We wonder about the magic of wishing on a star. We wonder if we've forgotten how to wonder. We just plain, old, forget.

Dr. James Hillman observes, "We dull our lives by the way we conceive them…"(5) We fill our days with the search for external reward, stimulation and validation. We sail through our cities well past the speed limit, plugged into books on tape, beepers and cell phones. Talk show hosts tell us how to fix our lives and make pizza. Songs of love and pain whiz through our psyches at mach speed. We are voyeuristic and bored, latching onto sordid newscasts and soap operas. We get excited over media sex and romance, while leading day-to-day lives devoid of passion. Our barometers are set to everybody else's standards. We talk ourselves into jobs that are safe but lacking in creative life force. We commit ourselves to relationships that are likewise. We tell each other we are fine, but inside, we are afraid to look. We are asleep and have forgotten who we are—then we ask our children to be like us. Christina Grof describes our dilemma:

> For thousands of years, mystics, philosophers, and poets have described human beings as having two essential components; we exist simultaneously as limited individuals who identify strongly with our bodies, our lives, and the ma-

terial world and as spiritual entities who are unlimited, universal, and eternal. We live with a
paradox: we are at once human and divine, limited and eternal, the part and the whole. We are
both the small self and the deeper Self. (27)

Edward Carpenter, a visionary social scientist and poet of
the late nineteenth century, writes that there is a vaster self
that can be reached past our ordinary consciousness. He describes his experience as being:

So great, so splendid...that it may be said that
all minor questions and doubts fall away in the
face of it; and certain it is that in thousands and
thousands of cases, the fact of its having come
even once to an individual has completely revo-
lutionized his subsequent life and outlook on
the world. (Ferguson, 31)

We are more than we think. Dr. Maria Montessori writes,
"It would be absurd to think that man...[would] lack a plan of
psychic development." She explains:

There is in the soul of a child an impenetrable
secret that is gradually revealed as it develops.... It contains within itself mysterious guiding principles, which will be the source of its
work, character, and adaptation to its surround-
ings. (Absorbent Mind, 19)

Then she warns, "...because of its delicate condition...the
psychic life of a child needs to be protected." (Absorbent
Mind, 19) But we do not protect this psychic life. We ignore
it. And when we ignore the power, direction and wisdom of

the heart, we overlook the breadth of majesty and sense of purpose that is ours. Dr. Hillman explains:

> ...there are things I must attend to beyond the daily round and that give the daily round its reason, feelings that the world somehow wants me to be here, that I am answerable to an innate image.... I believe we have been robbed of our true biography—that destiny written into the acorn. (4-5)

That 'destiny,' as Hillman describes it, is the calling of our heart, the innate direction of our soul that fulfills our being and gives our life deeper meaning, the journey that reconnects us to our passion and brilliance. It is our calling, our reason for being, the heart of our human experience. It is impelling. It yearns for the opportunity to live a much greater, more miraculous, benevolent and brilliant truth—to fulfill its soul's contract. It is our birthright.

Ours is a call to self-discovery, an exploration into life and all its possibilities—a sacred, creative, unpredictable, and sometimes even paradoxical adventure.

It is time to listen to the call, in ourselves, in each other, in our children—to connect with others who have heard their own voice echoing back through the cacophony of congested thoroughfares, drive-through windows and schedules too busy to keep. *Recover your passion! Discover your brilliance!*

It is time to collect all that we are, our stories, perceptions and dreams, the fragments of our lives, and acknowledge the magnificence and unlimited breadth of humanity that is ours, to build an environment of unconditional love that nurtures and protects, seeks and fulfills, that answers that call.

Our mental, emotional, physical, social, and spiritual awakening will shape the direction of the world's tomorrow. It is imperative and the time is now. We must remember, here in the present, all we are and why we are here:

We are here
to reconnect the higher functioning of our world,
not as we have constructed it in the past,
but as we deeply experience it
and know it to be.

We are here
to mend the barriers
that have kept us less than what we are.

We are here
to reintroduce ourselves to ourselves, to each other,
and to the capacities and forces
that truly lie within and without.

We are here
to lift the awareness of how we affect each other
and the physical world around us.

We are here
to gently assist in the already ongoing
and unprecedented conscious evolution of mankind.

Life demands we dedicate ourselves
to this higher purpose.

Now is the time.

This is the story of my family and the children who have given me wings and flight. This is our call to passion and brilliance. May it help ignite yours.

The Call to Brilliance:

- We are born with our divinely given gifts and willingness to give and receive love intact.

- As a seed contains the pattern for the whole tree, our being is encoded with the unlimited pattern of our brilliance.

- As a seed is directed by nature to grow into a tree, our motivation to explore and create is directed by the need to manifest these gifts.

- The desire to express this brilliance within the format of love is the fullest and highest expression of our being.

Who Will Be Left Standing?

"Ideas we don't know we have, have us," states archetypal psychologist James Hillman. M.C. Richards elaborates, *"Do we know what 'idea of human being' underlies the schools to which our children are sent? For you may be sure there is such an idea, however unconscious. We owe it to ourselves to ask Parsifal's question, 'What's going on here?' It is a step toward consciousness."*

I sit at Panera. An upscale café in Irvine, California. I watch as my daughter Erin and her friends prepare for their master's comprehensives. They are in the Ph.D. program in pure and applied mathematics at the University of California. Hundreds of students submitted their applications. Twenty-five were accepted. Thirteen are left. I applaud their passion, brilliance and tenacity, but I am saddened by a system that turns away young minds that want to learn.

They giggle. Like little girls playing with their *little ponies*. They share a secret. Then they grow silent. Something about 'the sufficient condition for equality of mixed partials.' 'The Bolzano-Weierstrass Theorem and Heini Borel.' Then a flurry of writing. They are physically here, but now they are gone, enveloped by their work. I find myself waiting for the next giggle. My gosh, they are beautiful!

Two more waitresses bring pumpkin 'muffies' (the top part of the muffin without the bottom) and another round of juice to the table.

I ask for a coffee refill. I know I shouldn't have it, but I ask anyway. I keep thinking about those little plastic ponies Erin used to dress up in play. They are still in a box gathering dust somewhere in the garage. I decided to keep them, unlike the Star Wars action figures we seem to have accidentally thrown away. One day, I know, those ponies will become collector's items.

I wonder about my daughter and her friends. How will the world measure their worth? They are so much more than anything we can auction on the Internet. Their hearts are in their study, but the system does not guarantee a reward no matter how hard they work—a system that will try to pit, sort and rank them against each other.

I look at my daughter. She is diligent and beautiful, long blonde hair tied up in a bun held by a pencil. No make-up. T-shirt and sweats. Who will see her for what she is worth?

I look at this group of girls. Students. Young women. Will they solve life's riddles through the mathematics they study? Will they bring positive new forms to life or will they unconsciously perpetuate old paradigms that no longer serve us? Who will they be? Where will their education lead them?

Education formats consciousness. It frames our perceptions of who we are and how we see the world. It teaches us how to interact. It shapes both individual and group reality through the paradigm it teaches. And it always has an agenda. Every educational system has an underlying agenda. Intentional or not, it will execute this agenda because it operates from and therefore teaches a perspective. Proceeding from a set of unspoken assumptions, it will perpetuate its hidden view of the world from generation to generation.

Educational systems aimed the upper class citizens of the Roman Empire toward the political arena, the uneducated ruling class of the Dark Ages toward the power structure of the Church, and the farm children of the 19th Century into the assembly line of the Industrial Revolution. Powerful enough to topple monarchies, create dictatorships and protect democracies, they create the model for our success, dispense hope and pass judgment.

Our current system is still geared toward supplying the workforce of the Industrial Revolution. Its intent is to separate an elite management from the masses—masses who are trained to serve them by following orders. Their function is to perform rote, mechanical and uncreative tasks. It is an antiquated system.

We need a system that fits the needs of today, the Information Age, an age that requires creative and innovative thinkers. We cannot afford to function as disconnected parts of an industrial assembly line. We are not machine parts. We are not merely cogs in a wheel. We are human beings and we need to function as whole, intact human beings creating and recreating our full potential. In fact, we need every internal resource we have to face our current challenges. We cannot afford to raise our children in a system that reduces them from whole creative beings with thoughts, feelings and perceptions to mechanical functions. These girls, too, are fulfilling some unseen function. Will they rise above?

An education aimed at providing a workforce for an industrial society that has long since changed its requirements is quietly alarming. It now creates more dysfunction than success. We are not the same society. The pace of life is faster.

The flow of information is greater by a magnitude we cannot begin to measure. The needs of industry are changing, and our needs as physical, emotional, intellectual and spiritual human beings are changing as well. In fact, both science and our own sense of spirituality have challenged the paradigms upon which we structure our daily living. Everything is changing. Even our children are changing.

All children are born with the seeds of their own brilliance. To be successful, we need to help them find, nurture and sustain the passion that leads to that brilliance. But that is not what our schools do and our children know this. On some level, they understand the paradoxes and contradictions we create by our adherence to an outdated educational structure. They sense the derailing of their calling, the smothering of their passions and the dousing of their brilliance. And they are disgruntled and disillusioned.

I think of my students. Thirty-five years of watching students. 'Students'—a euphemism for growing children. I can hear the voices of their parents, distressed, anxious and concerned. "Will he succeed? He has ADD." "She can't do the math. She never could." "He's bored and the teacher keeps putting him out in the hall. He is becoming disruptive. He's barely seven." I see the anger in the faces of the parents, the look of distress or malaise in their children's eyes. The parents of the kids who succeed are content, even proud, until the child loses interest. I can't say how many times I have heard, "We just don't understand it. Last year he was fine."

Most of our children are not content blindly following a path they have not chosen to a destination that is poorly defined, irrelevant and blatantly unfulfilling. They are sick of being tested, prodded and graded. Even those who are successful are increasingly buckling under a process that is oppositional to their needs. An educational system that attempts to manufacture self-concepts to fit the needs of an antiquated industry will engender the hostility and unrest of all its participants.

Our children are searching for their own mental, physical, emotional and spiritual integrity, but we sabotage their search. We fill their time with excessive homework from courses that are irrelevant. We dishonor the manner and time frames in which our little ones learn and grow. We process them through a system whose concept of human is deficient. We willingly submit our children to these constraints—and for what? All for the agenda of a system that is obsolete. And it has not changed since I was a child.

Flying on Dragonfly Wings

"The clue of our destiny, wander where we will,
lies at the foot of the cradle."

Richter

At five, I negotiated the eight bustling city blocks to the local elementary school. Like most children I went with an open heart, willing to believe what I would discover about myself and the incredible world around me.

The two-story school building loomed large, stony and ancient, a mini-version of an eastern Ivy-League college or perhaps a home for a giant. Two large square pillars flanked the imposing stone steps. But the lions that perched on those pillars had long since fled, leaving all little children unprotected.

I entered alone and vulnerable. Past the massive arched passageway and through the dark Gothic doors the hallway ceiling rose to a grand height defying the presence of a second story. To the left, the principal's office demanded attention. To the right, the attendance office sat waiting for its prey. And except during recess, those vaulted spaces echoed with silence.

Kindergarten brought many experiences including the opportunity for joy, innocence and the making of genuine friendships. The tenderness of other children welcoming each other by name, the ability to understand what was going on in a larger world, the confidence to know the routine, all these had lasting value.

I explored my creativity. I built block castles to the sky. I picked a sunlit alcove at the far end of the room to do my most glorious work: wooden block cities, villages and throne rooms glowing in the morning light—all built to the specifications of a queen. I felt powerful and creative, in charge of my life. But building time always terminated too abruptly, quickly swapping out my feelings of confidence and mastery with a sense of interruption, confusion, emptiness and disappointment. I was absorbed, intrigued, engaged and then I was robbed.

Young children, like seedlings, need protection. But unlike seedlings, they cannot be cultivated in furrows in a field. When we conceive of children, we must picture the soil surrounding each little root of each child as needing its own particular combination of nutrients. Each has its own requirements. We cannot grow children in batches. We must give children voice in their own direction. We must listen intently to both what they say and what they cannot yet tell us. This is how they learn who they are. This is how they grow. Rachel Kessler writes:

> When soul is present in education, attention shifts. As the quality of attention shifts, we listen with great care not only to what people say but to the messages between the words—tones,

gestures, the flicker of feeling across the face.
And then we concentrate on what has heart and
meaning. (Introduction)

But very little in school speaks to children's hearts, needs, motivations or desires. We fail to acknowledge their inner stories, ignoring the dialogue and innate direction of their being.

I yearned to read, but I was told I had to wait until next year. I wanted to play the piano that sat in the far corner of the room. It was not for children. I wanted to paint more, talk more and listen a little less. I wanted to know about things that weren't part of my day. I had questions about stories that didn't have time for answers. I had answers for questions that weren't asked and questions that couldn't quite be formed by words. I did not understand everything, but we 'moved on' anyway.

Inside every story evolves an inner story. Inside every life breathes an inner life. This is the life we are unconsciously living while we think we are doing something else. It is where we really do our work. It is the origin of growth and the source of our intellectual, emotional, physical and spiritual re-integration and blossoming. It is the life of the soul and it will lead us to our passion.

But instead of honoring and allowing our children to listen to their inner stories, to find their passion and brilliance, we fill their time and their souls with an external agenda—ours. We occupy their waking hours with activities that keep their attention focused elsewhere. Then we create an emotional environment, controlled by punishment and reward, that herds them into fulfilling our expectations for them. Soon, their inner dialogues grow softer, less distinct. Ultimately, that dialogue smothers and dies. John Dewey writes:

> The real child, it hardly need be said, lives in the world of imaginative values and ideas which find only imperfect outward embodiment.... The imagination is the medium in which the child lives.... The question of the relation of the school to the child's life is at bottom simply this: Shall we ignore this native setting and tendency, dealing, not with the living child at all, but with the dead image we have erected, or shall we give it play and satisfaction? (60-61)

Wanting to please the teacher, I learned to fake a lot. I began to forget the things I was curious about and the things I wanted to do. I learned to wait in quiet confusion and growing despair and resignation. I had visions of princes and princesses, of canvassing the sky with magic cloud paintings, of calling forth fairies and elves, and flying on dragonfly wings. I wanted to explore the universe, but I was told to 'sit down on the rug and be quiet.' I put my feelings on hold. And although there were no visible signs of distress and still moments of joy and camaraderie, I was shutting down.

When our authenticity is not honored, we hide. When we cannot grow according to our own blueprint, we grow emotionally, physically and spiritually misshapen. First, we lose touch with our integrity and then with our highest being. Joseph Chilton Pearce writes:

> What will be developed in the child is a capacity for deception as he tries to maintain some vestige of integrity while outwardly appearing to conform. Living a lie to survive a lying culture, the child forgets the truth of who he really is. (The Biology of Transcendence, 141)

Where misdirection, boredom and lack of integrity trample our connection to soul, life loses its magic and enchantment. We grow into unfulfilled lives of quiet desperation and disenchantment. Thomas Moore states that a disenchanted life is devoid of the spiritual food necessary to nurture the soul:

> An enchanted world is one that speaks to the soul, to the mysterious depths of the heart and imagination where we find value, love, and union with the world around us. As mystics of many religions have taught, that sense of rapturous union can give a sensation of fulfillment that makes life purposeful and vibrant. (The Re-Enchantment of Everyday Life, Introduction)

Without that enchantment we lose the capacity for joy. Disenchanted and disconnected from the life I experienced before school, I graduated kindergarten a very long year later and was promoted to the annex along with the other first graders.

The annex was a much later addition than the two-story monolith. It was modern, sleek and industrial, odd numbered rooms to the right, even to the left. Predictability replaced character. With true industrial efficiency, the school board pared down the design. The designers overlooked growing things like big, old climbing trees and the fantasies of children. An expanse of asphalt replaced a child's magic.

Disenchantment takes many forms. When our physical environment lacks warmth, delight, humor, creativity and a connection to nature, our souls follow suit. An industrial environment reflects an industrial state of mind. It is efficient, but sacrifices the calling of the heart. It reflects the concept of a human being lacking in divine grace and a view of humanity that has grown shallow and predictable. It creates an environ ment disconnected from the awe and mystery of life itself. It is the path to our spiritual extinction. Moore explains:

> It is not easy to discuss enchantment in a disenchanted society, one that suffers the lack of a deep, solid, communal fantasy life, because enchantment stands our usual values on their head. What is central in the hardcore, hard-working world of the disenchanted has little or no place in a soft life of enchantment, and what is important to the charm of daily life may appear as a distraction to those who are dedicated to the kind of seriousness that excludes enchantment. Yet there is no essential conflict between enchanted living and practical, productive activity; they can serve each other: one delighting the spirit of ambition, the other comforting the heart. (The Re-Enchantment of Everyday Life, Introduction)

It was now the end of the fifties and no one was going to help us find enchantment. We were growing up. We were to be young adults by the age of ten. Schoolwork was long and boring. It was supposed to be long and boring because it prepared us for work, and work was supposed to be long and boring. Work was to be done painfully and in silence. Work took an effort that demanded struggle and eluded joy. If we were to succeed as adults, we had better get used to tedium. We were earmarked for the workforce of the Industrial Revolution.

The Industrial Revolution was never designed for enchantment. Its intent was to change our society from a nation of farmers attuned to the beauty and cycles of the earth, to a nation of industrial laborers. But at first industrialists could not get farmers to successfully adjust to factory life. Farmers were too independent. So these industrialists turned their sights on children. They would train them. They would pass laws that made their training mandatory and they would call that training 'public education.' Alvin Toffler reports, "If young people could be pre-fitted to the industrial system, it would vastly ease the problems of industrial discipline later on." (The Third Wave, 45)

Mass education taught a basic curriculum of reading, writing, arithmetic and a few other subjects. It was not interested in cultivating souls, but in providing just enough basic literacy skills to enable people to read instructions and enough culture to homogenize the melting pot. But, to the industrialists funding and running public education, there was an even more important curriculum. It was covert. It taught punctuality, obedience and rote, repetitive work. It taught what was needed to place an obedient workforce into their factories. And today's curriculum has not changed.

Education today still consists of a carefully camouflaged and elaborate compulsory system designed to train our children for industry. As a result, our children are not really educated. To educate means to 'educe' or to draw out what is already within. This system is not interested in helping our children find out who they are or what they like to do. This system is interested in controlling them while they are young, so they will grow into adults who can be controlled. Toffler writes:

> Factory labor demanded workers who showed up on time, especially assembly line hands. It demanded workers who would take orders from a management hierarchy without questioning. And it demanded men and women prepared to slave away at machines or in offices, performing brutally repetitious operations.... Thus from the mid-nineteenth century on...schools ma-

> chined generation after generation of young people into a pliable, regimented work force.... (45-46)

Thomas Moore describes a true education:

> ...education is the art of enticing the soul to emerge from its cocoon, from its coil of potentiality and its cave of hiding. Education is not the piling on of learning, information, data, facts, skills, or abilities—that's training or instructing—but is rather a making visible what is hidden as a seed. (Education of the Heart, 1)

Our educational system dishonors the inner dialogue of the soul. It ignores it. And what we do not acknowledge will disappear from our consciousness, but not from our being. We feel that separation. Separating our children from their greater selves creates ramifications that outweigh the antiquated assembly line concept of productivity.

There was nothing in our education as children that honored the inner dialogue of our souls. Instead of helping us uncover our talents, interests and strengths, we were forced to memorize data for the sake of memorizing data. We might as well have learned a language from the moon—words, words and more words. Disconnected from personal experience, there was no way to process those words. School became a memorizing game: the teacher's words, the book's words, the words on the list. So, I learned to get pleasure from pleasing the teacher. I was a good student. I could memorize words.

But this focus on words actually inhibits a child's ability to think. Piaget's study of child development brought him to the conclusion that "thought [is] derived from the child's action, and not from his language." (Ginsburg and Opper, 7) Maria Montessori elaborates:

...education is not something which the teacher does, but that it is a natural process which develops spontaneously in the human being. It is not acquired by listening to words, but in virtue of experiences in which the child acts on his environment. The teacher's task is not to talk, but to prepare and arrange a series of motives for cultural activity in a special environment made for the child. (The Absorbent Mind, 8)

None-the-less, our educational system is built on the teacher's dissemination of information. Children are trained to listen to the teacher's words in return for the emotional reward of her approval.

When all of our activities are directed toward pleasing someone else, we eventually forget whom we are. We start to disconnect from ourselves without realizing what is happening. We are like frogs. Frogs will jump out of a pot if placed in hot water. But if frogs are placed in a pot of cold water and the water is heated slowly, they will boil to death. So it is with us. When disconnection is gradual we do not notice. Constantly denying feelings, trying to turn off the flow of our thoughts, unable to express ourselves, disabled from physical movement and unable to direct our own day, all lead to a disconnection of the heart. It is a form of mind control and punishment not unlike solitary confinement.

When we are cut off from ourselves our individual patterns of growth are violated. This violation creates reactions of anger, generalized angst, self-deprecation, depression, and malaise. It feeds a consciousness of relentless fear, hatred, greed, violence and callous indifference. It will never create inner peace. When we experience separation within, we can only feel, in a very profound sense, separation from each other.

Dr. Eric Fromm explains that this sense of separation creates anxiety:

> Children who have no say in the direction of
> how they spend their hours feel fundamental-
> ly incapacitated, walled off, rendered helpless.
> This helplessness, without the capacity to fix
> it, engenders anxiety, fear, depression and an-
> ger... guilt [and] shame over his separateness,
> all the opposites of a loving state of being. (8)

Dr. Rollo May explains how this sense of helplessness, the inability to achieve internally initiated direction, is not only self-destructive, but carries with it the potential for violence. May writes:

> Inner vacuousness is the long-term, accumulat-
> ed result of a person's particular conviction...
> that he cannot act as an entity in directing his
> own life, or change other people's attitudes to-
> ward him or effectively influence the world
> around him. Thus he gets the deep sense of de-
> spair and futility.... And soon, since what he
> wants and what he feels can make no real dif-
> ference, he gives up wanting and feeling....
> The human being cannot live in a condition of
> emptiness for very long; if he is not growing to-
> ward something, he does not merely stagnate;
> the pent-up potentialities turn into morbidity
> and despair, and eventually into destructive ac-
> tivities.... (28)

In school, we render the soul helpless, disconnecting it from the rest of the child and cutting off the inner dialogue that might bridge that separation. We keep our children from their passions. We keep them from their meaningful questions. When we ask them to guess which answers we are looking for, we disconnect them from their ability to think critically. By ignoring the affective, we tell them their feelings are unimportant and we bury their intuition. We insist on directing their thoughts. Then we direct their actions. We confine them to their chairs so their bodies cannot move. If they do not follow our orders, we give them labels and then we drug them. We keep them confused and off balance, their self-worth involved in a game of trying to win when the criteria are not clear and the rules keep changing. Expectations and rewards are arbitrary. The lives of children are reduced to a guessing game—trying to figure out what the teacher wants—what part of what to memorize and how it might be worded on a test. The sense of confusion and insecurity spreads like a virus through a child's life.

When we are alienated from our sense of self, it affects all our relationships. I kept trying to hide the gnawing feeling I might be the odd kid out—the one who was different. And in a system that consistently rewards conformity and punishes individualism, it was not an unreasonable fear. I wanted desperately to be liked by everybody, but the landscape of who liked whom was constantly changing. "No, I won't be your best friend, but if you are nice to me, you can come to my party." The lunch benches were hard and overcrowded. There was the perpetual question of "Who will sit with me? What did your mother pack? I smell tuna. Do you want some of my chips? How about the pickle?" There was an underlying sense of vying for friendships. And most friendships were unstable, depending upon the whim of the group at the moment.

In this atmosphere, most children look to an adult for emotional stability. In their need and optimism, they would like to turn toward their teacher, who, ironically, is often the source of their confusion. To a small child a teacher is a god, and when a teacher is kind, a child's whole world changes. Likewise, when a teacher criticizes or discredits a child's work, it changes that child's very perception of self. And when a teacher reprimands a child in anger, it falls like a death sentence. The damage is far greater than the initial feelings of hurt or embarrassment.

Most of us can recall at least one incident in school that left an emotional scar. I remember I loved art. I used to sit for hours at the kitchen table, listening to music and painting away the afternoon. I seemed to disappear into my work and then emerge feeling bigger after each session. But after this third grade incident, I didn't paint again until high school.

We were studying early California and made clay figurines of the people in the pueblos. It was now time to paint them. I followed directions perfectly. I laid newspaper on my desk. I got my paints and sat down quietly and quickly, excited about my project. It was a woman in a peasant top and full-length skirt. I was totally absorbed in my artwork. I dipped my brush into the pretty yellow paint. Her skirt was full. I meticulously sculpted each fold of the rich fabric, trying to emulate the pictures I had seen. I carefully painted her short sleeve top, adorning her slender neck with little dots of delicate beads. I painted the rich dark hair flowing down her back. I cleaned my brush and dipped back into the yellow paint making beautiful, long flowing strokes of striped fabric. Then I cleaned my brush again and felt drawn to the rich bright pink paint that lay beckoning on my palette. I began filling in the alternate stripes with great care not to impinge on the brilliant flowing yellow, when, out of nowhere, the teacher started screaming at the top of her deep lungs, "No! No! No!"

I looked up in terror and naiveté, wondering what had happened. I saw her terrible face, askew and still screaming. She lunged toward me. She grabbed the statue from my hands. She waved it in the air. She yelled, "Don't you ever do this again!" Then she looked down at me, the object of shame still held high over her head for all to see, "Didn't I tell you yesterday, don't use these colors! They don't go together on the color chart! Why weren't you listening?"

I had been absent the day before. And now, with tears streaming down my face, I wished I could just disappear. Christina Grof explains that when we hurt a child, we elicit fear, anger, hopelessness, victimhood, confusion, guilt, and shame. Each time, no matter how mild, it is a spiritual violation and not to be treated lightly. Grof writes:

> When we inflict suffering on others, we are assisting in the creation of profoundly blemished individuals. These individuals become adults who carry within them unrecognized wounded children. They are hollow men and women, cut off from their sense of worth and their source of inspiration. As their sense of cosmic loneliness deepens, it becomes secured into place. This, in its deepest sense, is spiritual abuse...(51)

Disempowering children robs them of their selfhood. Abusing children disconnects them from their own divinity. Joseph Chilton Pearce explains:

> A human nurtured instead of shamed and loved instead of driven by fear develops a different brain and therefore a different mind—he will not act against the well-being of another, nor against his larger body, the living earth. As a child we know we are an integral part of the continuum of all things.... We can and must rediscover that knowing. (The Biology of Transcendence, 261)

Children need to feel cherished and competent. They need to feel in charge of their own destiny. They need to be able to make the decisions and choices that directly affect them, keeping the channel to that inner voice open and effective. A child must be able to feel his own identity coming through the requirements of daily living. But children wear the labels we give them. If we see them in their highest light, their behaviors and actions eventually follow suit. If we tell them they are deficient, they will believe it, internalize it and act it out. They become what we tell them they are.

School made me feel small. It rarely made me feel cherished. But after school and on weekends I rode my bike and roller skated with my buddies. It was just my sister Cheryl and me, and lots of kids on the block. When we were not on our bikes, we were walking and we walked everywhere. Sometimes we climbed. We could traverse the entire length of the block without ever having to touch the ground it seemed. We would scramble up the old tree by the garage, over the shingled roof onto the supports for the wooden fence, across the block wall and down to the end of the world and back.

We understood our whole neighborhood and we were interested in everyone and everything. We knew who was baking bread or chocolate-chip cookies and who was yelling at whom. We knew when Mrs. Jenkins left for the market leaving Lannie's older sister, Miriam, in charge and when the dentist across the street came home. We knew when Andy's mom had to get a job and when Mr. Rhodes once again threw Mrs. Rhodes out of the house. We knew when the factory laid off men because Annie's dad was home cooking dinner. We knew it all. In this domain, we were kings and queens. We held the scepter on life.

Dr. William Glasser explains that a child is generally successful and optimistic prior to entering school because "...he used his brain to solve problems relevant to his life; he was optimistic because he had a lot of fun." (Schools Without Failure, 29)

I loved our little neighborhood. I felt empowered, sheltered and whole, but when I turned twelve, we moved to a larger house in a neighboring community. And although it was only about five miles away, it might as well have been a million miles.

❧ 3 ❧

Industrial Fluorescent

Two days have passed since my daughter Erin started studying for her test. I am sitting in a classroom on the university campus. Erin and a group of six students have decided to meet together to work out problems that might be on the test. All thirteen graduate students were invited. Only seven show up. One student walks into the room and announces there are now only twelve graduate students left.

These seven band together despite the fact their scores will be pitted against each other, and the test will determine whether or not they will go on. They focus on a 'contraction mapping' problem. My daughter stands in front of the group. The question is hers. She puts the problem on the board. The chalk squeaks. Nobody notices, except me. The drone of the air-conditioning of the empty building also goes unnoticed. School has been out for two weeks, yet these kids meet regularly and study. It is like sitting in a meat locker. It is cold. There are no windows and the fluorescent bulbs are the same as the ones in my office that give my students and colleagues headaches, industrial fluorescent. There is silence. Then one young man in the back figures out a part of the answer. Erin tries it again. She figures out the rest.

These kids do their work by a light that strains the eyes and gives people headaches. Yet, they persist. The floor is shiny white vinyl with small black specks. The walls are white as well. The chalkboard is a dusty black. Rows of individual desks and blue vinyl seats break up the monotony, but not enough. The desks are too small and restrictive. They were too small in grade school and they are still too small in graduate school.

A big white clock, round and trimmed in black, sits right over the blackboard. It follows us from kindergarten into the workplace. It occupies a position of prominence in the room. It can't be missed. It sends the message, "It's not what you learn or figure out; it's how fast." It's a race. It's competitive. There is a 'time-over' quality that makes it all about competition like a track meet.

This is a new building, but I bet the first industrial classroom looked a lot like this one. A million classrooms probably look like this one. There are no soft surfaces. There are no plants. There are no living things other than the students and perhaps the teacher. There is nothing to give this room warmth or a touch of humanity. I guess we are not really into either change or humanity.

Three of the students sit with their arms crossed around their chests, as if they were unconsciously defending their bodies. Another student, Elaine, addresses the board. She too poses a problem and the other students try to help solve it. They are each teacher and student. They all have questions and answers, and questions about their answers, but the test will not reflect their persistent curiosity. Neither will it reflect their ability to work as a team. There will be no way to measure this. Yet, their teamwork is their strength. With that skill they could solve the problems of the world. But instead, it will go unnoticed. Their ability to help each other will not be valued. Eventually the team will dissipate and its members will go in separate directions as the university pits and ranks each student against the other.

Suddenly, they break out in laughter! They figured something out! Although Josh says he still thinks he will flunk. They get excited! There is more laughter! Arms uncross. Stephanie passes a book around. Affect walks back into their eyes. Their excitement will not be measured on the test either —too bad. Without the reward excitement brings, why would anyone bother to discover anything? Excitement is its own reward. But we extract excitement from the learning process. Students are to be quiet, otherwise they are sent from the room. But without a teacher around to dampen their spirit, these kids are excited! The boys now lean forward as if ready to leap up to the board to help. Every kid in the room is riveted, pushing his or her whole being toward the solution on the board. Together they are sure they will get it. Silence…maybe not.

Another student approaches the board. They are running out of chalk. He scribbles the equation on the board and offers another possible solution. Four more students ask questions. They will sit in this classroom long past dinner until they figure it out. The only problem is there is so much more to learn in so little time, and no one really knows what will be on the test.

Josh moves from the rear of the class and finally steps up to the plate. His body is tall, thin and lanky, yet everything he has is going into that chalk. He shares what he knows in a slightly nervous, but enthusiastic manner. The chalk clips the board in short, terse strokes. He gets his point across.

Elaine writes away fervently, taking notes. She finds an answer in a book. They gather around. I do not understand what they are talking about. It is a foreign language to me. Occasionally, I catch a word I understand...'zero'...'coefficient'...but mostly it's another language.

I ponder the light. I think if we turned it off, some of the kids in the room would create their own. I wonder how they are surviving this system. What is the cost to psyche and soul? How is my daughter doing? How will this change her? Mostly these kids are tense and nervous. We are moving into another hour. I check out my daughter. Homeschooled along with her brothers, Erin is drawing on a reserve I can only begin to imagine. Her whole relationship to learning is different than mine.

Erin studied academics in a self-paced one-room schoolhouse inside a plumbing factory in a small rural town. Erin's perception of learning is that she went to school in a large lemon orchard. On breaks she climbed trees, fought lemon wars, built tree houses and ran zip lines across ravines. She kayaked in the drainage ditch, sold mud shampoo and built an entire city out of cardboard boxes complete with a government and monetary system. She did not distinguish between play and academic work. They both captivated her full energy and attention. Joseph Chilton Pearce explains:

> The compelling nature of play poses a problem for adults wishing to get the child to attend to adult notions of reality. The child's intelligence becomes invested in his imagined transformations of self and world, and these are singularly compelling. His awareness locks into fantasy; reality becomes that play. For the child, the time is always now; the place, here; the action, me. He has no capacity to entertain adult notions of fantasy world and real world. He knows only

one world, and that is the very real one in which and with which he plays. He is not playing at life. Play *is* life. (The Magical Child, 169)

Erin entered college at age thirteen. She took a full load, mathematics, art and computer sciences. She still played every afternoon in that lemon grove.

Now this process of studying for this test has also captivated her full energy and attention. I pray she is successful, as I do the other kids. I also pray that she does not lose the self-confidence, identity and personal integrity with which she grew up. I grew up in the center of Los Angeles and attended all those industrial schools. I have vivid memories of what it was like.

Donna Reed and the Birth of Mediocrity

"I would like to be able to fly if everyone else did,
but otherwise it would be kind of conspicuous."
Twelve-year-old girl, <u>The Lonely Crowd</u>
Reisman

Relocating five miles west to a classier area of town officially called West L.A., my parents bought a lot and built our house. I was twelve. We moved in on a plywood floor and one functional bulb in the dining room, so we could pass the building inspection in time, and I could start a new junior high in September.

This junior high was just a larger version of my elementary school. More asphalt. The history teacher hung a skull-and-cross-bones flag out the second-story window at lunch to announce a pop quiz. The alienation and isolation were the same only now kids were swapping stories about sex and who made it with whom. The P.E. teachers were merciless. The communal showers, one big room with lots of nozzles and absolutely no privacy, lacked not only dignity, but humanity. And in an environment where we had to maintain our anonymity, it was a blatant contradiction.

Nothing quite clicked. The home economics teacher was still reliving the fifties. The example Donna Reed set of the perfect woman running the immaculate household for the nuclear family defined her expectations. Unruffled demeanor (apron and pearls, managing the social venue of the family) was the measure of normal. Boys took woodshop. Girls took sewing. I would have loved to work in wood. Instead, I failed my gym bag project in sewing class. I could see Donna frowning as I knocked over the bucket of straight pins on the floor, tipped my chair and plummeted down, hind-side up, in a frantic effort to retrieve those little symbols of feminine handiwork and skill. I never understood exactly what either Donna or my teacher wanted.

Junior high made me anxious. Most of us still have nightmares about school or taking a test. We dream we forgot to read the book, we missed the instructions, we ran out of time. We live and relive the ongoing stream of anxieties, fears and small failures created at school for the rest of our lives. Joseph Chilton Pearce notes:

> Meanwhile, we legislate for stricter learning standards, "getting tough with kids," increasing homework and testing. It's interesting to note that testing is interpreted by all of us as a judgmental threat and shifts our energy and attention from the emotional cognitive brain and prefrontals to the R-system, which compromises whatever higher intellect we may have. In fact, being

back in school to take a test is a common night-
mare of adults. (<u>The Biology of Transcendence</u>,
113)

My schooling was no exception. It kept us too fearful, insecure, confused and busy to find our own direction. The
French teacher spoke a slew of French words to us. He refused to answer our questions in English. The math teacher
expected us to suddenly remember a solution we learned
twelve Tuesdays ago and hadn't used since. The English
teacher made us diagram literature to death. And the typing
teacher viewed her entire job and perhaps her 'raison d'être,'
as increasing our scores on timed tests. For an entire semester, we played beat the clock under the tutelage of her "Get-
ready, get-set, GO!"

At sixteen I escaped and started the tenth grade in high
school. I didn't like school and I didn't like many of the kids
—they had become too mean. I couldn't make myself interested in what I was doing just because the counselor plugged
me into some elective. Telling me if I worked hard, one day I
could go to college, didn't work for me either. I was no longer the awe-struck child in kindergarten who couldn't wait to
explore her world. Increasingly tired of being herded with the
crowd, I was burning out. Krishnimurti writes:

> Conventional education makes independent
> thinking extremely difficult. Conformity leads
> to mediocrity. To be different from the group or
> to resist environment is not easy... With increas-
> ing age, dullness of mind and heart sets in. (9)

My teachers did not notice my waning interest in school,
but my mother did. Hoping to rekindle my love for learning,
she enrolled me in three different art colleges while I was still
going to high school. It worked. It turned the darkness of the

school day into expectant joy. I went after school. I went during school. I went on Saturdays. Not since I was little had I become so thoroughly absorbed.

My love for painting had recaptured me. Spending long hours in our cold, dimly lit garage, swishing paint, creating relationships with colors, form, shape and hue spoke to me in a language I keenly understood, a language for which there are no words. No test could be written. No paperwork documented. No comparison could adequately describe this unfolding. It riveted my attention and filled my being. There was no way to measure and grade fulfillment. When I left high school each afternoon I was drained. When I emerged each night from the garage, I was reborn.

When an education speaks to the soul, issues of focus disappear. When the heart directs an education, passion steps forward to foster growth, productivity and fill our being with inner peace. When we are manifesting our brilliance, life is energetic and complete. We begin to meet ourselves straight on. Rudolph Steiner writes:

> Inner development is the education of soul qualities, spiritual qualities, ego strength, differentiation, will, thinking, feeling and breathing. The body itself opens from the inside. (Richards, 5)

But our educational system is not set up for this kind of growth and neither is the social structure we create within it. The social order of school forces a child to look outward instead of inward for validation. Based on competition instead of cooperation, it teaches our children to compete for grades, compete for peer approval and to discount their inner development. Then we tell ourselves we are 'socializing' our children.

What is the socialized child? If we look at the social structures of most high schools, we find emotional larceny and extortion. It is similar to elementary school where children try to buy friendships with extra bags of potato chips, cookies and pickles. In high school, the stakes are bigger. Many children seek peer approval by drinking as the crowd drinks, smoking, and participating in drugs and sex. This is the most visible price they pay for the external validation we have taught them to value. There is little in their day that tells them that a self-reliant, independent individual has value. The 'socialized' child endlessly seeks a sense of self-worth in the perceptions of others.

In high school, identity takes form in a group. My high school offered the typical social structure for that time, clubs and cliques—official clubs like the Drama Club—and unofficial cliques whose admission required the right sneakers and socks, the perfect sweater and the correct hair-do. There were nerds and jocks, surfers and socialites, rock groups and left-over beatniks. There was even the emerging Westside Story version of the gang.

But as the semesters passed, the climate changed. It soon became the thick of the sixties. The hippies stepped forward as the new anti-establishment peer group. Some of us traded the oppression of the strict social structure of the fifties for the mob mentality of the sixties. It was the same application of blindly following the crowd, just a different direction. Donna Reed and Life With Father had never seen anything like it. Symbol smashing was rampant. Starting timidly with the Beatle's bowl haircut, it gathered momentum to include flag burning. Angry drug music, bare feet and a serious lack of barber influence began littering the sacred halls, front lawn and walkways. But in spite of their sudden appearance, the hippies were just another group.

School fosters group identity, impersonal and devoid of individual integrity. It lacks the ingredients necessary for growing healthy, self-reliant human beings. Joseph Chilton Pearce writes:

With regard to enculturating our children, lacking all conviction otherwise, we move with total, passionate intensity. Convinced we must pass on this survival knowledge, we pound it into our offspring "for their own good" as it was pounded into us for our own good. Schooling is treated in a similar fashion—no matter how much pain schooling may have caused us, to save our sanity over having lost the richest, loveliest years of our life to the process, we rationalize that it must have been good for us! And we then subject our children to it in turn; they prove our point by becoming like us, confirming our worldview, joining our mass anxiety, and verifying it by coming on board. We have very little choice in the matter, but hope springs eternal that this time we will make schooling work. It never has. (The Biology of Transcendence, 121)

By the time I was a senior I was thoroughly disgruntled. It was clear; school was a hostile environment. Who was I? What could I *do*? And what did 'taking' classes have to do with anything, anyway? So, I stayed home to read the existentialists, Sartre, Camus and Simone de Beauvoir. For the first time since kindergarten I felt fulfilled. I was growing, discovering who I was in relation to the world. I was happy, but not for long enough. I finally took too many sick days and my parents refused to write another excuse. So one morning, I gathered up my books and marched myself into the attendance office, noteless and unarmed.

There I stood waiting patiently in line with forty other returning students. The office worker asked me for my note. I informed her I didn't have one. She repeated mechanically, "Bring one tomorrow." I took a deep breath. Then I told her there was no note. There was never going to be a note. My parents weren't going to write one.

I thought lightning had struck. The activity in the room ceased. The inhabitants froze. Behind the counter, the little man with the short gray hair, white shirt and bow tie sat down. The staff huddled in a corner and conferred. Two minutes later they pulled me out of line and pointing with a cool finger, asked me to "sit over there." Fifteen minutes after that I was escorted to the vice principal's office.

The vice principal, Mrs. Ray, was a humorless remnant of a human being. She made the stoic couple with the pitchfork in the painting "American Gothic" appear frivolous. Adjusting her glasses and narrowing her sights on me she asked me why wasn't I in school? I replied in a polite and genuinely courteous tone that I stayed home so I could learn something.

"And where were your parents?" she queried over her spectacles.

"My father was at work. My mother was home."

"She knew?"

"Yes, she knew."

"And what were you doing?"

"I was reading."

"Ah ha!" (For some reason she thought she had me.) "And WHAT were you reading?"

"Being and Nothingness by Jean Paul Sartre, The Second Sex, Simone de Beauvoir....The Stranger, Albert Camus...."

"Well," she flustered, "but how are your grades?"

"Half B's" I paused, "And half A's."

"Oh," she mumbled and walked out, unable to cope.

I returned to class.

Where have you gone Donna Reed?
When do I earn my pearls?

❧ 5 ❧

Blindfolded

It has been a good twelve hours since they started. Erin and her friends take a break. They share. Stephanie says that she has studied all day and has never felt so unproductive. Josh concurs. He reiterates. He is going to fail (he has never failed yet and Erin says that if Josh can't make it, none of them can make it). Erin shared the same feeling with me earlier this morning that Stephanie expressed; she felt singularly unproductive. I don't think she remembers that now. Each feels alone in their struggle until they share.

Elaine asks, "Is it true if you are a doctoral student you have to pass the test with a higher score?" Erin turns white. Stephanie isn't too pleased either. They have heard there were two different grading scales, one for master's students and another for the Ph.D. students.

Erin asks, "How many first-year students last?"

"Wait, there were thirty-five students," one kid says, "not twenty-five!" They feel like lambs at the slaughter. They are trying to name the students they know who are still in the program. Erin sends me a nervous glance. Even though she is still standing in front of the board, her hands are now crossed around her chest. Josh says he is, "so freaked out" about this exam. They don't know what to study. Nobody will help them.

Part of the test is a guessing game...what to study? Josh keeps wondering what life will be like if he can't do math anymore. Will it be over? Life? Josh has been up every night until six in the morning studying. He is afraid to go to sleep. Then he is afraid to wake up and face all the work he still has to do. One student has to go. Five remain in the room. Erin is back at the board. She solved the problem she posed. The third hour begins.

Our current educational system is designed to keep our children slightly off-balance and insecure, wondering what to do next. They are always at a loss as to what is on the test.

The test. It is a covert curriculum. It frames our children's self-concepts and feelings of self-worth. It tells our children that they will be measured and judged, what they do, what they say, what they think or feel, how and when. They will not know or remember all of its rules or applications until they trip over one like a land mine. And by then it will be too late. The five-year-old who steps out of line because he moves too slow, the eight-year-old who runs because she is excited, the ten-year-old who reaches out to touch the next child, the thirteen-year-old who bends over to pick up his pen during the test, the sixteen-year-old who accidentally brings the wrong folder to class—they all feel the test—the sense that the rules are ill-defined, hard to interpret and arbitrary.

Rewards and punishments are unfairly dispensed. They will forever carry with them the emotional assaults they feel at the hands of their teachers who have absolute power. There is no recourse. It is part of the test.

I hoped to raise my children in their formative years without that test—without the sense of insecurity and lack of self that compliance brings. I hoped to raise my children to find their passions and own particular forms of brilliance. I hoped my children would have a more compelling relationship to themselves and the world around them than I did growing up in the industrial fifties. I hoped for the best, because no one forgets the test.

ఛ 6 ఞ

How High Can a Dead Person Bounce?

"The fact that you are not yet dead is not sufficient proof that you are alive. Aliveness is measured by degrees of awareness."

Brother David Steindl-Rast

Testing kills the spirit. Not enough in that high school remained alive including me. So, I quietly graduated at the end of the year, packed up and sent myself to the University of California at Berkeley four hundred miles away.

It was 1967—Vietnam War protests, raging hippie-ism and storm troopers. Berkeley was the hot spot for it all. Being 'hip' was measured by a drug reality I found unappealing. Self-realization gave permission to do anything regardless of the consequences. Encounter groups shredded their participants to tears; lying dismantled on the floor was a 'breakthrough.' We were trying to find our individuality, but in spite of our desire, most of us were not any more intact, alert or alive than when we blindly followed Donna Reed like the rest of the crowd a decade before. The group still ruled.

And I participated. I went to student council meetings, political gatherings and animal rights happenings. I learned to bake bread, bead and macramé. I designed endless patterns of fanciful garments made of fabrics I would now shudder to buy let alone wear. I listened to the rhetoric on the street corners. I read activists' letters at magazine stands and found Laurel's "Vegetarian Kitchen." I also learned to meditate and sit in on protests at the same time.

One protest involved the illegal use of sound equipment. A small group of students had taken the equipment from the administration to voice their views throughout the campus. The administration disciplined the students. On the surface it was a relatively benign infraction, but in those days any issue had the potential to become explosive. The rest of the campus went on strike.

Speakers were flown in from all over the country to address the students. Martin Luther King's assistant spoke to a crowd in the student union—five hundred students sitting cross-legged on the floor all listening intently. He passed the microphone to the crowd to give us a chance to speak. One student made a speech accusing the administration of being dictatorial and violating the free speech movement by suspending the students who used the unauthorized equipment. The whole room stood up and applauded wildly. Hands clapped, feet stomped and caps were thrown into the air. Then everyone sat down.

The next student had the floor. He explained how the administration was well within its rights to take disciplinary measures as the equipment was taken without the administration's knowledge or permission. That—he explained, was the counterpart to theft. It was a violation of the law. Theft is illegal and if we establish laws to protect the innocent, but we break them when we feel like it, we are setting up an environment ripe for dictatorship. And that was a bigger violation of human rights because it breeched the very democracy we were defending. His speech also brought the house down. Once again the students stood up and cheered, clapping their hands and stamping their feet in approval. Then everyone sat down again.

This time, however, one lone student remained standing in the back of the room. Without the benefit of a microphone he addressed the crowd in a quiet, but audible tone. "First you applaud this guy, who said one thing, and then you applaud the other guy, who said exactly the opposite. How can that be?" And they applauded him too. So I got up and left.

I not only left the sit-in, I left the school, the city and the hippie atmosphere. I left my peer group and the whole persona created for us. I couldn't find where I fit in. I was neither Donna Reed nor Iron Butterfly. My stomach churned. My heart ached. A small still voice within whispered, "You're in the wrong story!" And as unpopular as the idea was, I went home.

Dr. Carl Rogers says that process of becoming involves "moving away from facades...moving away from oughts" (On Becoming a Person, 166) and meeting expectations to please others. It is a movement away from being other-oriented and a motion toward self-direction and autonomy. The autonomous person is responsible for her own actions and activities, deciding which behaviors have meaning and which do not. That person listens to an inner voice. Rogers explains:

> Often I sense that the client is trying to listen to himself, is trying to hear the messages and meanings, which are being communicated by his own physiological reactions. No longer is he so fearful of what he may find. He comes to re-

alize that his own inner reactions and experiences, the messages of his senses and his viscera, are friendly. He comes to want to be close to his inner sources of information rather than closing them off. (On Becoming a Person, 174)

Dialogue with our inner voice is necessary. Humanity has been carrying on a conversation with the voice within, the higher self, the inner teacher for thousands of years. Whatever we call it, this teacher within is integral to who we are. Rick Fields refers to it as "the spirit of Life that is always speaking to our souls." Fields writes:

The source of this voice—which may be without sound, and yet is heard—is called by many different names: the inner guide, guardian angel, spirit guide, the collective unconscious, or just plain intuition. (260)

It is our source of reconnection, one that breaks through all our internal bonds of limitation and self-doubt, one that must triumph if we are to be all that we are and do all that we can do. It is our source of authenticity, integrity and direction. So I left Berkeley and headed for my home in L.A..

This time I applied to UCLA, the University of California at Los Angeles. I was admitted to the Theater Department, where I soon fell in love with the performing arts. My new contacts in that department lead to outside studies with the historical giants in the field of acting: Lee Strasberg, Stella Adler and Jeff Corey.

Lee Strasberg was a legend. He helped bring the genius and insight of Constantin Stanislavski, otherwise known as method acting, out of Russia and into the American theater. Strasberg might be called the father of contemporary acting. A little man with gray hair, a soft-spoken voice and a slight

New York accent, he looked very much like someone's kind grandfather—but make no mistake, he was powerful because he was insightful. And he delivered that insight skillfully and truthfully.

Strasberg's gift was authenticity, how to stay in touch with that inner voice. He tried to awaken a sense of truth and faith in the reality of our own senses, calling us each time to the present. He taught the difference between the words 'to seem' and 'to be'—helping us each find the path to our own 'being.' He could not tolerate pretense. He showed us how to bring images to life through the truth of the soul rather than the over-worked stencils we mistake for authentic behavior. Interested in the inner life of the human spirit, the internal dialogue of the here and now, he brought us back to us.

I loved Strasberg's class, but it was over far too soon. At the end of the summer, Strasberg packed up and left for his home in New York, leaving an empty spot in his absence. I missed the intensity of the class. Wanting to pursue this further and trying to hang on to that feeling of being present, I auditioned for a colleague of his, Stella Adler. Unlike the welcoming, unpretentious manner of Lee Strasberg, Stella Adler displayed 'Broadway Class.' The Grand Dame of the theater, she was royalty.

Madame Adler interviewed her prospective students in a theater somewhere between Hollywood and downtown Los Angeles. It was old and musty and had the smell of 'make-it here or pack-your-bags.' I waited in the lobby until my name was called. An assistant opened the theater door and escorted me down the aisle from the back of the pitch-black auditorium to the one spotlight focused in front of the stage. There was a stool. He pointed to the stool and disappeared into the darkness. I was blinded.

First there was darkness and then there was silence—a long, long period of silence. Then out of the void came a strong and articulate, slightly stylized, theatrical female voice:

49

"And what is your name dear?"

"Resa."

"And how old are you, my dear?"

"Twenty," I thought I said.

And then I thought she said, "Do you want to be twenty all your life?"

I froze. It was a test and I did not know what she meant. "I'm sorry," I stammered, drawing on all the strength I could find. "I don't know what you mean."

There was another very long moment of silence and then I could hear the smile in her voice. "Do you want to be *tweny* (which I guess is what I had said slurring my words in the vernacular and leaving out the 't') or do you want to be *twenTY?*" she queried enunciating properly.

"Oh!" I exclaimed taking her hint, and this time, with perfect diction, I replied, "TWENTY!" And I was in! And in HER class, unlike Strasberg's large cattle call, there were only fifteen students.

Stella Adler's class led me to Jeff Corey's doorstep and it was an honor. He was, at that time, considered to be one of the best acting coaches in Hollywood. His class, too, was filled with professionals. But Corey was a real character. He was persistent and ruthless. He shouted passionately as he spoke, relentless in his pursuit of authenticity in himself and his students. It was not just the feeling he was interested in, it was the thought behind the feeling that counted.

In the middle of a presentation, Jeff Corey would stop the class cold: "What were you thinking while you were feeling that?" his big nose, angular features and bushy eyebrows framing his tiny piercing eyes. "Who are you in there?" every gesture, every interaction of his seemed to query. "Are you here? All of you? Could there be more? Let's look." He never quit. And he was never satisfied. I will always be thankful for his tutelage. I learned about having conscious interactions and the difference between faking feelings and authenticity. I learned about being present. I learned about an internal sense of truth. I once again listened to that voice within and I learned I had no desire to be an actor. Parker Palmer writes:

> The teacher within is not the voice of con-
> science but of identity and integrity. It speaks
> not of what ought to be but of what is real for
> us, of what is true. It says things like, 'This is
> what fits you and this is what doesn't'; 'This is
> who you are and this is who you are not'; 'This
> is what gives you life and this is what kills your
> spirit—or makes you wish you were dead.' The
> teacher within stands guard at the gate of self-
> hood, warding off whatever insults our integrity
> and welcoming whatever affirms it. The voice
> of the inward teacher reminds me of my truth as
> I negotiate the force field of my life. (30-31)

Not knowing exactly what I wanted, I turned once again toward school. I was looking for "my place on the porch," an idiom I borrowed from Carlos Castaneda. In his book, The Teachings of Don Juan: A Yaqui Way of Knowledge, Carlos Castaneda describes aligning with what is correct in a person's life, what is integral to one's being. Castaneda, doing a field study on the Mexican Shaman for a UCLA doctorate thesis, embarks on a journey of enlightenment. In search of truth, he finds his way through the desert to Master Don Juan's house. But the master will not work with him until Castaneda finds his own spot on the porch—the spot that feeds his life force and gives him energy—the spot where he can sit without fatigue. Castaneda writes:

> What he had posed as a problem to be solved
> was certainly a riddle. I had no idea how to be
> gin or even what he had in mind. Several times

> I asked for a clue, or at least a hint, as to how to
> proceed in locating a point where I felt happy
> and strong. I insisted and argued that I had no
> idea what he really meant because I couldn't
> conceive the problem. He suggested I walk
> around the porch until I found the spot. (17)

So Castaneda proceeds. First, he stands at the door in excited expectation. Then, he paces for an hour or more. As the
hours pass he squats, he sits, he rolls, he changes his position
still expectant in attitude. In some spots he feels nothing,
others panic, frustration, anxiety or just plain restlessness. He
tries to use his brain to figure out the problem, but to no avail.
Finally, in the wee hours of the morning, he falls asleep
curled up on the floor only to be awakened by the gentle
nudge of a pair of feet. As he looks up in surprise, he sees
Don Juan laughing above his head. "You have found the
spot," the master said. Castaneda reflects that he, "...did not
understand him at first, but he assured me again that the place
where I had fallen asleep was the spot in question...." (20)

Although Castaneda did not exactly know where to sit, he
instinctively knew where not to sit. The places that caused
him discomfort were obviously not where he belonged.
Castaneda continues:

> I asked him if each of the two spots had a
> special name. He said that the good one was
> called the sitio and the bad one the enemy; he
> said these two places were the key to a man's
> well-being, especially for a man who was pur-
> suing knowledge. The sheer act of sitting on
> one's spot created superior strength; on the
> other hand, the enemy weakened a man and
> could even cause his death. He said I had re-
> plenished my energy, which I had spent lavishly

the night before, by taking a nap on my spot.
(21)

Unlike Castaneda, I had not yet found my spot. I was still standing by the door, leaning on the post and sitting on the rail. You could count me among the walking dead. In this predicament, I fidgeted my way through the Theater Department, the English Department, the Art Department and any other department at UCLA that would let me in.

Eventually, I found my way to the Psychology Department. I hoped to explore clinical psychology, but instead I found the department focused primarily on research. The clinical and more humane studies were at another campus. So I participated in behavioral psychology experiments for information and extra credit. The question of the day was the expansion of human consciousness. Plato writes:

> Man is declared to be that creature who is constantly in search of himself, a creature who at every moment of his existence must examine and scrutinize the conditions of his existence. He is a being in search of meaning. (Anshen, xiii)

At that time, students were watching Uri Geller and later, Diana Gazes, bend spoons. Telekinesis was the topic of the Ed Sullivan Special. Mind was over matter. Some of us had rediscovered what the universe knew forever: life was energy, thought was energy, feelings were energy and how we directed that energy changed things. I saw pictures of Kirilian photography, the Kodak snapshots of the energy around our hands, the leaves of a plant or any life form. I saw the Kirilian photographs of Mr. Geller's fingerprints change hours after the photos were taken, and I sat in on UCLA's attempt to document telepathy. As the Dalai Lama notes, "The non-perception of something does not prove its nonexistence."(28)

So the psychology lab conducted experiments. It was all very methodical. One person sat in the center of the group. The rest closed their eyes and tried to envision details about the person's life, what he was thinking, doing, what his house looked like and so on. The findings were recorded and their significance evaluated. If the quantity and quality of information fell outside the laws of probability, beyond what conventional research considered random or accidental, the outcome was considered telepathic.

And there was much that was considered telepathic. The participants were able to see in their mind's eye the exact pattern of the volunteer's bedspread, the name model, year and make of the car that person drove, the exact date of his last dentist appointment and much more.

It was exciting, but the minute I stepped outside the doors of the lab, I could not relate this experience to the world I knew. It was as if there was a great rift in the universe, a private one and a public one. I could not find a clear path, so once again I moved back into the world of the commonplace. I transferred and ended up in the Education Department. I had no idea why. Roberto Assagioli writes:

> Man's spiritual development is a long and arduous journey, an adventure through strange lands full of surprises, difficulties and even dangers. It involves a drastic transmutation of the 'normal' elements of the personality, an awakening of potentialities hitherto dormant, raising of consciousness to new realms, and a functioning along a new inner dimension. (250)

But the classes in the Education Department at that time had nothing to do with awakening potentialities. They had to do with classroom management and discipline, and very little else. I learned about techniques for controlling groups of children. I learned how to mold behavior by rewarding children for doing what I thought was right and by withholding reward for imperfect performance. I worked in a kindergarten classroom. Every Friday I robbed these children of their constitutional right of due process—I tested and graded them. By the end of the year, I had become prosecutor, judge, jury and executioner. I no longer liked who I was or what I was doing, so I transferred out of the Education Department. I was due to graduate and I was lost.

I sought advice. I talked to friends. I dialogued with my teachers. They all told me to talk to school counselors, but the counselors were not helpful. One suggested I go into oceanography because it was the up-and-coming field and I could make a living at it. Another suggested architecture because there was an opening in the department. Then I ran into a professor who came up with a novel idea. He said, "Do what you do best. Do what you love!"

At first, I couldn't think of anything. I tried to recall the classes I had taken. I tried to list the professions I knew. Nothing worked. I sat there feeling like an empty balloon. Then an image started to form. I remembered the beautiful dresses I had sewn in Berkeley. I remembered how I felt when I was designing them. I had a bizarre idea. In spite of my junior high school sewing class failure, I would go to graduate school in costume design!

It was two weeks before the application deadline. I found the head of design for the Theatre Department. Our paths had never crossed before. I introduced myself and asked if I could show him my portfolio (I didn't have one). Would he still be there in about two hours? Then I raced home, tore down my closet, grabbed every piece of artwork, scribble, craft and dress I had ever done—armloads of unorganized, crumpled, poorly presented examples of varying degrees of competency and doodles, and headed back to his office. It took about six trips to unload it all. I piled my work everywhere, on his desk, chair, floor—above his head. Looking back, I'm surprised he tolerated the confusion, but it must have made an impression.

Three out of fifty applicants were accepted, and I was one of the three. Not only was I accepted, I was hired as a teaching assistant. Shortly after that, I was given my own classes to teach. The following year, I was asked to run the department and continue teaching while the head of the department was on sabbatical. If I had been more alert, I would have noticed synchronicity weaving its wonders, opening the path I was supposed to follow. Instead, it took two years for me to finally understand why I was really there. It had nothing to do with costume design. I loved teaching. I loved teaching, because I loved learning. My whole journey of trial and error, searching and probing, switching disciplines, pointed me toward my true passion: I wanted to be THAT kind of teacher—the kind that was constantly learning.

I remember my father turning pale as I announced I wasn't leaving UCLA, but headed back to the Education Department. I wanted to teach. I felt impelled to teach. I was passionate. Parker Palmer talks about subjects that chose us:

> Many of us were called to teach by encountering not only a mentor but also a particular field of study. We were drawn to a body of knowledge because it shed light on our identity as well as on the world. We did not merely find a subject to teach—the subject also found us. We may recover the heart to teach by remembering how that subject evoked a sense of self that was only dormant in us before we encountered the subject's way of naming and framing life. (25)

By this time, the Education Department had expanded and offered a new holistic division of education. R. Griffin (1981) defines a holistic education as:

> ...an education which seeks to provide for the development of the student in mind, body and spirit. It is an education which aims at the integration of elements: self and world; mind and body; knowing and feeling; the personal and societal; the practical and transcendent. It sees the enrichment of the student's self-understanding and the enhancement of the student's sense of self-worth as providing the basis for the realization of these goals. (Wilson, 41)

The Los Angeles Unified School District at this time was also trying to move in a more holistic direction. It had just opened a series of alternative schools. These schools were housed in old storefronts, behind churches and in any space available within the area they served. I had the good fortune to visit a fifth grade creative writing class. It was held in a loft under the eaves of an old mansion that housed the school.

In that dimly lit space, devoid of books and tables and many of the trappings we associate with a real education, these children learned to write. Teacher and students sat in a circle on the floor of the attic and discussed where they wanted to live, in what, how, why and when. Each gave an oral description of his or her ideal living situation with great care and attention to detail. They were open, honest and focused. Then they wrote. There were no complaints and no one wanted to be interrupted. They were busy exploring, creating and relating their personal inner worlds to the external world they shared. Dr. Carl Rogers describes this type of experiential learning as having qualities not often tapped in current structures:

It has a quality of personal involvement—the whole person in both his feeling and cognitive aspects being IN the learning event. It is self-initiated. Even when the impetus or stimulus comes from the outside, the sense of discovery, of reaching out, of grasping and comprehending, comes from within. It is pervasive. It makes a difference in the behavior, the attitudes, perhaps even the personality of the learner. It is evaluated by the learner. He knows whether it is meeting his needs...The locus of evaluation, we might say, resides definitely in the learner.... When such learning takes place, the element of meaning to the learner is built into the whole experience. (Freedom to Learn, 5)

When this type of creativity comes from the inside out, when it is self-initiated and meaningful, it connects us to our greater selves. As Julia Cameron explains:

Creativity is the natural order of life.... When we open ourselves to our creativity, we open ourselves to the Creator's creativity within us and our lives.... Our creative dreams and yearnings come from a divine source. As we move toward our dreams, we move toward our divinity. (3)

To connect to our greater selves, we must shift perspective from thinking our children are empty vessels to be filled, to seeing them as already complete and engaged in the process of blossoming from the inside out.

Marilyn Ferguson writes about this connection to a bigger, more transcendent self. She says that there have always been those who, based on their own experience, believed we could change the human condition. We could transcend that condition by expanding our narrow and limited consciousness through a shift in perspective and therefore perception:

> Only through a new mind can humanity remake itself.... Open your eyes, they were saying, there is more. More depth, height, dimension, perspectives, choices than we had imagined. (45-46)

She explains that long before the threat of nuclear war or ecological extinction, visionaries warned of the dangers inherent in the path we were following:

> They feared for the future of a people without a context.... Humankind, they said, might recognize the subtle veils imposed on seeing; might awaken to the screen of custom, the prison of language and culture, the bonds of circumstance.... We are spiritually free, they said, the stewards of our own evolution. Humankind has a choice. We can awaken to our true nature. Drawing fully from our inner resources we can achieve a new dimension of mind; we can see more. (46)

Now, a group of educators who thought they could raise the bar of conscious learning had made it into teacher training. They gave us an opportunity to learn about ourselves, not just through theory but experience. It was a new curriculum. Two to three hours a day, two to three times a week, we broke into discussion groups. These groups were designed to explore our own consciousness so that we might facilitate greater possibilities within our students. The process was unforgettable. It initiated me into the mysteries of growth nurtured through relationships and much more. I was introduced to the works of Carl Rogers, William Glasser, Eric Fromm, John Holt, Jerome Bruner, Neil Postman and Charles Weingartner and many other insightful thinkers, and the world remained open and fresh. And I remained driven, excited and ecstatic.

Postman and Weingartner posed the question, "What's worth knowing?" John Holt investigated the tendency of children to create their own structures in pursuit of the freedom to learn. Eric Fromm dove into the deeper issues of what's at our core and Dr. Glasser proposed a system of growth without failure. I was moved. I went transpersonal.

A transpersonal education is not a method; it is a perspective. The methods are as limitless as our imaginations. The perspective focuses on "the transcendent capabilities of human beings." Marilyn Ferguson defines the process as one in which:

> ...the learner is encouraged to be awake and autonomous, to question, to explore all the corners and crevices of conscious experience, to seek meaning, to test outer limits, to check out frontiers and depths of the self. (287)

This approach bridges the dogma of a strict, rigid format and the chaos of a lack of structure driven predominantly by emotional criteria. It is more humane than a traditional structure and more intellectually vigorous than other alternatives. It is holistic, attempting to gather up the whole person within a much larger definition linked to much greater possibilities. Ferguson writes:

> Transpersonal education is the process of exposing people to the mysterious in themselves —and then getting out of the way so you don't get run over. (287-288)

Rogers describes his own experience with this process as being transcendent:

> This whole train of experience, and the mean-ings that I have thus far discovered in it, seem to have launched me on a process which is both fascinating and at times a little frightening. It seems to mean letting my experience carry me on, in a direction which appears to be forward, toward goals that I can but dimly define, as I try to understand at least the current meaning of that experience. The sensation is that of floating with a complex stream of experience, with the fascinating possibility of trying to comprehend its ever-changing complexity. (On Becoming A Person, 154)

Rogers was impassioned. And so was I! I finally left the university after eight years, with a Bachelor of Arts and Master of Fine Arts in Theatre Arts. I had full minors in English and psychology, earning elementary, secondary, community college and university level teaching credentials in multiple subject areas, including a specialization in reading.

But I left sensing there was more, a lot more.
I left longing for the possibilities.

Love Rekindles the Inner Spirit... but What Keeps It Alive?

"In everyone's life, at some time, our inner fire goes out. It is then burst into flame by an encounter with another human being. We should all be thankful for those people who rekindle the inner spirit."
Albert Schweitzer

Love rekindles the inner spirit. It is our greatest connection for learning, our finest vehicle for growth and transformation. In <u>Sacred Scriptures</u>, Timothy Freke writes:

> Love is the Way.... Our essential nature is love and love is the way to awaken it. The Hindu Mundaka Upanishad teaches that the self cannot

be known through thoughts, but only through love. To awaken this love is the goal of life. Love reveals to us a permanent truth beyond the transient nature of this world. (92)

Dr. Joan Borysenko, cellular biologist and psychotherapist, writes:

People who have near-death experiences return not only with the sense that love is the most important thing, but that love awakens the desire for wisdom. They say that love and wisdom are the only two things we take with us from this life, because they are the substance of our souls. (213)

A loving relationship is the foundation of all meaningful learning. Love is our basic nature. But we fail to recognize this core truth within our search for identity. A journey of self-discovery is a journey of relationship, a journey of love. To make that sojourn, we need each other.

Every time we interact, every time our paths cross in any form, we learn who we are in relation to each other; we learn about love. We measure our value and identity against our ability to love and be loved. Every story is a love story, regardless of the content, because it teaches us about us.

I was twenty-seven years old, out of school and about to be married. It was a beautiful wedding. I remember saying, "I do," amidst banners of flowers and white satin lace. I dieted for three months vowing never to eat chocolate again. I recall the smell and crinkle of the tissue wrappings of new underslips and corsages, and seeing miles of white veiled netting weaving through images in the many-mirrored dressing room. I was hoping they'd save me an hors d'oeuvre. Pictures of ageless women in long white tea dresses and a gentler era filled my mind, and I could smell the orange blossoms and the newly mown grass. I was full of hope and love and naïveté. (Years later—three children, four dogs, two cats and a horse later, I would tell my daughter, "When you say I Do, REMEMBER to say I DO WHAT? What is it I do?") The two little curls at the side of my forehead wouldn't relax.

Love draws us together. Love is our link to each other. The invisible grid that binds, love is life's relationship to itself. Without love, there would be nothing to connect us to each other. We would have an empty world full of strangers. There would be no families, no friendships and no reason to ever interact. Love provides answers to those questions lodged deep within our hearts: "Who are we? Why are we here?" Without love, we are cut off from ourselves.

My groom's name was Dennis. Tall, dark and handsome, he had come to rescue me as he paced nervously outside the garden wall. I loved his moustache. His white tux glistened in the warm July sun.

Relationship in Latin means referre, relatum, to bring back. Through our relationships with each other we learn to bring love back into our lives.

The night before our wedding I had a dream Dennis and I were playing Romeo and Juliet, leaping together from balcony to balcony throughout the corridors of time. We were married July 25th, 1976. We will always leap together.

Love should be the lens through which we view all life. Yet, we have taken love in its many forms out of almost all our expressions of living. We have limited it to our closest family and friends. Bringing feelings of attachment, of concern or love into our public life and institutions is not considered 'professional.' We have a nonverbal agreement to leave these feelings at home. They are not to be brought into public, not into the workplace or any other social institution—not even school, the place we entrust with our young.

But without love in our schools, teachers whither, children remain unengaged, and learning is a chore. Teachers wonder why they chose this profession and students look for excitement elsewhere. Without love in our schools to rekindle the inner spirit, everyone in the system is transformed from a blossoming human being into a management problem. Maria Montessori writes:

> ...this love, which is the gift of every tiny child who is brought into our midst—if this were realized in its potentialities, or if the fullness of its values were developed, our achievements, already so vast, would become immeasurable.... Love is conceded to man as a gift directed to a certain purpose, and for a special reason.... It must be treasured, developed and enlarged to the fullest possible extent. (<u>Absorbent Mind</u>, 293)

Without love to ignite that spark of passion and brilliance, we cannot discover who we are.

❧ 8 ❧

On the Tracks

I am sitting at my desk in my office at school. I run a home-school program for a local school district. We are fortunate in that this program has the blessing and support of all of its superintendents and the school board. The program is full of love, warmth and compassion and the families in it are finding passion and brilliance at every turn. But the district is big and not all families are as lucky.

The third mother this week walks in with the same story. This one is angry. She anticipates that I am just like the person who fought her back at her daughter's high school. As she moves into the room, I see a young girl, about fifteen, crouched behind her. She is thin and shadows her mother. Her taut fingers cling to the edge of her mother's shirt. Her eyes hide behind an overgrown hedge of bangs. She doesn't want to be here. As the mother advances, the daughter releases her grasp, swings around and ducks back into the hall. She does not make it two feet past the door.

Mom is challenging. O.K. What does she have to do to legally pull her child out of that school and teach her at home? Am I going to try to stop her? What does she have to do?

I try to calm her down, but she is not listening to my words. She lunges forward, face red and neck tight. Perhaps she is afraid that if she listens, I will knock her down. Perhaps she feels it is either her victory or mine. An image strikes me. I am standing on a railroad track facing an oncoming locomotive. The engine is not fast, but persistent. I brace my arms and feet—right leg back, left leg forward. My right hand is positioned like a stop sign. I am not superman. I am not trying to derail or stop the train. The best I could hope for is that the train sees me before it hits. I would like to explain.

Dear locomotive,

Although I, too, find myself on the tracks, I do not work for the railroad. I would like to help. I appreciate the problem. I understand. You think you need the track in order to move forward. You cannot conceive of any other way. Yet, the track is your nemesis. It is limiting. It restricts your direction and keeps you traveling in circles. What to do?

I think I can help.

Sincerely,

Resa Brown
Mom First, Homeschool Coordinator Second

I look back at the mother. She says she has other kids, but this child panics the moment they enter the school parking lot. Her heart races, her pulse soars, she breaks out into a sweat and cannot move. Nobody knows why… It is the test.

Mom sits down. Her eyes well up with tears despite her anger. She has been trying to get her daughter extra help in reading and math through this district for years. No one has helped. No one has listened to her. It was district triage and her daughter was not considered deficient enough to warrant help.

Now the child is lost and scared to death. Her grades have been slipping. Her anxiety grows nightly. She does not understand what is happening in the classroom. She freezes. She cannot keep up with the assignments and homework. They can't get her out of the car in the morning. She doesn't make it past the parking lot and into the classroom without a panic attack. Their pediatrician wants to put her on medication. Mom says, "Enough is enough!"

I think of my eldest son, Stephen. He would never have been able to 'keep up.' Neither would his brother, Matthew.

The test is not about what they know. It is the way to hold growing human beings emotionally captive by making them dependent on a system of arbitrary rewards and rules and punishments. The system defines their identity and feelings of self-worth. It keeps them off balance. The longer they are in the system, the worse it gets. I look back and wonder, when I was a teacher, what damage did I do?

9

You, Me and a Positive Relationship

"A positive learning climate in a school for young children is a composite of many things. It is an attitude that respects children. It is a place where children receive guidance and encouragement from the responsible adults around them. It is an environment where children can experiment and try out new ideas without fear of failure. It is an atmosphere that builds children's self-confidence so they dare to take risks. It is an environment that nurtures a love of learning."

Carol B. Hillman

It was a beach community. My students had the smell of fresh air, seaweed and suntan lotion. They reminded me of summer all year long, of my own childhood at Santa Monica beach, transistor radio and Coppertone oil, face down on an old beach towel. Only I was the teacher now.

School is our first major connection to love in the outside world. It provides the social structure within which we interact. It creates the framework of experience that tells us who we are and how we feel about ourselves in relation to others. It is the backdrop for measuring our ability to love and be loved on a stage bigger than the family unit.

My first job in the K-12 structure was in a middle school. It was brand new and designed to be an improvement in education. Careful planning had gone into the physical plant to facilitate student management. The architecture was innovative. Classrooms radiated around a large assembly room. Each room had moveable walls that folded back on tracks in the ceiling. Teachers could create a small intimate space or a large multi-purpose classroom at their discretion. The environment was climatically controlled. There were a lot of brightly colored orange walls. No windows. The architect had eliminated fresh air and sunlight. The teachers eliminated the rest.

The designers of the building and the school board that approved its innovative but ambiguous concept never consulted the teachers. And no one consulted the children. The teachers ignored the creative structural design. The kids ignored the teachers.

The teachers were uncompassionate and highly resistant to change. They viewed themselves as they had for the last fifty years, as data entry technicians. They believed their job was to input information, test the results and evaluate the outcome. It was impersonal and scientific. They ignored creativity. They ignored humanity. They ignored the effect they had on their young charges. Emotions were viewed as abnormalities. The relationship between teachers and students was reduced to managing paperwork and mitigating or eliminating any reactions that got in the way. The kids would have preferred a window.

Intentional or not, school creates the template for our identity and self-worth. Dr. William Glasser says the single basic need we have is for identity. Identity is based on our relationships. A successful identity is based on the sense that we are someone special, important and worthwhile in relation to others. Feelings of love and self-worth are integral to our sense of self. If we are well treated, we feel good about ourselves. If we are treated with disdain, we doubt our value. When we are continually measured, judged, reprimanded and told we fall short, we feel bad about ourselves. When we feel bad, we develop identities of failure that rarely disappear. We will carry that identity and those feelings into every relationship and every endeavor for the rest of our lives.

Most teachers, however, do not realize that they are building the identities of hundreds of children every year. Many of these teachers have taught thirty years or more. Their reactions to their students were preprogrammed and reinforced. Teachers believed they already knew who was going to walk through their classroom doors and how they would respond.

Seeing children through a pre-constructed lens, the teachers' expectations fulfilled themselves. Attitudes and judgments based on first impressions of haircuts, clothes, language and even handwriting all factored into the teachers' treatment of their students. In the teachers' minds, children could not all be wonderful. There had to be a curve. Some children had to be more successful than others. The teachers could perceive no alternative, and they managed the classroom to produce that result. Only a small percentage of children would get the best scores. Children were evaluated against each other, making competitors out of friends. Grades, based on this competitive evaluation, showed up two or three days later after the class had moved on to other assignments and the children had no idea how to learn from their mistakes. It was a charade. Papers were passed back full of undecipher able red marks and a letter grade that gave the recipients no information. It only conveyed a defective identity. It never taught them how to correct their errors. Most children were unsuccessful most of the time and did not know why.

The execution of this constant scrutiny and evaluation teaches self-preservation instead of openness and receptivity to growth. The evaluation is not a collaborative venture between teacher and student. It is solely and arbitrarily dispensed by the teacher. This destroys any relationship of trust between student and teacher. It creates an underlying guardedness no matter how congenial the relationship may appear on the surface. It turns the teacher into someone who can dispense emotional pain. It creates an environment of separation, distance and fear. The student is at the teacher's mercy. Dr. Glasser writes:

> By…accepting each child's thinking…and by utilizing his mistakes as a basis for future teaching, we have a way of approaching the child that supports him. The present system of accentuating his mistakes tears the child down and makes him unable or unwilling to think. (Schools Without Failure, 144)

Within a critical environment, a child's receptivity is replaced by fear of judgment. Fear does not create a good learning environment because learning involves taking not just intellectual, but emotional risks. To do that, there must be trust. Fear and trust cannot occupy the same place at the same time.

When we provide non-judgmental environments in which to explore, children and adults alike are not afraid to take risks. In an environment of trust we open our hearts, as well as our minds, to new information and possibilities. When we get closer to each other on the outside, we get closer to ourselves on the inside. Our identities become more authentic.

Only then do we find the passion and brilliance that is ours. Only then do we all grow.

But teachers are not trained to build nurturing relationships with our children. Dr. Glasser observes that teachers are just taught to use an old psychiatric model of noninvolvement and emotional distance to separate themselves from their students. This paradigm is detrimental to everyone's well being. It creates relationships that magnify the sense of loneliness and isolation many students already feel. In The Lonely Crowd, David Riesman describes the traditional role of the contemporary teacher as removed and inaccessible. He writes:

> As schools became more plentiful…the obligation to train the child… falls upon the teacher. But the teacher does not work close to the child's emotional level. And the teacher regards her job as a limited one…. The physical setting in school reflects this situation. Seating is formal—all face front—and often alphabetical. The walls are decorated with the ruins of Pompeii and the bust of Caesar. For all but the few exceptional children who can transcend the dead forms of their classical education and make the ancient world come alive, these etchings and statues signify the irrelevance of the school to the emotional problems of the child. The teacher herself has neither understanding of nor time for these emotional problems, and the child's relation to other children enters her purview only in disciplinary cases. (58)

An emotionally sterile and judgmental environment will never create a good learning environment no matter how innovative the intent. William Ayers explains.

> Teaching is a human activity, constrained and made possible by all the limits and potential that characterize any other human activity. Teaching depends on people—people who choose to teach and other people who become students, by choice or not. There are these two sides to teaching, and on each side there are human beings, whole people with their own unique thoughts, hopes, dreams, aspirations, needs, experiences, contexts, agendas, and priorities. Teaching is relational and interactive. It requires dialogue, give and take, back and forth. It is multi-directional. This explains in part why every teaching encounter is particular, each unique in its details. (16)

No innovation, no structure, no method, no curriculum can create contact and communication. Only people can do that. To create a learning environment where our children can have successful identities and feel safe and secure enough to open their hearts to growth, we must create relationships that open our hearts to love. Jeannie Oakes and Marty Lipton write:

> As Vygotsky and other socioculturalists demonstrate, people learn in relationships—that is, social and cognitive development are inseparable. Consequently, a caring classroom relationship is part of a 'search for competence,' and, as it is a relationship, there are two people searching…. The relationships between teachers and students and among students shape academic learning, [and] intrapersonal learning… (252)

I left at the end of the school year, when my contract was up. But at a time when school districts were cutting back and teaching jobs were scarce, I had no problem locating my next job. The next district had openings they could not fill. It was very different from the more popular laid-back atmosphere of the beach. It was a war zone.

East of downtown Los Angeles, this high school had once been the center of an old-line upper-class community. Most of the children in this area had grown up and moved away. The remaining children who lived on the estates back in the hills were sent off to private boarding schools. As the upper class student population dwindled, district lines were redrawn to include the population increase in surrounding communities. These poverty stricken areas were refuge for the immigrant poor. The lives of indigent children are not often discussed in child development classes. Poverty communities never quite make it to the syllabus. The turmoil, angst and fears of their daily realities should not be overlooked.

We may label them 'students' having euphemized the depth and vulnerability of their private lives, but these kids had adult responsibilities. They had little time to grow as children. Parents gone pre-dawn looking for work, no food for breakfast, uncooperative younger siblings left in their care, made them less than eager and largely unprepared for school in the morning. Many missed their first period classes because they just couldn't make it on time. Some missed whole days because the sitter never showed up or the daycare facility suddenly shut down without warning. They were constantly robbed of their energy and enthusiasm for the day. When they finally did arrive at school, they were often too tired or too hungry to study. Confused and distracted they bungled through the day. Life forced them into early adulthood; teachers infantilized them—all creating a split in their identities, self-respect and spirit.

Evening was even worse. By nightfall the tensions of the day permeated their overcrowded dwellings making little room for personal space or emotional calm, let alone homework. The students faced violence on the streets, abuse in their homes and turmoil in their hearts. The structure of the school ignored these realities.

My sister was going through her doctoral training in psychology in a college suburb in the Midwest. She worked with children and often talked about childhood 'disorders.' The contrast was vivid. The children I saw didn't have the opportunity to have a 'disorder.' They were too busy trying to survive.

And school wasn't any gentler on them. Penalized and repremanded for missing homework assignments mislaid in the midst of episodes of domestic violence, English assignments posted with failure, endless reams of mathematics computations drilled into children who badly needed hugs instead of points—all created an environment ripe for frustration and violence. The classes the school offered were irrelevant to the needs of most of these children—children who were still trying to find their place in a hostile world. School should, at the very least, provide a safe shelter, a daily ear and a chance for children to relate their day in school to their days and nights outside—a chance to give a child voice and be heard.

Time at school would be better spent finding and supporting children's strengths, rather than focusing on their weaknesses and pounding out their failures. It is a toxic environment. At the end of the school day, very few children left feeling better than when they arrived.

And a toxic environment is poison for everybody. The teachers were mean, hostile, defensive, disgruntled, frustrated and forlorn. They picked on the kids, picked on each other, gossiped behind everyone's backs and created their own pecking order. Then everyone gave them power—the kids, the parents and the community.

But their careers didn't start out that way. Many teachers arrived at that school with their hearts open—willing to love, wanting to cherish the relationships they would build with their students and colleagues, hoping to make a difference. Instead, they found a system that was almost as indifferent to their needs and hostile to their presence as it was to their students'.

The seasoned teachers were always on guard, defending their departmental positions. The newest teachers got the worst assignments, the most difficult classes, and duties like hall patrol during volatile periods of high tension. New teachers were put in situations they neither had the skill nor the support to win. Under these circumstances the assistance of a more experienced teacher would have been helpful; but rather than trying to fix problems, school officials preferred to ignore them.

Unrest and malaise, repression and hostility were rampant. There were food fights, street fights, knife fights, and gunfights—but there were still student body elections. The administration insisted on business as usual, so the kids took the election posters still stapled to hallway walls and set them on fire. Then they set the bushes on fire. After that they set the trash cans on fire and flung them three stories down the stairwells. The flaming trash cans hit the basement. The smoke triggered the automatic fire alarm. The emergency sprinkler systems went off. The basement flooded. And the best the administration could do was to summon the janitor to mop up the mess.

My classroom was in that basement. It had high transom windows that opened onto the ground floor outside. I was told to keep the door to the classroom locked. If I smelled smoke, I was supposed to tell my students to climb onto the counters and crawl out the transoms before the room filled with water. Try delivering those instructions with a straight face.

By the end of the year the administration finally figured out how to correct the problem—they turned the sprinklers off so the basement wouldn't flood when the fires hit.

Within this scenario, no one was really happy, not the teachers, not the students locked into their classrooms and not those retaliating. When fear is rampant, needs go unmet, relationships deteriorate, students rebel and teachers react.

Dr. Glasser has constructed a model that identifies five basic needs on which good relationships and strong, healthy identities are built: "love/belonging, power, survival, freedom and fun." (Quality School Teacher, 19) When student and teacher have a satisfying relationship, genuine love and compassion have an opportunity to grow. When there is collaboration, when both student and teacher have a voice, there is power, freedom and trust. When there is unconditional love, which cannot co-exist with the practice of grading children, there is security and self-fulfillment. When there is intimacy, there is belonging. When there is laughter and genuine joy, there is fun. When we create environments that nurture solid, unconditionally loving, empowering relationships, the benefit is not just to the individual, but to us all.

When we create an educational structure whose goal is to satisfy our basic need for love within our relationships, we transform our experience of who we are and how we perceive the world. We nurture a state of well being that promotes self-fulfillment, joy, wonder, gratitude, cooperation and compassion—all the attributes of inner peace. When we experience inner peace, we treat each other better. We replace climates of violence with enlightenment and compassion.

An institution for human growth cannot ignore the human relationships on which all learning is built and be effective. If we continue to send our children to the educational structure as it currently exists, we will continue to struggle with the problems we have created within that structure. When our children cannot develop an identity through love and self-worth, they have only three options. They can withdraw from a society that deprives them of their basic needs, they can rebel against it, or they can comply. Compliance is the most deadly because it masks a child's true self and destroys the child's integrity and will. The greatest tragedy for a compliant child is that no one knows something is wrong. According to Arthur Jersild:

> The compliant child...moves with the tide, so to speak.... He yields...the compliant one may meekly accept everyone else's verdict as to what he should learn or think.... But this compliance is a means of self-protection, not a form of self-fulfillment. (33)

Jersild claims that children who incorporate this strategy are playing an assumed role, one that does not reflect their real selves. To deal with their situation, they begin a process of self-alienation. Dr. Karen Horney writes that this maladaptive strategy becomes integrated into a 'pseudo-identity' through which the child adopts, "less than honest strategies for dealing with others." (Jersild, 34)

The truth is, it's not only the students who adopt this strategy of compliance and self-alienation. Teachers also feel trapped in a system that masks their identity and attacks their integrity. William Ayers writes that in spite of the image of the dedicated, caring teacher, many schools disempower teachers, pre-specifying their thoughts and constraining their activities. He explains:

> In large, impersonal systems, teachers become obedient, they conform, and follow rules...we [teachers] are expected to deliver the curriculum without much thought, and control the students without much feeling. Students are expected, in turn, to follow the rules and go along with whatever is put before them. The key lessons for everyone in such a school system, top to

> bottom, are about hierarchy and one's place in
> it, convention and one's obligation to it, and un-
> questioning passivity in the face of authority.
> (19)

The district was run by politics. The personal agendas of those in charge had little or nothing to do with the welfare of either student or teacher. There was animosity among the ruling lords, and students and teachers were caught in the crossfire. The principal asked for innovation; the Head of the English Department ordered a pre-canned curriculum and methodology. Following the dictates of the supervising department, there was no room for creativity, deviation or experimentation. The two sets of directions contradicted each other. It was a petty chess game and we were the pawns. But even pawns can learn.

In the time I was there, I became skillful. I figured out how to get young adults to hand in their knives without anyone getting hurt. I dodged gunfights between rival gangs. I put up rolls of paper along the hallway leading to the art exhibit, so the kids would scribble their graffiti on the paper instead of on the paintings. I took my husband with me for protection whenever we had an event after school hours. I missed the Christmas dance, when they beat up the boys' vice principal in the lavatory, and I was absent the day the teachers' windshields were shot out in the faculty parking lot.

So when Dennis and I had an opportunity to move ninety miles up the coast and two hours away from the violence, I enthusiastically resigned and took the next teaching position that came along. It was in a cozy continuation high school with a faculty of four and a student body of sixty. These kids had failed both the traditional high school and the local alternative school. This was their last chance before they either dropped out or were thrown out of school altogether. They came to us drunk, stoned, distraught, labile, hostile and fearfully quiet, or just lost, but their problems were far more internal than the stark realities of East Los Angeles.

I taught the subjects I loved, English and art. Attendance was taken by the hour. The goal was to get students to arrive at eight o'clock in the morning and stay until lunch. After lunch, there was one-on-one time, parent conferences and help from other professionals like psychologists and speech therapists. I had time to evaluate my students on a daily basis, time to plan and invent new solutions to meet each child's individual needs.

My art class was an immediate success, but almost no one showed up for English. They didn't like to read. They didn't know how to read. They didn't want to read. And they hated writing. That pretty much killed an English class. So I tried to think 'outside-the-box.'

The kids liked to 'hang out.' Knowing this, I replaced their desks with a few couches and some old, over-stuffed armchairs. Then I bought twenty copies of Carlos Castaneda's search for truth among the Yaki shamans. I hoped it would speak to their search for identity and integrity, or at least open up a dialogue.

My students began by reading out loud. They took turns. It worked for about fifteen minutes. Reading was laborious, and for their peer audience so was listening. So, I read—full of the enthusiasm and fervor of an ex-drama student.

Attendance soared. The eight attendees increased to the full fifteen with a few extras. I cancelled art as an hour by itself and opened the room up to anyone who wanted to listen, including those students who wanted to draw or paint while they listened. I used Castaneda's series as a vehicle for every lesson possible from reading, word attack skills, literary analysis, spelling and journal writing, to discussions on sociology, history and of course, philosophy. There was greater attendance, fewer kids showed up stoned or drunk, and above all, there was enthusiasm in the morning.

I loved my job. I felt empowered, creative, trusted and worthwhile. I was going to work there forever. Then, three months later…after looking the principal straight in the eye and telling him I had no intention of starting a family and leaving the school…my husband convinced me, 'it was time.'

PART II

Flying by the Seat
of Our Pants

10

Vulnerable

"**Pregnant.** (preg'nant) adj. 1. having a child or other offspring developing in the body. 2. fraught, filled, or abounding (usually followed by with): *a silence pregnant with suspense.* 3. teaming or fertile, rich (often followed by in): *a mind pregnant in ideas.* 4. full of meaning, highly significant: *a pregnant utterance.* 5. great important or potential, momentous: *a pregnant moment in the history of the world.*"

"**Pregnable.** (preg'na-ble) adj. 1. Open to attack."

Random House Dictionary
2nd Edition Unabridged

The school year ended in June. It was now August and I was hot and nine months pregnant. I was expecting our first-born and looked forward to returning to my students six weeks later.

Meanwhile, Dennis and I had been living an enchanted life. We were two working adults with two incomes, responsible only to and for each other. We had a brand new tract home in the suburbs. We had each other and a dream. I looked at his tall frame, cherished his handsome, stunning features and thanked heaven he was in my life. (I still do). We talked and laughed a lot. (We still do). We had energy for each other, totally absorbed, undistracted energy. And life was simple. (Never again!) Dennis met me after work for a quick game of tennis and then dinner out. The house was always clean and there was plenty of time to spare. I joined a gym for women and spent the afternoon lounging by the pool. It was the first and last time we ever lived like that.

Then, one night, it hit—the transformation. We were at my mother's house having dinner. I thought I had gas. I was running my fork back and forth through the mashed potatoes when I realized something else was going on. I didn't feel so hot. I stood up, walked out of the kitchen, staggered down the hall to the back bedroom and curled up on the bed. I wasn't sure why. Our baby would not be arriving for another couple of weeks. The doctor said so that morning. So I left his office, went back to the pool and swam a mile. Now I had gas.

Dennis came running after me down the hall. I wanted to be left alone…I wanted him to stay…I wanted to be left alone. The poor guy didn't know whether to come or go. Then I snapped at him. Then he left.

Halfway down the hall, he turned on his heels and came back. "Are you in labor?" The pain hit. I missed the first two phases of labor and went right into transition. We barely made it down that hall. We hardly made it to the car. I was sure we weren't going to make it to the hospital.

Panicked, I yelled at him for driving too fast. Then I screamed at him to hurry. Frustrated, he forgot to get on the freeway. Then he stepped on the gas.

We sailed into the hospital emergency loading zone. He hit the brake and ran for a nurse and a wheelchair. I focused on the dash and tried to breathe. Two male medics showed up with a gurney. I looked at the prospect of standing all that way up and then actually rolling over and laying down on that gurney and decided they must be crazy. I'd have the baby in the car. At least I wouldn't have to move. Dennis showed up with the wheelchair.

We made it into the emergency room. I wanted to kick the admission's nurse who kept us in her office as she insisted I remember my social security number and insurance carrier. They let us up the elevator to the maternity ward anyway.

We made it to the birthing room. I decided to have the baby in the wheelchair rather than face the prospect of moving again. Two attendants, four strong arms in white, descended on me. The next thing I knew, I was on the bed focusing on the tall fir tree outside the window.

Dennis coached me through every contraction. Each breath I took, he took. He counted his way through every second for me. Five hours later our son, Stephen, was born.

Who was inside this blanket I held? Where did he come from? What does he feel? What does he think? So tiny, so completely helpless and dependent! I was overcome with love. I looked down to share this moment with my husband and found him by the side of my bed, on the floor—sound asleep. We left the next morning to go home to learn how to be a family. Stephen Covey writes:

> Love is a verb. It's also a commitment...the most fundamental promises we make to other human beings are those we make to the members of our family—in our marriage vows, in our implicit promises to care for and nurture our children. (Seven Habits of Highly Effective Families, 99)

To Our Stephen:

First there was nothing, then there was you. There was hope and anticipation, a query of the unknown and the slightest flutter deep inside my womb. There were walks with your father, his hand on my stomach trying to catch the trail of your movement, trying to communicate. There was humming and singing and even reading. There was your startled kick as I leaned across the dryer to turn it on; the noise startled me too. There was the resting and caring and a change in diet—the watching of weight and calcium and protein and fresh things. There was the moment of labor. The wondering what will happen next. The immersion in your delivery, my soul enwrapped around yours, listening, undulating—feeling the rapture, the ecstasy, the involvement in the pain of the phoenix giving rise to form anew. There was love all around without separation from your struggle for emergence. You and I, one form about to become two. And then there was you. And for your Dad and me, there was only you—our energy, our focus, our perception of life itself. You gave us meaning and life renewed. You made us parents.

My six weeks of maternity leave from school was up. Do I apply for a six-month extension? I ran ads in the newspaper for caretakers. I talked to friends for referrals. I called every agency I could find. I did not want to give up the life I had built for myself at school. I did not want to leave my baby to daycare. No one could love this child like I could. I couldn't wait to see my students. I was at war with myself.

The decision to stay home was tough. I was afraid. I knew how to run through the noise of a busy schedule. I didn't know how to sit home in the quiet and silence of the day. I was used to being up at six and at school at seven. I was used to moving fast.

At home, I was lost, anxious and confused. In the quiet and stillness, I had to face myself. Life slowed to every breath, and I found myself listening to all the spaces in between. There was no television. We didn't want one. There was no radio. We hadn't gotten around to buying one. There was no noise, no distraction, just Stephen and me. I cleaned the house, mindful that there was a sentient being in that infant seat. No one was knocking on my door telling me what a wonderful job I had done on the kitchen sink. There was no dust or grime review. By the end of the day, the house was dirty again in the next flutter of activity. Erma Bombeck's voice kept echoing through my head —something about the epitaph on a housewife's tombstone. "Here she lies. She cleaned."

But I was cleaning more than a physical house; I was sweeping out internal clutter and debris. I let go of my career and identity in a world that recognized people by their job description. I just was, without title, external reward or recognition, without expectation of the next event, the next hurdle, or the next challenge and certainly without glory.

The immediate needs of an infant, the nursing on demand, the cuddling, the cooing, the eye-to-eye contact during this most intimate of times, preempted almost every activity. There were days when going to the bathroom and getting a shower was a challenge. Getting out of the sweats I slept in was impossible. I could no longer set a goal and have any certainty I would achieve it, because I chose to put my baby first.

And when my husband came home at night, I was hard pressed to tell him what I did or what had happened. I felt ineffective, but I was being made whole.

❧ 11 ❧

The Hidden Curriculum

Return to the present. We are back at Panera. It is eight forty-eight in the evening and my daughter and her friends have been studying all day, the seven of them. Around them people eat, but these students do not notice. They are riveted to their studies. They are again teaching each other, figuring out the answers. I can't believe they are not starving.

I order a Fuji apple chicken salad for myself. The four-by-six inch flier propped up on the table announces this new salad. It reads, "A crisp and refreshing new mix makes its debut"…it's talking about the salad. I look over at the kids. So carnoot! The ad continues, "Our new Fuji apple chicken salad offers a festival of flavors and textures…" I look at the kids again. I see three different races, an indeterminate age span and two distinct sexes. They come from at least two different states and seven different colleges. When will they be allowed to make their debut? When will they have passed their rites of passage? Who will be allowed to bloom? My daughter orders a bowl of bean soup with cheese. We eat at a table away from the other students. I feel bad. I am the only mommy there.

Another hour passes. They must be starving. I walk past the other diners to the cashier. "A box of pastries for the table please...and throw in some extra knives so they can share." There is enough for everyone.

I carry the pastries back past the self-absorbed diners. I put the box on the center of their table. Eyes light! They dive! But they are polite, cutting the muffies in half. There aren't seven of each flavor. They are mindful of the mixture. They care about each other.

I watch their faces lit by the low, overhanging lights. They are all crowded around one book, all seven of them. The light is soft. It casts beautiful shadows across these gentle faces. I recall an old nineteenth century oil painting, where the surgeons are all gathered around the operating table. The artist has captured the character and personality, the sense of earnestness and absorption, reflected in each face. I wish I had a camera. I think I will never forget these kids. They have my heart. Josh says he is going home to play a mindless video game and recharge his brain. Elaine thanks everyone. The group breaks up. They all thank Koe. He helped and it wasn't even his comprehensive. Erin and I stay a little longer. She continues to study for the test.

I think of Erin's brothers. Stephen is in graduate school at UCLA in computer electronics. He is weeks away from finishing his master's thesis. Matthew just graduated UCLA with a Bachelor's of Science in Mathematics/Applied Science Management and Accounting with a Specialization in Computing. Not bad for two kids who would have been labeled dyslexic, dysgraphic and having ADHD had they been processed through our regular school system. Stephen didn't read until he was nine. He entered college at twelve. Matthew didn't read until he was ten, and then he entered college a year later at eleven. Had they been sorted, tested and labeled when they were little, they would not have had the confidence to excel. They would have been put in remedial classes and resource rooms. Their behaviors would have been molded to defeat, their minds forced to follow the format and their bodies pinned behind their desks. Their failures would have been reinforced in report card after report card. They would have lost touch with their true identities—the particular genius each child has at birth. They would never have had the opportunity to discover their passions and brilliance.

I think about the comprehensive, the test Erin and her friends are trying to pass. There is so much to study, so many possible permutations and ways of coming to an answer; there is no possible way to study with any certainty of success. If they studied day and night for the next ten years, they could still not possibly guess what would be on the test. So for them, what is the test? They face fear and anxiety. Their ability to pursue this passion for math is precariously balanced on how well they guess what to study. They put their lives, their identities, their self-confidence on hold—all for this test.

The hidden agenda: the test. It is intentional. It is subtle because we never focus on it. It is clever. We focus on the curriculum of skills and content. We think THAT is the test. We are mistaken. We hardly ever focus on the behavioral control of our children—a form of testing and conditioning that is reinforced daily—a form that will dispense their self-concepts and frame their sense of self-worth. What does it mean? What are its ramifications?

Alvin Toffler coins it our "covert curriculum." (45) It is trained into our teachers. It is drilled into our children. John Gatto quotes the National Institute of Mental Health report:

> Education does not mean teaching people to know.... [It means] "teaching them to behave as they do not behave.... Schools were behavioral engineering plants.... (<u>The Underground History of America</u>, 284)

Leslie Owen Wilson refers to it as the operative curriculum:

> ...what surrounds children in schools and to the organization, the structure, the rules and regulations...competition, quiet, order, sequence, sitting still, accepted standards, behavioral rules and programs, compliance...and so on. (19-20)

It is real. The hidden curriculum never changes. It remains remote, unseen, yet highly operative. It shapes behavior in ways that are profound. It creates children who do not know how to listen to their own hearts. It makes our children feel fragmented and incomplete. It keeps them guessing and on guard. What is O.K? What is not? They will never completely know because the criteria and applications are always changing. It warns them that something they do will be wrong, penalized, punished and ostracized. It will cause them pain. It will reflect a deficient self. Eventually, some of them will rebel.

It is the test—an illusive test. There are many layers. It is not about multiple choice or essay. It is much, much larger, harder to capture and more difficult to define. From the minute our children walk through those kindergarten doors, they sense the test. The test tells them that something about them is not O.K. or there would be no test.

Where's the Instruction Manual for This Kid?

"Giving birth is little more than a set of muscular contractions granting passage of a child. Then the mother is born."

Erma Bombeck

In a restaurant, Jenny, my cousin's two-year-old daughter, under my watchful eye, threw the bowl with cereal and milk back over her head and hit a passing waiter. The waiter dropped his tray and frightened Stephen, then three months old. Stephen wouldn't stop howling even though the commotion stopped. I felt helpless. The other diners were quick with commentary. We left and I retreated back to the comfort and security of our living room, unwilling to negotiate the grown-up world too soon again with a baby. Three more months passed. I had much to learn.

By the time Stephen was six months old, my husband noticed a serious deficit in our parenting. The issue, socialization—mine. Leaning over my shoulder as I changed another poopy diaper he whispered, "Maybe you need to get yourself out of the house on a regular basis before it's too late."

Taking Dennis's advice, I found myself in a "Mommy and Me" class. The group was held in a multi-purpose room. The tables and chairs were pushed to the side. Lying on blankets in a circle on the floor were eighteen contented babies. The women were all socializing. Breaking into the circle was like crashing into a wagon-train encampment. There was just no room for strangers; so I started a second circle of one—plus baby. I hoped to make friends anyway. I was naive.

Instead, I found everyone was an expert with an opinion. The group formed its own little self-supporting consensus— the woman on her fifth baby, the lady with newborn twins, the visiting grandparents who hadn't seen a baby in thirty years. Even the mother whose child was only two months older than mine had something critical to say.

Each had heavy emotional issues about parenting: what to feed a baby first, when to wean and potty-train, whether or not to use a pacifier. The 'family bed' raised the ire of almost everyone. Should parents allow a child to sleep with them? We did. We never thought twice about it. Nor did we care what anyone else did. They NEVER did. There was zero tolerance for deviation. But this is part of our educational culture.

In school, we learn that different means wrong. From the time we are little, we are taught to do the same things, in the same way, at the same time as everyone else. We learn to walk in a line and sit in a row. Our school system is geared toward keeping us in step. Creativity is discouraged—it is too unpredictable. Individuality is frowned upon. And our relationships follow suit.

Teachers use emotional blackmail to get us to color between the lines. We learn to apply the same tactics to our relationships. We judge other people as we were judged and we respond with the same disdain our teachers did. A step out of line is intolerable and an emotional reaction swiftly follows. Joseph Chilton Pearce writes:

> When we accuse or judge another, it has the same effect on us as being judged ourselves. Any judgment we make, no matter of whom, registers in the heart as a disruption of relationship, and the heart dutifully responds on behalf of our defense, shifting neural, hormonal, and electromagnetic systems from relational to defensive. Our sensory system reflects those shifts in its source material and the environment we experience changes accordingly, although perceived as the usual natural phenomena of our world to which we respond as usual. Creator and created are giving rise to each other, we are judged as we have judged. (The Biology of Transcendence, 128)

These relationships do not nurture love and trust. These are relationships that turn the innovators of tomorrow, the healers, the scientists, the artists, the explorers, into either passive followers or those who rise to the top by merciless attacks on others. We do what we know. And these women were no exception. They personified judgment and disdain, which they used on each other and taught to their children. Pearce explains:

> We...having been restrained and judged since birth, automatically judge others, restrain them

if possible, and teach our children to do the same. (The Biology of Transcendence, 257)

Stephen and I stayed in the class anyway. The months passed. Each week the other parents and I sat in that circle, now with our toddlers on our laps. Every mother was so proud, working with her child, clapping to the beat of the music, jingling those bells and tambourines, looking and listening to the big picture storybook.

But Stephen was no longer interested in looking at a book. By the time Stephen was walking, he was pure kinetic motion. He would not sit during circle time. And, of course, there was that evil eye from that group of moms who formed their own consensus. They made it perfectly clear that a child who did not sit still was destined to unruliness—which, as everybody knows, leads to criminal activity. The implicit emotional deductions were outrageous.

In spite of my best efforts, Stephen never remained in my lap anyway. He squirmed. He wriggled out of my loving grasp like a wrestler out of a half nelson. He couldn't care less about jingling bells and had no interest row, row, rowing his boat gently down the stream. He was off and running, over to the windows, tugging on the pull cords, listening to the clatter as each blind slat crashed into the next. Then he was over at the workbench, examining every tool, twisting, turning, pushing, pulling and prodding whatever he could find. Then he was under the table, digging up unlimited wads of used bubble gum, pieces of lint, dead bugs and other treasures. Under the carpet, behind the furniture, around the corner, wherever he went, I was mortified.

When I tried to bring him back to the group, he cried, struggled and screamed. We gently fought our way through every circle time. Finally, the teacher quietly pulled me aside. I thought she was going to ask us to leave. Instead she said,

"Why don't you just let him explore? It seems to be what he needs."...It was a new idea for me.

Dr. Glasser explains, "Our ability to start to satisfy our needs before we know what we are doing or why we are doing it is one of nature's strokes of genius." (Schools Without Failure, 28)

And Stephen was busy satisfying his needs. He was being drawn toward something I did not yet understand. He was moving toward becoming uniquely Stephen. Dr. Margaret Wheatley writes:

> Life moves toward wholeness. It seeks coherence.... Every self makes sense. It creates a world and an identity that feels coherent to itself. From infinite possibilities, it chooses what to notice and how to respond. All living beings create themselves by this sense-making process of perception and response. As we look at any living being, we are observing its particular coherence, the logic it has used to create itself.... (A Simpler Way, 90)

Stephen continued to be the great explorer. This child took everything apart—every toy, construction set, mechanical device. Whatever held anything together was fair game for his little fingers, but by now we were learning to work with him.

So, when Stephen dismantled the door handle of my sister's brand new car before she finished buckling him into his car seat, we were no longer alarmed. As he offered her the disconnected part, she thanked him, asked him to help her reconnect the handle and then moved his car seat to the center of the car away from harm's way.

When I entered the family room and discovered the children's table dismantled and scattered across the floor, I took the same tactic. I told Stephen how clever he was, asked him to show me how he took apart the legs and elicited his help in putting them back together. Then I explained that maybe the table was not for taking apart, but I would help him find things that were.

We were never angry. We made a conscious choice to assist Stephen, to work with him in the particular direction he needed to grow, even if it did involve dismantling the things around him or flew in the face of popular parenting. And taking things apart was definitely on his path. Later he would take apart phones, small appliances, sound systems and professional computer systems all at an early age, all on the path to his own genius. Wheatley explains:

> Partnering with life, working with its cohering motions, requires that we take life's direction seriously.... This direction cannot be ignored or taken lightly.... Like all life, we learn to side-step the fearful minds that keep us from the great cohering motions which give meaning to our lives. (A Simpler Way, 103)

As time went on, our path of 'partnering with life' appeared to be a solitary one, at least within that "Mommy and Me" group. By the time Stephen was two, the women in the group started talking about making their children independent and snubbing those parents who weren't. We train each other in this paradigm and then police those who stray.

This quest to foster independence took on a vengeance. Parents pulled security blankets from toddlers, stripped babies of their bottles, threw out beloved pacifiers and threatened to cut off thumbs. Children were plucked out of their cribs and flung into twin beds. Older siblings were sent off to overnight camp. No source of familiarity and comfort was left untouched.

But 'independence' is really a euphemism for separation. We separate our children from the very things that give them a sense of intimacy and security. We push them out of the nest earlier and earlier, and then we wonder why there is a rift between our teenagers and ourselves.

Interdependence is an entirely different way of interacting. An interdependent relationship occurs when two or more whole, solid, centered human beings cooperate with each other so that everyone's needs are met. An interdependent relationship is built on trust and intimacy. Interdependent relationships are nurtured within the protective walls of an unconditionally loving family.

'Independent' relationships create polarity and conflict. They imply that the only way to be 'whole' is to be separate. They create a sense of self-centeredness. They underline the necessity to take care of oneself because no one else will. They promote self-preservation. They separate people from each other. They are bound to create disharmony and rebellion. They do not facilitate meaningful growth.

The drive to force our children into independence is a form of brainwashing foisted on us by the masterminds of the Industrial Revolution. Largely unaware of where this practice comes from, we still push our babies out of the cradle in its name.

Before the end of the nineteenth century, the multigenerational, extended family was the center and support of our day-to-day existence. To accomplish the goals of the Industrial Revolution, industrialists had to break up loyalty to this social unit. They invented the smaller, more vulnerable nuclear family and then redefined growth as separation or independence from the family.

This wedge was necessary to free the parent to work long hours in the factory and to train the child in school to the new paradigm. Generations grew up learning a set of values and ethics different from that of the family's and more compatible to the objectives of industry. Alvin Toffler writes:

> To free workers for factory labor, key functions of the family were parceled out to new, specialized institutions...family structure then changed ...to accommodate the requirements necessary [to fit] the new techno-sphere. (44)

Participation in the larger, more supportive family unit was seen as subversive of economic success. We are the poorer for this loss of comradeship, support and love.

By the time Stephen was two and a half, most of the mothers in the group had unknowingly succumbed to this industrial paradigm. They put their children into preschool and daycare. Some of the mothers went back to work whether they needed to or not.

Dennis and I prioritized our values, redefined our needs, and figured out how to keep me home with the kids. It was economic suicide and the industrialists would have been appalled, but children only grow up once. And thanks to the loving and unconditional support of my husband, I was able to participate. Nothing was going to separate and divide our family.

The Industrial Revolution has never been a humane movement; many of its goals conflict with those factors that nurture the soul. Love brings us together. Yet, the industrial paradigm creates separation, excludes love and calls that division between family members 'growth.'

Growth is better defined as the capacity to strengthen our relationships, not break away from them. Growth demands greater communion, greater responsibility to heart—to our families, our friends and our communities; the greater the love, the greater our consciousness, our compassion and the sense that we all affect each other and need to act with that in mind.

Love is our finest vehicle for growth. But thanks to our industrial format, our society excludes love from its paradigms. It pushes love as an operational force out of our institutions and out of our consciousness. It does this because love brings us together, and together we are far too powerful to be manipulated.

ভ 13 ঞ

What Doesn't Kill You
Will Make You Stronger!

I see myself in the eyes of my young children and I remember my love affair. I reach out on wintry-cast silver afternoons and struggle back to the beach. Back to the sand. Back to where I launched my babies to the trust of the wind and the benevolence of the tide. I empty myself in an attempt to re-member the lessons of the summer: the sense that true growth is partnered with love and patience, and understanding flows from sources least expected.

We sailed. Or rather they sailed and I watched from the shore and then I turned my back to listen, to sense the heat of the sun on my breast, to cast aside my fears. If I cannot help them, I will not hinder them.

I read my book. I take a nap. I am seduced by the need to sleep, to forget, to unlearn. Out of the depths of my reverie I am beckoned by their callings, "Mother, come swim to us. Mother, come see what we can do."

I pick up my life jacket. It is a long walk now to where they have sailed. They have journeyed swiftly, two sails and a nursery-rhyme-full of wind.

Can I catch them? The sand is hot and strenuous. My path is obstructed by the unaware and the self-absorbed. My children call. I track the tilt of their sails and the wake of their preambles. The sea is a Sunday holiday of swimmers and windsurfers. My children navigate from their hearts.

"Mother, swim, mother swim, you can do it." If they say I can, then I shall. The water engulfs my trepidation. The seaweed slows my efforts, but my children still call. The shore shrivels behind me and the boats loom large.

Out of the spray forge my young ones, bow straight ahead towards my soul. "Watch out!" I cry. "You're going to kill me!" "Faith, mother," they retort, "and reach for our hands." A sail under full wind knows no mercy.

I reach out, but fear entwines my grasp and wedges its way between my heart and the hull of their ship. "Mother, too far!" cast their cries as they pivot to pass again. "No!" I scream. "I'm going to die!" "No!" sang their songs, "You're going to live!"

Two, three, four passes. I resign myself to forces I do not understand. Our hands clasp. But I am not yet in the boat. The weight of my past pulls the edge of the boat to the waves, the sails now parallel to the water. My jacket is hooked on the side of the craft.

"The boat will capsize!" I scream. "No," smile my children. "Take off your life jacket, mother, so you can live." "No, we will all die." "Faith, mother. We will all live." I fling my jacket to the sea. Dancing, pulsating with life, the sails aright. My children and I soar. I love. I learn.

Motherhood for me was a quiet, understated, revolution—a cleansing of the soul. It was at the same time pushing my limits and building strengths I never knew I had. It required I be aware, centered and in the moment. It demanded I focus on the needs of another human being who could do nothing without me. A baby is. A baby loves. So, my baby taught me 'to be' and 'to love.' And within this new form of schooling, I learned about unconditional love and patience. I learned how we could be so much more for each other, in our homes, in our workplaces and in our schools. Within unconditional love we find our greatest integrity.

But when we remove that integrity from our institutional structures, we create a humanity that can't find itself. We create school systems that raise our children to ignore the voices of the heart, teenagers who rebel because they are trying to find themselves, and adults who feel unsatisfied and disconnected. If, as adults, we have lost the integrity of our heart, how can we expect anything else of our children?

I applied for a six-month's maternity leave, extended it to a year and then two. Then I quit to be a full time mom—no money, no restaurant evenings out, no fancy meals, not even convenience foods, no help, no vacations, no wardrobe changes, no savings account, no financial security—just lots of debt and one very happy, unusually cooperative, but active, two-year-old who was interested in taking everything apart. And we all grew.

Stephen was less than two and a half when Erin was born. A letter to our daughter, Erin:

Our Dearest Erin,

You were born one bright and sunny afternoon. Your birth was a pleasure and a delight; you greeted life after only forty-five minutes of the birthing process. Your father immediately took you inside his strong and loving arms. He cradled you, gave you your first bath, played with you and then returned you to your mother's side, where you nursed and went to sleep. We have always cherished every moment with you. Four hours after your birth, we packed up and went home to grandma's house, where your brother Stephen could hardly wait to hold you. Now, about five hours old, we placed you in his arms while he sat on the couch. He loved you and kissed you up and has always referred to you as 'his baby.'

At no point from the time you were born until the time we left the hospital did you ever leave our side, and at no point will you ever leave our hearts.

Every birth is different. Every child is unique. Erin was alert from the beginning. She was intense, determined and thoroughly present. Erin insisted on spending the first two years of her life in a backpack on my back. Stephen touched and took apart everything. Erin watched. Everywhere I turned, everything I did, Erin perched, chin on my shoulder and watched. And even though she preferred the view from the top, whatever life was going to bring, she was ready. So at age two years and three months, she became the sister in charge of her older brother, Stephen, and her new baby brother, Matthew. A letter to Matthew:

Our Dearest Matthew,

Managing two other children under the age of five may have kept us from recording your early years, but not from noting the twinkle in your crystal blue eyes. That twinkle was there from before your birth. You were caught turning somersaults in the womb the week before you were born. We saw your smile on the sonogram. Wherever you went, everyone knew your name because we were always calling it; an entertainer, a performer from day one, if it was cheered on, you repeated it.

Your brother took things apart and your sister watched everything. You were a collector. You collected rocks and put them under the pad in your car seat so you could sit on them. You collected twigs, bugs and cuttings from plants. You collected friends and you still do. You have endeared yourself to all who have known you. In spite of my best efforts, your initial introduction to life was from the perspective of your two-year-old sister and four-year-old brother. We are blessed to have you.

Our children present the finest of lessons. The family unit is said to be holy because it is the template for the work of the divine. All interactions no matter how seemingly insignificant, minute or inconsequential, teach. Each second-to-second event provides a lesson and an opportunity for growth no matter what face that lesson brings: patience, humility, tolerance, charity, forgiveness, anger or self-control—ultimately, it's all about love. For when love is the active driving force, all learning is possible.

Dean Ornish, M.D. writes that our physical, emotional and spiritual survival as individuals, communities, a country and perhaps even as a species depends on the healing power of love, intimacy and relationships:

> I am not aware of any other factor in medicine—not diet, not smoking, not exercise, not stress, not genetics, not drugs, not surgery—that has a greater impact on our quality of life, incidence of illness, and premature death from all

causes... Love and intimacy are at a root of what makes us sick and what makes us well, what causes sadness and what brings happiness, what makes us suffer and what leads to healing. If a new drug had the same impact, virtually every doctor in the country would be recommending it for their patients. It would be malpractice not to prescribe it. (2-3)

Ornish continues:

I am a scientist. I believe in the value of science as a powerful means of gaining greater understanding of the world we live in....Science can help us sort out truth from fiction, hype from reality, what works from what doesn't work, for whom, and under what circumstances. Although I respect the ways and power of science, I also understand its limitations as well. What is most meaningful often cannot be measured. What is verifiable may not necessarily be what is most important. As the British scientist Dennis Burkit once wrote, 'Not everything that counts can be counted.' (4)

Love is our greatest guide, our strongest connection to learning. Love is not quantifiable. It cannot be tested or graded. It is much greater than the feeling or experience of emotion with which we use to identify it. Love is our finest teacher.

Love heals. It casts out fear. It melts away the darkness revealing clarity and light. In Gifts From a Course in Miracles, the authors describe the Course's definition of healing relationships as replacing fear with love:

> Relationships offer unique opportunities for learning, healing, and awakening. It defines healing as 'to make whole.' It emphasizes forgiveness of both others and ourselves as a path toward establishing true communication, experience love, and [recognizing] our true Self in each other. (73)

When we change the reflections, preconceived constructs, images and expectations we hold for each other, we free ourselves to be whole and heal.

Healing relationships come in many scenarios: Life with three children under the age of five was like living inside a washing machine, which, incidentally, was always running. Sometimes I wondered if it was even possible for things to get more chaotic. I tried to imagine what it was like to have five, six, seven or more children and salute those households that manage that miracle. But it seems to me that all any parent can give is one hundred percent of his or her time, energy and focus. It doesn't really matter if it goes to one child or is divided among many. Spent is spent. Exhausted is exhausted. And devoted is pervasive, but not necessarily 'in control.'

We thought we were raising Stephen. We carefully monitored his interactions with his environment, realizing that with each encounter he was forming indelible impressions about himself and his relationship to the world. This almost worked until there was more than one child. Stephen, at age two, turned around and tried to raise Erin. And by the time poor old Matthew came along, we had a full house and Matthew had to face an inconsistent, immature, self-appointed committee of underage policy makers.

Life is never exactly as we imagine. Dr. Glasser talks about 'quality pictures,' the images we carry in our minds that affect our interactions with each other:

...the reason we perceive much of reality so differently from others has to do with another important world, unique to each of us, called the quality world. This small, personal world, which each person starts to create in his or her memory shortly after birth and continues to create and re-create throughout life, is made up of a small group of specific pictures that portray, more than anything else we know, the best ways to satisfy one or more of our basic needs. (Choice Theory, 44-45)

Fulfillment of these pictures is what drives our relationships and interactions.

I needed love, order and peace, and the feeling that I could create these things for my family and myself. I pictured my three small children all seated around the child-sized table and chairs in the family room near the fireplace—the fire warming the hearth, their smiling faces awaiting lunch as we sat down to homemade soup and sandwiches on a misty winter's afternoon. But try as hard as I could, I could never quite make it work because my children, like all children, had their own pictures in mind.

To begin with, the fire warming the hearth was an accident waiting to happen. My children were active explorers and there was no way to block its access unless I sat there and did not move. I also had difficulty keeping the three of them in one spot long enough to eat together. I served Stephen first because he was the eldest and he did not need as much supervision as the other two. By the time I gave Erin her food, which was only minutes later, Stephen had gulped down his lunch and was gone. He was still kinetic energy in motion, up and running before the baby's soup had cooled. By the time I sat down to join the survivors, Matthew was bathing in chicken soup, the table and floor were a mess, and my boiling point was rising.

Children strip us of our armor. They are masters at creating frustration. Accepting myself clearly, seeing myself not as I had envisioned, but as I was in the moment, was a challenge. Each interaction held a mirror to my soul, showing me my strengths and weaknesses.

I was frustrated by the chaos they created. The toys, the confusion, the energy that spun through our house should have been reported on the six o'clock evening Storm Watch. But under it all, I held myself responsible. I should, I told myself, be able to live up to my own expectations. I should be able to have a more orderly house. I should, with all the talking and modeling of good behavior, with all the ways I worked to fulfill their needs, have children who fought less and were better at putting away their toys.

In times of stress and chaos my husband would say, "What doesn't kill you will make you stronger." Time after time, I had to learn to be patient and temper my feelings. I had to reach past the frustration to find and react from a place of unconditional love. I had to grow, but it wasn't easy.

I modeled correct behavior until I was blue in the face. I remained calm until the last child started the last fight, and beaten by fatigue, it was over, and I was angry, and I didn't like being angry, and I didn't like myself for being angry— and I wasn't too fond of them either at this point. And, on occasion they stopped their bickering, united in their stunned perception of "What's gotten into mom?"

What 'had gotten into mom' was that nothing quite worked the way I envisioned. I was always reaching for an elusive sense of peace and order. Managing my life, their lives and the house was a challenge. I bought large wicker baskets. Then I tried to teach my kids to sort their toys according to trucks, dolls, building blocks and art supplies, putting each in the appropriate basket. When that didn't work, I put all their toys in bins and locked them in one large closet. The hook and eye latch was set at the six-foot mark. Somehow, something always happened. The latch broke. There was a distraction in the other room and in the two unguarded seconds the baby toddled into the closet and tipped over a shelf.

Life was not perfection. My kids were not perfect and neither was I. But I loved them. And, in spite of my exhaustion and frustration, I learned to cherish and laugh at the disorder they inevitably brought. And, in time, I learned to laugh at my need for order and perfection. And eventually, I learned to accept myself, as I accepted them. And now, we can all laugh together...most of the time. Carl Rogers writes:

> And when I can come out wearing no armor, making no effort to be different from what I am, I learn so much more—even from criticism and hostility—and I am so much more relaxed, and I get so much closer to people. Besides, my willingness to be vulnerable brings forth so much more real feeling from other people who are in relationship to me, that it is very rewarding. So I enjoy life much more when I am not defensive, not hiding behind a facade, just trying to be and express the real me. (<u>Freedom to Learn</u>, 228)

When we accept ourselves for all that we are, we abandon internal criticism and judgment. We create an internal environment of love and trust that allows us to create an external environment of acceptance for all. We give up the need to judge each other, because we accept ourselves. Only then can we grow.

And we did grow, in our own peculiar manner, in a way I could never have envisioned—toward passion and brilliance.

❧ 14 ❧

Flowers, Paper Plates and Fresh Barbecued Albacore Tuna

I am back in Erin's apartment. She has been working since eight o'clock in the morning. It is now mid-afternoon. She has moved only two feet from the couch to the floor and back again. I ask her if she would like some lunch. She will not stop. I will serve her the soup and corn she requested on the floor where she sits. She looks up for one more moment. "You know," she says, "I really love doing this. I do not dread a summer of doing math all day. I look forward to it. One day, I hope, I will be able to contribute to it…to find something new that will help applied mathematics. I just love doing it."

The test is in two days. All her neighbors know. She lives in a small little community a few miles from the university. She lives over a flower shop. The neighbors on her block live over or behind little shops as well. It is enchanted. She lives on an island four doors from the water and the ferry to the peninsula. Outside her window I can hear children laughing on their way to the beach. This morning, when I took a walk, I saw legions of little red and blue people making their way to the ferry. They were headed to the ocean side for the Junior Lifeguard Program. They laughed and giggled along the way. They were energetic and enthusiastic. And although it was only barely past seven o'clock in the morning, no one appeared to be sleepy or sluggish. This was not the same group of kids I saw walking to school a few weeks ago. These were happy children.

There is a knock on the door. The florist has a bouquet for Erin. They have brought her flowers daily since they heard she was studying so intently for her rite of passage. It is their contribution to her struggle and her joy. Bells of Ireland, roses and sunflowers all deck her living room. Yesterday, they brought up two bouquets in one day. Last weekend, another neighbor brought up a dinner of freshly caught and barbecued albacore tuna. He brought enough for Erin and the two other students who were here at the time. He did not forget the corn and mashed potatoes. His wife sent paper plates and napkins. Everyone sympathizes with 'the test.'

Most of us remember the terror and sense of helplessness the test brings. I had two dreams this week, hoping that Erin would be allowed to continue in this program.

In the first dream, I am in a car waiting for a parking spot at a little corner strip mall. In the dream, I discover I must have fallen asleep because I wake up to find I am blocking traffic, both behind and in front of me. I see a tow truck getting ready to haul my car away. I leap out of the car and explain to the man that I am sorry, I must have dozed off. He continues to secure my car to the tow truck. He does not appear to hear me. I do not know what he wants. I do not know what to say to him to make him stop. I do not understand the rules of the game. I am obviously not as capable as the other drivers waiting to get into the parking lot. Somehow I have failed the test. I implore him to release my car, telling him it would have been the third time it was towed this week. At first, he appears deaf to my pleas. Then, he finally releases my car and I drive away in a fearful sweat, but unfettered, freeing myself from his judgment and the grip of the test.

In the second dream, I am helping my daughter prepare for something. We are in a large mansion and we are hurriedly running around trying to get things done in time, although I do not seem to understand what it is we need to do or by when. The doors and windows of this huge house are all open and it has become nighttime. All of a sudden, a committee of judges appears at the doorstep and tells us time is up, the test is over; we have failed and we have to leave. I block them from entering, closing the sliding doors before they can throw us out. I am terrified they will not allow my daughter to blossom and be successful. I hear myself pleading, "Not yet! Not yet! Please give us a second chance. We are not done yet!"

❧ 15 ❧

Third Time's a Charm

*"There is nothing either good or
bad but thinking makes it so."*
                        Shakespeare (<u>Hamlet</u>, II, 2)

I woke up one morning and realized I was laboring under a misconception that whatever I did for Stephen, I could and should do for Erin and Matthew. I was wrong. Our children had different needs at different times and our family dynamics were always changing.

Getting to a "Mommy and Me" class for Erin did not work. It wasn't right for me, and I am not so sure it was right for Erin. At the very least, I had grown. I no longer cared about the issues the class discussed. I had already begun to rely on my own experience and I was gaining perspective. I was not concerned whether Erin tried banana or cereal first; I was busy retrieving the food Stephen had stuffed in his cheeks from the dog's dinner bowl. I was not worried about weaning Erin; I had already seen Stephen wean himself when he was ready and I knew first hand that the same internal drive for growth applied to everything a child did—including potty training. I did not care whether or not I gave my child a pacifier; Stephen had a pacifier in his mouth constantly for one month and then spit it out and never wanted it again. Erin wouldn't have any. And we forgot all about pacifiers by the time we had Matthew.

Erin was Erin. She was, and has always been, her own little world of perfection. Intense, self-confident from the beginning, she knew exactly what she wanted. She crawled for a while and at about seven months of age picked herself up and walked around the furniture. She not only dressed herself by age two, but knew exactly what she wanted to wear and in what combination. She walked young, talked in full sentences early and read well by the age of four and a half. She took care of herself, her brothers and us. If she had been born first, our whole path would have been different. We would have taken her interactions with life as the norm. We would have pursued a more traditional approach to schooling because Erin could handle anything. And we would have wondered what was wrong with her brothers, who read late and weren't as focused. Erin's self-sufficiency paved the way for her baby brother Matthew.

By the time Matthew came along, we had become relaxed parents. When Stephen was an infant, I ground his baby food, freezing it in ice cubes and keeping on hand batches of freshly frozen ground chicken, broccoli, carrots and sweet potatoes. When we had Erin, something had to go and it couldn't be Stephen, so I substituted ready-made baby food for homemade when we were out of the house. By the time Matthew came along, we were very, very busy. In fact, no one has any memory of ever making, buying or feeding Matthew baby food. He must have survived sitting on our laps, scrounging off our plates and other table scraps. We just can't remember.

Matthew was and still is a character. He has always broken the rules on child development. He could walk at twelve months, but preferred being closer to the ground, so he crawled for an additional six. (Years later he would dance internationally.) Matthew also developed not only his own sounds but also his own language. The only one who could understand him was Erin. He talked. She interpreted. Everyone was very happy.

Then one day, a speech therapist working for our local school district overheard him. She insisted we have him tested. We did and the pressure was on. Even though Matthew was only three, the government already wanted to take charge.

The speech therapist told us that he may never talk like a normal person. If he did, it was likely to be really slow. This would affect his ability to do well in school. She strongly urged, even threatened, to place him in a special government preschool for severely handicapped children. She reported to her superiors. They demanded we put Matthew on a bus at eight in the morning even though the school was less than ten minutes from our house. They claimed that the 'separation' was better at the doorstep. They would return him at three.

We declined. We didn't want separation. It was that old industrial theme: children should be separated from their parents. We disagreed.

Clearly feeling they needed to protect him from us, the authorities labeled us 'in denial.' Then they sent the district psychologist to our house without our permission to assess whether or not we were negligent parents because we refused to turn over our child to their system. We weren't. And we didn't. And that ended that!

Expecting children to all be alike forces them into a straitjacket of acceptability and squeezes them into a narrow channel of possibilities. We need to have faith in the way our children grow and not compare them or penalize them for their differences. We need to watch and guide them in a way that honors these differences. We must not treat children as defective for 'falling out of the mold.' Children all develop differently. Any teacher or parent can see this. Any structure that ignores this fundamental truth is doomed to fail.

So, we found a speech therapist who wanted to wait a year to see what Matthew would do on his own. By that time, he was already speaking rather fluently and was ready to work with her. She modeled the way he made his sounds and helped him with his sentence structure. Today he talks swiftly, fluently and with great finesse. His social skills are charismatic and his verbal ability is terrific. In fact, there are times when we wish he would just be quiet—at least for a moment.

A heartless, impersonal, self-conceited system tried to label Matthew slow, delayed, dyslexic, dysgraphic and speech delayed. Had we listened to them, he would never be the shining star he is today. When we label children, our relationships proceed from those labels. We start to treat our children in a way that substantiates and validates what we perceive as the problem instead of correcting and moving past the difficulty. Labels are a prison sentence. They keep us from seeing what is actually before our eyes and prevent us from identifying when the situation changes. They put us in a rut that impedes growth. Both the labeler and the labeled start responding to each other in kind. When we abandon the habit of seeing each other through labels, we will all have room to grow.

௸ 16 ௸

Trying to Stuff an Odd
Shaped Child into
a Square Hole

*"...self-assertiveness is rewarded as far as competi-
tive behavior is concerned, but is discouraged when
expressed in terms of original ideas and questioning
of authority."*

Fritjof Capra

Finally, the day came. Stephen was ready for kindergarten. I
felt panic and separation anxiety. I believed it was a character
deficiency. In a society that demands independence, I was
guilty of wanting to keep my baby home within the protective
walls of our family.

None-the-less, Dennis and I went to observe our local kindergarten. The class had thirty-three five-year-olds and one

adult. Nature would never have been so cruel. And this adult had limited personal resources. Whatever had enticed her to become a teacher had long since faded. She was at a loss, thirty years in the same classroom, following the same routine. This is not what she had envisioned when she started teaching.

As the bell rang, she gathered up her young charges and transformed them from an energetic school of tadpoles into a group of bored frogs. With an unspoken dictate, she demanded their energy, robbed them of their internal direction and then made them sit. We could say she was not in touch with her students, but this was only the symptom, not the source of her difficulty. She was not in touch with herself. Martin Buber writes:

> The good teacher...must be a really existing man, and he must be really present to his pupils; he educates through contact. Contact is the primary word of education. (Rogers, <u>Freedom to Learn</u>, 101)

But she made contact with no one. Her presence was not compelling. Neither were the relationships she created. She had the children sit in a half-circle for share-time. But the teacher herself did not know how to share. Turning to the child on her right she requested he show the class what he brought today. The rest of us could not hear her and she did not care.

At first, the child tried to share the seashells he brought with the other children, but sensing the teacher's lack of involvement, the child stopped trying. The teacher ignored the other children until she sensed the fidgeting and squirming, which she handled with a feigned, kind, but crisp, "Boys and girls, please sit still!" She exuded the attitude it was their job to be interested in what she was doing and not her job to find what was interesting to them. If they weren't interested, it was their fault; they obviously needed to try harder.

As the hour progressed, I looked at the thirty-three kindergartners sitting in a circle on the floor. Watching the energy in the room, I felt my chest constrict. I sat in a pint-sized chair and smiled approvingly at all the little kids sitting quietly in perfect order in their places on the mat. I didn't know what else to do. The morning sun filtered through the windows and hit the tables where the children were not. The institution was in order, yet it missed a feeling of well-being and sense of wholeness. It gnawed my soul. I was vaguely conscious of my breathing.

The teacher posed on the big chair at the edge of the circle. The children were situated so the windows were not in view. She spoke to them with a very controlled, formal and false sweetness, like an actress who was hired to play her impression of a kindergarten teacher. She offered the children nothing of her real self. She, with great professionalism, exposed nothing. She made little eye contact with anyone, looking at everyone, yet hidden from view. She talked at them, never to them. She had forgotten how to listen with any sense of empathy. When she asked them questions, she did not want to know their answers or opinions. She had a single answer in mind, each time—hers. The children realized it was a guessing game and that their own thoughts and feelings were unimportant. It was obvious to everyone; this was perfunctory.

Then she asked the next child to stand up and share something with the circle. This child, having learned from the first that the other children were not important, talked only to the teacher, hoping for an emotional reward. The teacher was there, but she had heard it before and did not listen. As a result, the class felt uninvolved. Even the child who was talking seemed to sense his teacher's lack of interest and fidgeted. The other children started to squirm. I also squirmed and Dennis, who felt it improper to squirm, started to itch.

More important than the subject matter, this teacher taught each child that he or she was unimportant. She conveyed it by her lack of attentiveness, lack of empathy and lack of compassion. Her behavior told them they were not important enough to warrant these reactions. Because she was not conscious, she had no idea how her lessons landed, but the children will accept her attitude as true statements about who they are for the rest of their lives. They will develop self-concepts lacking the full measure of their worth. And just like their teacher, they will learn to turn off and shut down. She will pretend to teach; they will pretend to listen. Everybody learns to pretend. Parker Palmer writes:

> Teaching, like any truly human activity, emerges from one's inwardness, for better or worse. As I teach, I project the condition of my soul onto my students, my subject, and our way of being together. The entanglements I experience in the classroom are often not viewed from this angle; teaching holds a mirror to the soul. If I am willing to look in that mirror and not run from what I see, I have a chance to gain self-knowledge—and knowing myself is as crucial to good teaching as knowing my students and my subject. (2)

The session came to a close. The teacher's interaction was mechanical. She knew what to do next because she had done it many times before, regardless of the needs of the children in the room. Turning on the record player, she set the children on automatic. Her relationship to these children was negligible. Her recipe was predictable—too many children, a box of crayons, a pile of coloring books and a long-awaited nap.

The children seemed to feel an overwhelming sense of boredom. She exuded a sense of despair. As she laid her head down on her desk, we took the hint and left.

The next school we visited was a traditional college preparatory school. It prided itself on academic excellence. Long concrete steps led up to the front door. It reminded me of my own elementary school experience, a formal two-story building surrounded by a chain-link fence confining the old familiar blacktop, tetherball, four square and a sandpit beneath the jungle gym. There was an administration building with secretaries' offices, front desk, cubicles and phones ringing off the hook—not to mention that newly mopped institutional smell.

"May we see your kindergarten?"

"Certainly. Second corridor down to your left and then across to the third building."

"Thank you."

As directed, we quietly let ourselves in the back door of the kindergarten classroom. The teacher didn't seem to notice and the kids didn't care much either. "They must get a lot of observers," I remember thinking. As our eyes grew accustomed to the gray light, the structure became clear.

It was a large class, twenty-eight kids, and the children were regrouped by some level of achievement. The teacher stood at the front of the room, wrote on the board and worked with a table of six children. These were the chosen few, the kids the teacher identified as the 'top of the class.' An aide sat across the room and drilled another table of six; these were the next in line. Of the sixteen remaining survivors, about a third sat quietly by themselves and worked on something involving a pencil. Another third squirmed at their desk, stared at the ceiling, the floor, and the outside window framing a pristine view of the blacktop. The remaining six students were dead, but that didn't seem to matter—the pick of the crop had already been chosen.

The administrators talked about academic excellence. Everything they did, they explained, aimed at that title. The teachers, they claimed, were vigilant. But looking around the room, it seemed to me the system was rigged so only 'the top few' could attain this level of excellence. Academic excellence was really about who was more excellent than whom.

Most kids would not attain academic excellence, despite what anybody said or what the teachers thought they were doing, because of the administration's stubborn adherence to the bell curve—an artificial model of success. It was all about the curve.

The bell curve creates a hierarchy of self-concepts. It is a pre-determined grading scale that guarantees only ten to twenty percent of our children will ever truly feel successful. The rest are told they are only average or less. Most kids will feel defective because they will perceive themselves to be at best no one special. No matter how hard they try, the curve will always be the same. No matter how high they raise the bar, the same eighty-percent will be less than the others. The ranking this school receives will only affect the self-concepts of the teachers and administrators. No amount or quality of work will change the outcome for the students if there is a curve. And in our traditional educational system, as it was created, there will always be a curve.

Next we turned to Maria Montessori. She did not believe in the bell curve. She saw every child as brilliant. But when we finally found the Montessori school we saw listed in the phonebook, it was not what we expected. We made our way past the rickety fence and the front yard booby-trapped with skates, shovels and leftover lunches into an old converted house. The living room was littered with activity and voices and bodies jumping off the wall and off the couches, but we couldn't find any help over three feet tall. Shoving, hitting and crying, petty theft and extortion were the mass themes of the moment. It was a curriculum of neglect. It gave the adjectives 'self-paced' and 'alternative' a bad name. It was definitely not Montessori, despite its advertising. Maria would have been appalled. Eric Berne writes:

> People are born O.K. Taking the position 'I'm O.K., You're O.K.' is the minimum requirement for... lasting emotional and social well-being.... (C. Steiner, 1) The 'I'm O.K., You're O.K.' life position is the position people need to have in order to achieve their fullest potential...[but,] it is not intended to promote the notion that all of people's actions are acceptable. The existential position, 'I'm O.K., You're O.K.' is a point of view about people apart from their actions and power.... (C. Steiner, 3)

Eventually an adult cleared the path. She was supposed to be in charge, but before we could ask her any questions, a parent showed up and asked to take her child home. The teacher's eyes glazed over. "What child? What was her name? Was there a four-year-old named Tiffany here?" She wasn't sure. We promptly apologized for being at the wrong address, cautiously backed out the door and continued our search for a true Montessori.

The driveway up the hill to the next school was impeccably landscaped. The building sparkled of clean, fresh, white paint. This is better, we thought. A receptionist who inquired of our intentions greeted us at the front door. She escorted us through the sleeping preschool room, twenty-four napping four-year-olds lined up in orderly rows of six, two teachers and an aide.

The kindergarten room had one very loving teacher and eighteen five-year-olds. First, there was the pledge of allegiance followed by quiet and a spelling test. Quiet was a problem, at least for our son. He was never quiet. He never ran out of something to say. And then there was the 'spelling test,' twenty-six long words. Stephen didn't even know the alphabet. How could he handle a spelling lesson? We needed a less academic environment for our son so we kept looking.

This next school was a lot better for Stephen than the others we'd seen, even though it, too, was not a perfect Montessori. There were no grade levels to either push him forward when he wasn't ready or hold him back when he was. There were no grades. Maria Montessori never believed in labeling, ranking or forcing her children to compete against each other. She believed in creating an environment that honored the uniqueness of each child. She believed that all children had within them the blueprint of their own identity and the ability to find that identity as nature intended. And she trusted that given the opportunity, they would. Dr. Montessori writes:

> Every man has his own creative spirit that makes him a work of art....The end product...is like a masterpiece which an artist has kept in the intimacy of his studio and into which he has poured himself before showing it in public....This fashioning of the human personality is a secret work of 'incarnation.' The child is an enigma. All that we know is that he has the highest potentialities, but we do not know what he will be. He [will] 'become incarnate' with the help of his own will. (The Secret of Childhood, 31-32)

So, we promptly enrolled our son. We especially liked the structure. Every morning, the children had an opportunity to explore two-dozen learning centers. Each center had a different set of manipulative tasks and skills. Stephen, however, would only work on the manipulatives that involved taking something apart or putting it back together. He meticulously avoided anything that had to do with letters, sounds or reading. The teacher noticed, but had no efficient way to redirect this imbalance. In her frustration she secretly labeled him 'slow' and then passed the information to the other teachers, but not to us. Dr. Glasser observes:

> Very few children come to school failures, none come labeled failures; it is school and school alone which pins the label of failure on children. (Schools Without Failure)

Now, Stephen was in what would have been the third grade and still did not know how to read. He was eight and struggling with "the fat cat sat on the mat." Years later, in an interview, Stephen describes the experience:

> "I remember that the reading group scared me. I remember sitting at a table and everyone was reading and I just didn't."
>
> "What did you think about that? Or how did you feel?"
>
> "If I took you and sat you in an Aborigine tribe and handed you some rocks. And everyone around you was banging the rocks together and you didn't feel like banging the rocks together and weren't sure if you liked banging the rocks together, how would you feel? You didn't want to be banging the rocks. You had the rocks in your hand...you weren't sure why people were banging the rocks...kind of interested in the expressions of people's faces as they were banging the rocks...it was altogether rather unappealing. You just kind of sat there thinking 'what am I doing here?'"

"But were you O.K. with it or was it an issue?"

"No, it wasn't an issue. I didn't notice that I was the only one not reading, I just thought that I was just further down the line than they were. I didn't think I was behind them, I just thought that they'd been there longer."

If Stephen had been in a traditional classroom, he would have been penalized for failing to 'keep up' because his work would have been graded. Comparing his work to the work of other children would have been detrimental to his sense of self. He would have gauged his self-worth based on what everyone else was doing, never getting past the comparison and judgment. The self-concept Stephen would have formed under this scenario would have disabled his access to his own talents. He would have conceived of himself as 'less than' the others, making it difficult for him to tap into his own internal passion and brilliance when he was ready.

Stephen made it through kindergarten and two other classrooms until he met his last teacher there, Brian. In our first parent-teacher conference, Brian indicated that he thought our son was very smart. He explained that the kindergarten teacher thought Stephen was slow and how he disagreed. Brian continued to explain how the other teacher backed off, believing Stephen was unable to read. Perhaps Stephen was now ready.

In December of the third grade, Stephen was ready. He zipped past the kindergarten reader and through the fourth grade reading book by June. Then he skipped to a college level book that same summer. As I walked into the living room I found him reading Greek literature to Erin and Matthew. And although he did not get all the pronunciation right, he understood what he was reading well enough to explain it to his younger siblings. I was ecstatic! I thought we had his education set...I was wrong. Life is movement. And just when things were going well and I felt I could relax, the property on which the school was located was sold for commercial development and the school closed. We went back to one of our original alternatives, the more academic Montessori.

17

How Late IS Late?

Back to the present. A parent calls my private practice. Her second child, Zachary, cannot read. He is in kindergarten. It is the third month of the fall semester. The teacher, in the district he is in, has issued a formal warning stating he may not pass kindergarten because he is not progressing at the same rate as most of the other kids; he is not learning his letters fast enough. The principal has called a meeting. It is a 'power' counsel. Sitting in on this meeting will be the district psychologist, the school counselor, the teacher, the resource specialist and mom. They will attempt to intimidate Zachary's mother, proving once again they are the 'experts.' They will prove that a parent cannot begin to know as much about her own child as they do. When they do, they will consider the meeting a success. (As both mother and expert, I vote for the mother.)

Meanwhile, my client is upset. Her child's life flashes before her eyes. He is five. Will he have the same struggles in life she and her husband have had? He is only starting and already he has failed. She is tearful.

We talk. This is her second child who is a 'late' reader by state standards. But I did not get her first child, Travis, until he was in the second grade. And we have just spent six years, twice a week, undoing the damage to his self-concept created by the school's artificial race. Travis is just beginning to believe he might be a good reader.

We have a better chance with Zachary, because we are starting earlier. But the bottom line is this; the child will read when he is ready. The hope is to counter the negative 'I'm not as good as the other kids, I'm not as smart' messages he is getting in school.

I know this family well. I have been working with them for years. Travis has a big heart, but he has had to regain his self-esteem. Every time he heard an adult tell him he couldn't read, he told himself that must be true. Then, when he really could read, he still kept hearing the little tape in his head telling him he was not a good reader. That tape blocked his progress. It is still not over.

Zachary, too, is golden—bright eyes, crystal blue and shining, long blonde bangs and a bowl-shaped haircut. He should have been the poster child in overalls out in the field with a crisp red apple in his hand, big smile on his face and a message that reads "Organic Produce...Fresh and at it's Finest!" I wonder how long we can save his glow.

Zachary's teacher is unhappy with him. He doesn't want to sit still. He squirms He fidgets. She puts a letter on the board and asks the class to repeat the sound, B...B as in ball. (There is no ball there.) Zachary's eye's glaze over, but rising to the test he makes the B sound with his fellow classmates. He has learned to memorize things that make no sense to him. He has given up his autonomy, common sense and integrity in less than twelve weeks. He is pretending to know what this adult, whom he has no relationship with, wants him to know—but he doesn't have a clue.

Zachary sits at the edge of his seat. He stares intently at the board. But when the teacher puts up five more letters and then puts up a B again, Zachary does not remember the sound. He does not remember, because it never made any sense to him in the first place. And a week later and a month after that, he still does not remember, even though he still sits on the edge of his seat, staring intently.

So I work with him. We meet at the café at Borders bookstore. We talk about the B sound; then we go touch all the books. They begin with the B sound too. We move; Zachary learns best that way. (So much for labeling kids with ADHD when all some of these kids really need is to get up and move). We walk down the aisles touching the books and repeating the B sound. Then we find pictures of things that begin with the same sound…bee…ball…bike. *He* finds them in big picture books. *He* drives the process. *He* wants to know. He has not yet shut down. The next week we do the same thing…One sound, B…not twenty. We take it at his pace. It makes sense to him. He walks up and down the aisles on his own, finding B for book, also for butterfly and bat and many, many other words.

Then I ask him, would he like to know what that sound looks like on paper? His eyes light up. We draw the letter together, my hand over his. The next time we meet he shows me lots of letter B's on lots of pieces of papers. Also C's. He's added another sound with some help. And so it goes until eventually the alphabet makes sense to Zachary. No problem. Then one day, he starts to read. He reads all the titles on all the books he passes going down the aisles in that bookstore. And if he doesn't know the big words, he sounds out the letters…and he just won't stop.

School sends home another letter. They want to hold him back again. He's not writing paragraphs and his handwriting is terrible.

The most salient feature of our educational system today is that it that finds a reason to keep most of our children from being successful. John Holt writes:

> Finally the schools, as they separate and label children, a few winners and a great many losers, must convince them, first, that there must always be a few winners and many losers, that no other human arrangement is possible, and secondly that whether winner or loser they deserve whatever comes to them. Only thus can we be sure that the winners will defend the system without guilt and the losers accept it without rancor. (25)

We have become so conditioned to this system that we do not question it at all. We willingly submit our children without much reflection or hesitation. Whether they win or lose, we are desensitized. But we can choose a better way. We can choose to have all kids win in their own manner and in their own time frames. All we have to do is take back our power and do it.

18

Love, Mathematics, and Middle School

"Our children are in motion. We happily note their changes and herald them as growth. In ourselves we seem less willing to notice, but we too are in motion, evolving and changing through our lives."
Margaret Wheatley

Children change. Now that Stephen could read, we enrolled him in the more academic Montessori school. But I had changed too. This time, instead of being the uninformed parent I was in the prior school, I joined the teaching staff. I taught art to each of the classes and ran an after-school arts and crafts program. And like any involved parent, I spent a great deal of time at the school helping out, filling in and, whenever feasible, aiding in the direction of Stephen and Erin's education.

Erin had now entered the Montessori school at what would have been the first grade level. Matthew was in a nursery school six blocks away. When he was done at twelve, he stayed with me when I taught or he went out on the yard to play with the other children. And we were all there together.

Stephen immediately made friends with two of his old "Mommy and Me" buddies, David B. (the owner's son) and Billy. The three of them explored their way through the day, creating perfume out of leaves, flowers and patches of the side lawn. They learned first hand that all organic material rots, but under different circumstances and in different combinations. They initiated the activity. Their teacher, Barbara, managed to turn it into an exploration of science, the sign of a gifted teacher. Joseph Chilton Pearce explains:

> While the child plays on the surface, the great work goes on beneath. Regulatory feedback, conceptual construction, and synthesis, all the mechanics of learning, are nonconscious procedures. Awareness is the end result....When the intentions we press on the child are in flow with his intent, he learns quickly and joyfully because then it will be his play with us. Interaction is play, but action and reaction are work. The biological plan is aborted when we invert this genetic plan for learning. That is, to approach learning consciously, we think we or the child must do the work of learning, but that is a biological impossibility. The greatest learning that ever takes place in human mind—a learning of such vastness, such reach, such complexity that it overshadows all other learning—takes place in the first three years of life without the child ever being aware of learning at all. (The Magical Child, 168)

Undaunted, however, I thought I would help them out and make the learning process 'better.' I thought they needed lots of help. Neither Stephen nor David B. could spell. And Stephen's handwriting was atrocious. It looked like a child's half his age. And Stephen couldn't remember his math facts, but Billy and David B. couldn't either. So I scheduled a time once a day to work with them.

We started with multiplication tables. I focused on anything that involved multiplying a seven, eight, nine or twelve. But drill as hard as we could nothing worked. By the end of each day they seemed to know most of their math facts; by the next day, it was gone. Barbara walked around muttering something about 'a dead horse.' Years later, Stephen and I had this discussion:

> "Do you remember trying to learn your math facts?"
>
> "Yes, I remember the only way to get us to actually learn our math facts, you had to sit us down and not let us leave until we remembered at least some of them."
>
> "Did it work?"
>
> "No. I still exactly remember the same set I remembered before. I mean, honestly, I know six times six is thirty-six. O.K. I remembered a lot of the math facts and then you made us remember many of the others and then I knew them for a couple of weeks and forgot them, but I still remember the original ones that I knew before you sat us down that morning to do it."

In spite of Stephen's inability to remember his times tables and my interference, we had two great years there. But the school was unable to add a sixth grade. There was not enough room. Just when I thought everything was running smoothly, I once again had to look for an alternative.

This time, however, Stephen directed our search. He wanted to see the local junior high, so I called to make an appointment.

I explained that I had a son who would be of the age to enter their school next September. I wanted to find out more about the school, the curriculum and the teachers. The woman who answered the phone paused and said "Hmmm...just a minute. I will give you to the secretary." I repeated my request. The secretary paused and said "Hmmm...the district has a brochure on the curriculum requirements and we are trying to get together a few pieces of literature to add to that for registration in the fall."

Silence followed.

I tried to explain again that I would like to come out and SEE the campus, OBSERVE or MEET the teachers, PERUSE the textbooks and DISCUSS the school in general with someone.

More silence. "Hmmm..." she said. "Well, you'll have to talk to your child's counselor." (My child isn't even enrolled yet and already he has a counselor?)

"Fine," I said. "Is this counselor there now, or do I have to make an appointment?"

"Just a minute please." Once again there was a long period of silence. "You can come on April twenty-fifth at seven thirty in the evening to the parent orientation AND THEN if you have any questions you can ask a counselor." (It was February.)

"Your school may be able to wait until the end of April, but I can't! WHO can I see NOW? I would like to observe the school and some classrooms."

"BUT NO PARENT EVER OBSERVES THE CLASS-ROOMS. IF THEY DID WE WOULD HAVE THREE HUN-

DRED AND FIFTY PARENTS ALL OVER THIS CAM-
PUS!"

As the decibel level in our conversation rose, I thought, but
did not say, "If you had three hundred and fifty concerned
parents all over YOUR school, you'd probably have at least
three hundred and fifty excited, motivated students which I
BET YOU DO NOT!"

Instead I lowered my voice, apologized for getting a little
edgy and asked, "Whom may I speak to now?"

Silence. "Well...sometimes," she said, "we have a parent or
two, especially if they're from out of state..." She paused.
"My husband was a counselor and he once had a couple from
New York come out and ask if they could see the students. He
told them (she chuckled) 'Why? They look just like your students!'" Chuckle, chuckle. Silence. "You can talk to the principal. He will call you back."

"Fine, when may I expect a call?"

"Just a minute," she said. "He will call you back today."

We set a ten o'clock appointment for Friday morning with
the principal. To our surprise, unlike the office staff, he was a
kindly gentleman full of warmth, compassion and understanding. He had no problem walking us through the campus. He
showed us at least a dozen classrooms in operation.

He said the school was well organized because of its strict
infrastructure. When students walked into each classroom,
both the homework and class assignment were on the board.
Each student had an agenda book and was responsible for
copying the whole assignment into the book each hour. The
teacher initialed what the child wrote was correct. A parent on
the other end initialed that he or she saw it each day. The
teachers prided themselves on how well the system worked.
Everything was perfectly planned and executed. The principal
emphasized that the most direct path to success was in
following the plan. The system wasn't about learning; it was
about compliance.

He explained that 'smartness' did not count as much as the ability to be well organized, responsible and follow through on all the dictates. The entire school was run on a demerit system. Every student received a hundred points for just showing up. Then for every 'behavioral infraction' the child lost points. Children lost points for facing the wrong way in class, for forgetting a book, for being late, for missing homework assignments, for, by the teacher's discernment, not paying attention or talking as well as fighting on campus. There were no distinctions made between points lost for forgetting a homework assignment and beating up another child. It was all about compliance.

Stephen and I went home and thought a long time about what this man had said. Learning to follow directions is very different from learning to listen to inner direction. This was a big shift from the Montessori philosophy of growth from the inside out. We discussed the issues at length and I came up with the following conclusion:

Learning to follow directions does not educate inner wisdom. No matter how good a program sounds, if it does not nurture learning from the inside out, it disconnects our children from themselves. We cannot raise our children like this. I would not raise Stephen like this.

When compliance is more important than listening to conscience, to inner direction, to personal integrity, we raise a generation of citizens who blindly follow orders. We create a society ripe for dictatorship. We raise a society lacking in heart and compassion, because children who are raised in an environment that disconnects them from their own conscience also become disconnected from their own compassion. Children who grow up in a compassionless environment, one that is all about compliance to the exclusion of everything else, grow up to be compassionless adults. We do what we know. Stephen and I would find a better path—a path connected to the direction of the heart. Dr. Stephen Covey writes:

Educating the heart is the critical complement to educating the mind. In the words of American educator John Sloan Dicky: "The end of education is to see men made whole, both in competence and in conscience. For to create the power of competence without creating a corresponding direction to guide the use of that power is bad education. Furthermore, competence will finally disintegrate apart from conscience." (First Things First, 180)

Educating the heart depends on emotional integrity. This does not happen in a system that is all about sacrificing that integrity in the name of compliance. Compliance will not nurture integrity. It will mask and penalize it.

When I talked to Lori, the owner of the Montessori School, about what we had seen, she suggested we 'homeschool' our children. I had never heard the word 'homeschool' before. I did not know what it meant. But I did not want my son raised in an environment that ignored the direction of his heart, so I said, "Let's go!" I had no clue what that would mean.

PART III

School at Home

What's a 'Home School'?

"Children are searching for the real meaning of life. We believe in their possibilities to grow. That is why we do not hurry to give them answers; instead we invite them to think about where the answers might lie. The challenge is to listen."

Louise Cadwell

This was the eighties and although homeschooling had been around for decades, it was still not very common. There wasn't much going on in our area, so my friend Lori, owner of the Montessori school, and I took the day off and drove to a small community about fifty miles away to attend a home-school meeting. The nondenominational meeting was conducted in a small recreation room behind a church in a semi-rural part of town. The room was full of women who had made the decision to stay home and educate their young, even though it was not economically feasible for many of them. There were a lot of very old cars in the parking lot and children running around in well-worn T-shirts. The adults sat in a circle.

The organization was a grass roots support group. There were no dues, no requirements and no curriculum. One of the newer moms had just pulled her nine-year-old son from school. Now he was bored at home. Accustomed to being told what to do, where to go and when, he was at a loss for direction.

The other mothers chimed right in. Some said their children were also bored when they were first pulled from school. At school they never had to dip into their own resources to find activity and direction. They were well trained. The teacher told them what to learn, what projects to do and when.

Released from this regimen, these children needed a readjustment period. For many, that meant boredom (and no T.V. to fill the void). Some recovered quickly, but it took many a full year before they rediscovered what they liked to do.

Children, however, who had never been to school were still as self-motivated and internally directed as when they were toddlers. If they were bored, they did not turn toward or rely on an external source for entertainment. They used their boredom as a springboard to experiment and find new avenues to fulfill their needs. These were children who had learned how to learn.

Looking around the room, I noticed that the children who had never been to school had a different quality about them. It was the same look that surrounded small babies, one of innocence and unconditional love. These children did not need to put on hardened armor to protect themselves from the cruelties of other institutionalized children, the unpredictable and painful judgments of the teacher or the lack of humanity of the system in which they found themselves. These children had loving, solid relationships all day long with their teachers who were their parents and siblings. They were confident when they talked to adults. They were kind to each other.

They knew how to resolve conflict. The older children respected and took care of the younger and even vice versa. But above all, they seemed to emanate a sense of unlimited love and compassion.

It is only through love and compassion that we experience any kind of meaningful growth. It is only through love and compassion that we get closer to each other and, in turn, find out who we are. Arthur Jersild writes:

> Compassion is inextricably linked to acceptance of self and of others. It is the ultimate expression of emotional maturity. It is through compassion that a person experiences the highest peak and the deepest reach in his search for self-understanding....Why is compassion so intimately tied to understanding and acceptance of self and others?...First, to understand another person we must be able to realize not simply what he is thinking but also what he is feeling. It is not enough to know what is in his mind; it is essential also to know what is in his heart. (125-128)

We cannot know what is in someone else's heart until we have felt what is in ours. I thought about creating an education directed by love and an internal sense of conscience instead of school's absolute adherence to blind compliance. I thought about the compassionate environment my family could build and I contacted a local homeschool group:

To Whom It May Concern,

> I am applying for coverage under your legal umbrella. I feel compelled to protect my child from entering a system that will make him com-

pliant and keep him from becoming all that he truly is. I want him to experience the love and compassion, the passion and brilliance, which are his birthright. I want to do this with him.

Sincerely,
Resa Brown

We did homeschool and it changed our lives.

Love and compassion should be the lens through which we view all life. Its range of influence should extend past our narrow definition of family and friends to all interactions and experiences everywhere. For the sake of generations to come, we must focus our attention on love, not compliance. We must focus on love in its widest, grandest of forms as the key to our being. We must connect to love in all forms holy. It is our greatest understanding, our finest teacher. Love is what remains when all else fades away.

When Erin turned seventeen, she spent the summer in Israel. Part of her eight-week sojourn was a five-day trek, backpack and sleeping bag shoulder-slung, into the barren Negev Desert. One morning, she broke away from her still asleep companions for a morning jog. She ran along the shore of the Dead Sea until her campsite departed from view. All she could sense was an encompassing searing heat and a small, warm breeze. As she turned around, all she could see anywhere was desert—no people, camping gear, cactus, sagebrush or tumbleweed—just sand, everywhere.

She could count what she saw on her fingers: miles of sand, a cloudless sky, one bush, two birds, a goat and the water so full of salt it was devoid of all life. In that moment, the birds and the goat turned toward her in kinship with life. She felt a contact, a connection, a relationship. In that moment, she understood all life was holy. All life was sacred. And in that timeless instant, she had touched creation; in that space beyond time, she had been touched by the eternal hand of love. As the <u>Course in Miracles</u> explains, there is only love. All else is an illusion.

When we acknowledge love and compassion as the vital, physical force of existence, when we let that force, rather than blind compliance, direct the nature of our existence, when we let it build the structure of our reality and secure the stability of our world, then we will remember who we are and why we are here. Our essential nature is love. The Dalai Lama explains:

> Some people believe human nature is aggressive. I do not agree with that. I believe that from our birth until the last day the involvement of compassion and human affection is a crucial factor in our lives. (iii)

Furthermore, compassion and passion go hand-in-hand. Our ability to be deeply compassionate is directly connected to our ability to feel deeply, to be passionate. The dictionary definition of passion is "a strong amorous feeling or desire; love, ardor." Jersild describes this connection:

> To be compassionate means to partake in passion: the passions of others, the passions that arise within oneself. It means to participate in feeling rather than simply to view it as a spectator might. It is a way of entering into emotional fellowship…Compassion is stronger than anger, mightier than love, more powerful than fear. It gives the measure of a person's strength as a human being. It is not the emotion of the weak. It is the hard-gotten property of the strong. (126)

Passion is the fuel of love. When positively channeled, passion directs our being towards a greater identity. Emanating from a Greater Source, it cannot tolerate falsity or lack of integrity. Awaiting relationship, it yearns for interaction. It hopes for intimacy, trust and the ability to share its gifts with another. It fills our being with compassion and beauty. It calls us home in truth, clarity and dignity. As Jean Houston writes:

> Why must we have a passion for reality? Why must we love and desire and be filled with metaphysical ardor? Because these passions set up in us the momentum for bringing new forms into being...
>
> Love is the form that gives life to the process and is itself increased by its own endeavor. Love becomes quite literally all. In states of coherence one is marrying oneself on all levels. Love then takes the next quantum leap and one loves all others in one's immediate reality. This then moves to an all-encompassing Love of all and everything. And so love becomes the most powerful agent for the fielding and forming of reality. In love the lenses fall away. In love one forms all formings.... *In love one arrives home at last.... (200)*

❧ 20 ❧

The Top of the Heap

I sit at Panera again. I am alone, except for a sourdough roll left over from lunch, a half-empty bottle of water and a warming glass of iced tea. I have been here all day with the exception of a brief errand. Erin and I came at seven-thirty this morning to join her other friends in study before their one o'clock test—the first of two. The next will be tomorrow morning at nine o'clock. They had better wake up functional, not easy for kids who are used to studying late into the night. They will need a running start.

Elaine called everyone the night before to see if they were all right. She made a special call to Erin, who had a migraine from three-thirty in the afternoon to seven o'clock that evening. When Erin's migraine had passed, Erin bounced back on her feet and started over. "Reset," I heard her tell herself, as she pulled out her books and looked for her algebra notes.

So, here I sit at Panera. Fondling my iced tea. I would contemplate the tea leaves if I knew how—but there aren't any. The clock ticks. How are they doing? I dropped four of the girls off at their test just before one o'clock. Stephanie was telling everyone to close their eyes, take deep breaths and relax their limbs. Phebe was talking about how her parents are praying. I offered to drive the four of them so they wouldn't have to hassle with parking. There is some anxiety as I don't seem to be moving through the parking lot fast enough.

SO…Now I again sit here at Panera, waiting for the call, waiting for someone to say, "Come get me…or us." Two and a half hours for a test. That is how long they will have to do a lifetime of mathematics.

It is three twenty-seven. So far, no phone calls. Is that a good sign? I could get up and put more ice in my tea, but somehow I'm glued to the time posted on my cell phone. How will it be for them? How will it be for my daughter?

It is a function of the test to create an elite few who succeed and can give orders to the rest who have failed and have to follow. Once our children are trained into the mindset of the test, this system sets about the arduous task of sorting them like lemons. There are A grade, B grade and C grade lemons. Some lemons are just plain old rotten. That would have to be the lower twenty to thirty percent. So we create a system that ensures these results. We ignore the inconvenient truth that all children can do well given enough time and assistance. Instead we pit them against each other in a race, letting only the fastest finish the race and receive the award. But we are talking about children. We are not betting at the racetrack. We are talking about the future of our world. And fast does not necessarily mean proficient, thoughtful or insightful.

I listen to arguments supporting the "No Child Left Behind Act," whose methods of evaluation leave more children 'behind' than ever before. This act requires that all children succeed by some standard that lumps them all together at the same time. This Act requires that all children be 'tested'— and tested equally. But if we really want our children to demonstrate their skills, we must let them do so individually, in their own manner and within their own time frame. It is back to that round, white clock with the black trim poised over the blackboard. It is still a race. The act should really be called "No Child Left Behind Ready-Set-Go!" It leaves no time for passion let alone brilliance.

If Passion
Hits You over the Head,
How Will You Know?

*"Several beautiful children were born to Aphrodite
and Ares.... Eros, their little son, was appointed god
of love. Although nursed with tender solicitude, this
second-born child did not grow as other children
do, but remained a small, rosy, chubby child, with
gauzy wings and roguish, dimpled face. Alarmed for
his health, Aphrodite consulted Themis, who oracu-
larly replied, 'Love cannot grow without Passion.'"*

Late Greek Myth

Homeschooled. We aimed for passion. Instead we tripped
over commotion in the early morning and hit panic as the day
moved on. It was the first day after Labor Day, after a warm
and wonderful beach-filled summer when everyone we knew

packed up and suddenly returned to school. Now we were left alone, in the living room, to face our destiny.

I had the same feelings I had when Stephen was an infant. What do I do with him? How do we find meaning and insight? How do we fill the day and avoid busy-work? Do we fill the day? I was slightly anxious. We had no curriculum, no plan and no support group: No one I knew would even think of doing this.

In fact, I didn't even think it through well. I had neglected to clear enough time to get anything done with Stephen. I still had to get Erin and Matthew to school. Matthew was enrolled in the Montessori kindergarten and Erin was in her second year there. That meant Stephen and I had to dance around their drop-off and pick-up times. Dropping them off was not always timely. I still taught the after-school arts and crafts program. It was difficult to just pop in and leave. Something had to be put away. Someone needed to talk to me about something. Something always happened.

We would return home and then, half a day into it, we had to go get Matthew and bring him home. And a couple hours later we had to go for Erin. And even though the school was only ten minutes away, that was a lot of ten-minute chunks back and forth, and back and forth. I was critical of a school day that interrupted a child's passionate focus through a scheduled change of subjects, and here I was doing the same thing, breaking up our day.

As we practiced this ridiculous schedule, I worried Stephen's day was starting too late. He spent too much time waiting around for me. Maybe he wasn't getting enough done. Maybe this was a ridiculous idea. Maybe I was a ridiculous mom. Maybe…maybe…maybe…and so on ad infinitum.

So we became innovative, at least we tried. Math facts in the car. Spelling, in the car. (Forget handwriting in the car.) Listening to music and discussing the lyrics within a sociological context, in the car. Philosophy on the off ramp. History at the stop signs. There is no end to what you can do when you blunder full-speed-ahead, internally panicked.

A few months into it, we added a classmate, Tracy. Tracy's mother did not like their local school, so Tracy joined us one morning at eight. But Tracy had only gone to a regular public school. She expected regimentation and automatic structure. Stephen and I were still bumbling around the living room looking for paper. He was fine with no structure. He had been raised in a Montessori environment where much of his day had been self-directed. In fact, all his life, Stephen had been actively working against externally imposed structure. As much as I complained, I began to realize Stephen had a skill Tracy needed to rediscover.

Day one, I took Tracy and Stephen to the public library to figure out what there was to know and what out of that was worth knowing. We rented portable tape recorders and took a self-guided tour. When we got to the social sciences, I stopped the tape and asked what the term "social sciences" meant. Stephen spewed out in rapid succession any and every buzzword or term he had ever heard about anything. He did not have the slightest concern whether he was right or wrong.

Tracy, on the other hand, would not venture a single guess. Tracy had learned in school that it was not O.K. to take risks, because risks were penalized, ostracized and marked down. Teachers do not want new, creative, answers; they want the answer in the teacher's manual. They do not have the motivation or inclination to explore alternative possibilities and open new doors, particularly if it is not on the test. Tracy was well schooled. If she were not one hundred percent sure, she would not take the risk. That should have been a clue.

As the month progressed, many differences showed up between Tracy's five years of traditional institutionalized schooling and Stephen's Montessori background. For instance, I suggested we learn some new vocabulary words followed by an informal spelling test. Stephen and Tracy responded in completely different ways. Tracy was most insistent on studying the list, taking the test and then marking how many answers she got wrong at the top of the page. For her, the whole point of the test was to reduce the number wrong. She was not even interested in how many were correct. Stephen, on the other hand, insisted that I give him the test BEFORE he studied. That way he would know which words he didn't know and would only have to study those. He couldn't care less about his score.

Tracy was more internally disciplined than Stephen. She was ready to start immediately on whatever it was as long as I gave her an assignment. If I didn't tell her what to do, she was lost. Stephen was never lost, even when he didn't know what he was doing or where he was going. Stephen meandered his way into doing something. He tinkered around until he found what he wanted to do and then nothing could pull him away. Stephen figured out a way to make the process work for him. He was thoroughly absorbed. Tracy, on the other hand, had internalized the forty-minute hour, the average amount of time most schools spend on one subject. You could set a clock by Tracy's attention span. The minute she started to fidget and lose interest, I knew the hour was almost up. Any time spent past that hour was excruciating. Her attention had been trained and focused to a school schedule. Furthermore, she was still waiting to be told what to do.

Tracy was only interested in the end result. Stephen would have benefited from a little focus on the end product. Tracy needed to learn to be absorbed in the process of exploration. Stephen knew how to explore. Tracy was far more organized and Stephen could only benefit by his exposure to Tracy's sense of order. Together, they made the perfect student.

We are all born with the skill of self-direction. We come into this world with the innate drive to discover and create. When Tracy was a baby, no one could stop her from learning and growing. As Dr. Glasser has observed, try to stop a two-year-old from exploring. It is not possible for long.

So, what happened to Tracy's unceasing drive to learn? Her school trained it out of her. When she turned five, she entered kindergarten, where they put a stop to her exploration. They confined her to her seat and made sure her focus was directed away from any internal sense of what to do. They aimed her attention completely towards the teacher. They destroyed her sense of balance between inward inquiry and the passionate drive to explore the outer world. They gave her the implicit message that the ability to acquire information, without being given an assignment, lay outside her reach. They told her she was not smart enough or mature enough or old enough to explore on her own. They told her from now on, all information would be dispensed by an adult source, and they took away her power and control. They allowed her ability to search to atrophy like an unused muscle, and then they complained she was unmotivated to memorize the information they gave her and perform the tasks they doled out. And they didn't just do that to Tracy; they do that to almost all our children.

Tracy had only gone to her local public school. Six months later, Tracy was back in the same institution. We couldn't make it work for her.

But it was not easy for us either. With Tracy gone, Stephen and I were forced to face each other. All Stephen wanted to do was program on the computer. When I tried to steer him towards other subjects—including what I thought were important skills like math and English—I watched this otherwise thoroughly absorbed child start to unravel at the seam. It was almost impossible to get him to attend to the subjects that were not on his agenda for that day. After a while, I could see that something else was going on. Dr. James Hillman notes:

There is more in a human life than our theories of it allow. Sooner or later something seems to call us onto a particular path. You may remember this 'something' as a signal moment in childhood when an urge out of nowhere, a fascination, a peculiar turn of events struck like an annunciation: This is what I must do, this is what I've got to have. This is who I am. (3)

He continues:

Each person enters the world called. The idea comes from Plato, his Myth of ER at the end of his most well-known work, the Republic.... The soul of each of us is given a unique [soul companion] before we are born, and it has selected an image or pattern that we live on earth. This soul-companion...guides us here; in the process of arrival, however, we forget all that took place and believe we come empty into this world. [It] remembers what is in your image and belongs to your pattern, and therefore [it] is the carrier of your destiny. (7-8)

For centuries we have searched for the right term to identify this 'call.' Christina Grof cites it as:

...the deeper Self...the Self, the creative energy, the force of love, the Divine Mother, our Buddha nature, the Tao, Cosmic Consciousness, the Great Spirit, the Christ, the Beloved Within, our source of inspiration, our higher power or God, just to name a few. (22-23)

Hillman writes:

> The Romans named it your genius;...the Christians your 'guardian angel.' The Romantics, like Keats, said the call came from the heart, and Michelangel's intuitive eye saw an image in the heart of the person he was sculpting. The Neoplatonists referred to an imaginal body, the ochema, that carried you like a vehicle. It was your personal bearer or support. For some it is Lady Luck or Fortuna... In Egypt, it might have been the ka or ba with whom you could converse. Among the people we refer to as Eskimos and others who follow shamanistic practices, it is your spirit, your free-soul, your animal-soul, your breath-soul. (9)

The Native Americans have referred to it as your spirit guide. It has been called the higher self, the inner teacher, the voice within, or simply identified as intuition. Whatever it was, it was tangible and persistent. Hillman claims:

> A calling may be postponed, avoided, intermittently missed. It may also possess you completely. Whatever; eventually it will out. It makes its claim. The [soul companion] does not go away. (8)

So I gave up and tried it Stephen's way. Once again I found him on the computer, but he couldn't explain to me what he was doing. All I saw was the cursor rapidly bouncing from one screen to the next. I had no clue if what he was doing was valuable or not. As far as I could tell, he was just pressing buttons. Of course, he was happy, but I was not. We could always go back to math facts, but then we would both be miserable. Out of frustration, I wrote a note to myself:

> Today, I decided I wasn't going to waste any more of my life or his nagging Stephen into being organized and completing his projects in the same decade that they were started. Of course, the problem is mine, because although I stress the importance of process, I personally don't feel I have done my job unless I see a finished product at the end of that process.
>
> Still, I am learning that this homeschool process, and that is what it is, a process, involves dealing with both MY idiosyncrasies and HIS. It is in a sense a merger of two imperfect human beings and WE NEED TO LEARN TO GET ALONG TOGETHER AS WE ARE! (What a wonderful training ground for a marriage!) I AM NOT GOING TO BE ABLE TO CHANGE EITHER HIM OR MYSELF, and HE IS NOT INTERESTED IN THE PROCESS OF CHANGE. THEREFORE, HE HAS TO LEARN TO LIVE WITH ME, AND I HAVE TO LEARN TO LIVE WITH BOTH MY SHORTCOMINGS AND HIS!

Dr. Hillman talks about a psychology of childhood that views a child's behavior, including those behaviors we might consider less than functional or even maladaptive, as belonging in some way to the child's uniqueness and destiny. It is as if the child is breaking through his own barriers to uncover and manifest his or her brilliance. Hillman explains:

> Given with the child, even given to the child, the clinical data are part of its gift. This means

> that each child is a gifted child, filled with data
> of all sorts, gifts peculiar to that child which
> show themselves in peculiar ways.... (14)

When I recovered my composure, I gave Stephen a time grid on which to plot his schedule. The grid was marked in half-hour increments from eight o'clock in the morning to nine o'clock at night, Monday through Friday. I tried to get him to block out sections of time in which he could log exactly what he was doing. I felt we were out of control. I wanted him to fill in traveling time, tennis lessons, gym lessons and Boy Scouts. These were immutable because the time for these activities was set. Then I devised two categories: projects and skills. I defined skills as spelling, math computation, Spanish and bookwork that did not require a high degree of interaction. I isolated these things so Stephen COULD work on them without me when he wanted. Projects were everything else.

Working together, we managed to define two projects. One was to figure out how to buy a new car. It included product research, leasing and banking information. The other was to construct a giant life-size paper mâché sculpture of a horse using wire, newspaper and white glue. The schedule would be up to him. All I really wanted him to do was plan out the week and fill out the grid. But instead of describing a specific task, he just put the word 'electronics' into all the project spots.

I was frustrated. Electronic what? I wanted him to define the project, maybe even state an objective. I had given him plenty of examples. That was it! How could I let him sit there and randomly play with circuit boards, wires and batteries?

"SO," I asked in an irritated manner, "electronic what?" "What IS the project? WHAT are you trying to accomplish?"

"Oh," he said calmly and matter-of-factly, "I want to tap into your phone line."

"Great," I said. "Do that on your own time with your buddies. We'll make a third category and call it 'friend time.'"

So, once again, I asked him to identify a specific and well-defined project. He talked to me about a program he'd like to write on the computer that translated symbols into words. "Fine," I said briskly and penciled that into all the time slots we had previously erased, grateful he was working on something I could understand.

The next day, Stephen read the <u>Tripod Trilogy</u> from seven o'clock to ten o'clock in the morning, which wasn't on the schedule at all. He read through car time while we took his siblings to school and through a half hour of waiting time in the parking lot while I took care of business in the office. When we came home, he worked on his translation project, programming straight through from ten-thirty to three, eating lunch as he worked. So much for our carefully allotted time schedule! I could not exactly tell what he was learning, but I was learning about internal drive and passionate focus. I was learning that when positively channeled, passion reunites us with our own brilliance. I was learning about a 'calling.' Once again I could not pull him away from his task. Dr. Hillman concludes:

> ...we must attend very carefully to childhood to catch early glimpses of the [soul companion] in action, to grasp its intentions and not block its way. The rest of the practical implications swiftly unfold: (a) Recognize the call as a prime fact of human existence; (b) align life with it; (c) find the common sense to realize that accidents, including the heartache and the natural shocks the flesh is heir to, belong to the pattern of the image, are necessary to it, and help fulfill it. (8)

This time in my frustration I wrote a letter to a friend:

Dear Ellen,

I really looked forward to homeschooling Stephen. I anticipated a year of great exploration. We would go beyond the basics of the three R's and explore our way into government offices, courtrooms, businesses, banking institutions and more. We would discover the secrets of the universe together. Instead, I spent the year tripping over the way Stephen learned.

To do a page of mathematics took twenty minutes or two days. Once Stephen understood the process of a particular mathematical operation, he was no longer interested in the specifics and, to him, unimportant details of calculation. He took twenty seconds to do a problem and four minutes to get to the next problem. He squirmed. He fidgeted. He took apart his pen and explored the spring. He counted how many filaments were in the bulb of the nearby lamp and played with the mechanics of the switch. He paced the room while his mind raced to ten other things. He could understand obscure algebraic equations, but he was not interested in multiplying seven times nine.

Stephen was in anguish. Forcing him to focus on details or to learn in a linear fashion from step A to step B to step C drove him crazy. He needed to understand the 'Gestalt' or overview in a process indigenous only to Stephen. I waited impatiently for an end result and we rarely produced one. I did not experience him as cooperative. He did not perceive me as helpful. He wished he could please. I wished I could nurture better. He suspected I was right. I suspected I was wrong. He was frustrated and so was I.

I spent the year agonizing over my inability to direct and balance Stephen's curriculum, let alone get him to clean up his room. Then I remembered an experience we had when he was no more than two years old:

Dennis and I took Stephen to Malibu Creek Park. Our purpose was to take our first-born back into the hills to observe nature. We parked our car in the parking lot, walked about twenty feet down the gravel road when Stephen stopped. He sat down and started to play with the gravel. As patient, loving parents, we waited five, ten, fifteen minutes while our son sifted through the dirt. None-the-less, we were anxious to move on to the great out-of-doors and share the wonders of nature with him. He would not budge. Dad tried to lift Stephen. He screamed. He kicked. We put him down; the dirt enraptured him. We gave him five more minutes. He wouldn't budge. We tried to coax him. He wanted us to stop.

Finally, Dad figured out we were in Stephen's way. We knelt down to see why this child was so enthralled and at his level, we found a universe. We found a world of brightly colored mountains of stone, colonies of bugs, islands of grass and other growing things. Twenty feet into miles of parkland, Stephen had uncovered the whole experience in a manner that had meaning for him.

Sometimes, when I feel like Stephen is wasting his time programming that computer, I try to remember this incident. I try to see it from his level. I try to remind myself that maybe he is getting everything he really needs, for now, right where he is, in his own little world, pursuing his passion.

Thank you for listening,
Resa

❧ 22 ❧

Dancing into Life
—but What About
Workbooks?

"Life is in motion, 'becoming becoming.' The mo-tions of life swirl inward to the creating of self and outward to the creating of the world. We turn in-ward to bring forth a self. Then the self extends out-ward, seeking others, joining together. Systems arise. Extension and desire organize into complex and meaningful forms...."

Margaret Wheatley

Life is an orchestration between the inward search for mean-ing and the outward quest for experience and information, the two creating and recreating, supporting and deepening each other.

I remember our first steps. It took courage and practice. Dancing into life when you are used to regiment, externally created structure, or even textbooks, workbooks and taking classes, is initially challenging. We had to learn to abandon these crutches. We had to move into the world and let creativity be our guide.

We started timidly in the living room:

Stephen and I drew a horse on graph paper using pictures of horses as a resource. Then we used a grid to calculate and reconstruct a life-size representation. First, we drafted an internal wire structure (five feet tall and six feet long) to support it. Stephen then covered the structure with newspaper, attempting to stick to the form we worked out on the graph. The project took about two solid weeks. He paper mâchéd seven-eighths of it. By the third week we ran out of steam. The six-foot horse hung around, however, in our living room for another five or six weeks waiting for its finishing details. Finally, Dad quietly escorted it to the garage.

We moved to the study:

Stephen created a computer program of his version of Etch A Sketch®. Then he used the code to form Hebrew letters and tried to make the letters correspond to the English symbols on the keyboard. He made the letters move like a type-writer from the right side of the screen to the left (Hebrew), but he couldn't keep the computer from breaking up the word at the end of the line. We put this project on hold.

We included the kitchen table:

Perusing the Sunday paper, Dad found the L.A. Times Stock Market Competition. We enrolled. It was only a paper chase. No money was actually required. Stephen picked $10,000 worth of stock spread over five different industries on the New York and American Exchanges. He picked these stocks on the basis of current events by researching both the front page and the business sections of the newspaper. We traced the progression of the stocks over a six-week period, correlating the position of the stocks with current events in the paper. We finally sold the stocks at the deadline date for a nine-hundred-dollar loss.

We went stir-crazy and frequented the library:

Stephen and I went to the library to figure out what was worth knowing. We explored the shelves until Stephen picked subjects he liked. We spent many weeks researching "what's worth knowing." We took and prioritized notes. We made graphs to explore data. We formed hypotheses and supported them with appropriate information. Then Stephen formed his own conclusion.

We engaged friends and teachers:

Stephen and David B. explored marine biology, geography, chemistry and mathematics with a retired scientist. They played tennis with a tennis coach, took gymnastics at the local gym for kids and briefly studied Spanish with a credentialed teacher who was at home raising her kids. They also took apart telephone and sound systems and any other piece of electronics, the more complex the better.

Stephen went to Tracy's mother's store every Friday for three months and learned how to run a retail store. He also accompanied them to the vet, who donated his time twice a month to give them a forty-five minute class on the anatomy, common diseases and general health care of canines.

We went out into the commercial world on our own:

I took Stephen to Costco for an economics lesson. Stephen figured out how much Dad needed to earn annually to support our family, calibrated it down to the hour and created a budget. When Stephen emerged from his calculations he gave us an allowance of $200 in food and then he went shopping. When he emerged from the food aisles, he had spent $270 in food and $30 of our $50 biweekly miscellaneous budget in snacks, even after putting back $13 in taco chips and nacho sauce, and $9 worth of Cajun buffalo wings. He could not explain the discrepancy; we went back to the drawing board.

I had Erin and Matthew join our adventures:

Later that afternoon I tried a similar, scaled down version of economics and math, this time including the two younger children. We went to the supermarket. I gave each child two dollars and asked them to buy as much nutritious food as they could find for that amount. Then I set them loose in the store.

Matthew headed for the pet aisle and fixated on a collar for the cat at $1.49. That was all he wanted to buy and he insisted on keeping the change. Erin objected to the PINK color (after all it was HER kitty) and threatened to refuse to let him put it on the cat IF HE DID buy it! Matthew burst into tears and insisted I take back the two dollars because there was nothing else in the store he wanted. Erin capitulated; if he really wanted to buy a cat collar, he could buy a BLUE one (at $3.49). Then she stormed off to pool her resources with her older brother. I told Matthew to just get the BLUE one (I gave him an extra $2.00) and not worry about the price." (So much for the lesson.)

But Erin and Stephen were still working the problem. They quickly figured out that two heads were better than one and four dollars were better than two. Upon much deliberation they bought the following items—which they considered necessities:

- One wash cloth with a goose on it $1.49 (for mom)
- One bottle of strawberry kefir (liquid yogurt) $.99 (for Dad)
- One 16.oz can of green beans $.39 (we never ate canned vegetables)
- Three large carrots at $.90 per lb., total $.39
- One cucumber $.49
- One individually packaged slice of cherry pie (listed as "fried pie") $.33. (Heaven only knows what was in this!)

They were very proud of their purchases, even though they were eight cents over budget. We continued our journey.

We made more play dates:

Stephen went to his cousins', Adam's and Jenny's, orchard to play. There they built tree houses in the ravine, played games in the twenty acres of lemons, and invented mechanical devices with Adam in the barn. Adam and Stephen invented a water pressure system using a 'rubber dinky.' I did not know what it was for, but they really liked it. They switched a valve and the rubber dinky went streaming forward because the water pressure was amplified through a system of pipes. They also built a valve from scratch for an air compressor and experimented with various siphons.

As time went on we sought community service:

Stephen and his best friend David B. rigged the sound system for the Christmas show at a nearby community church. First they figured out how the church's sound system worked.

Then they ran microphone lines and adjusted sound levels using the amplifier and equalizer. They organized who was going to wear microphones, when and what kind. Then, they ran the sound system during the show. After the show, their curiosity got the better of them and they took the whole system apart re-connecting components and adding features "to make it better." It was their gift to the church. David B.'s parents graciously offered to cover the $300 in repair costs as a school expense.

We finally stopped trying to direct Stephen's education:

Stephen wanted to make a bionic arm, but we couldn't find information on how to construct one. I was ready to drop the project when he picked up the phone. I thought he was clowning around. He called his friends for advice. When they couldn't help, he called his uncles. When that failed he called Dennis's office and unbeknownst to us, asked his father's colleagues for help. Someone referred him to someone else and pretty soon he found an electrician and a systems analyst who would work with him to collect data and materials on making a functional automated arm. He never actually constructed that bionic arm, but he learned at a very young age that people were his best resource.

Our voyage was so intriguing, I pulled the other two children out of school and we began to homeschool as a family. But, in spite of my degrees and credentials, I was really not prepared to work one-on-one with three kids at the same time. In an attempt to control the chaos, I quickly reverted back to workbooks and texts.

First, I started with grade-level appropriate material in the areas of reading, writing, spelling and mathematics. But grade levels are a publisher's concoction. Mathew, for instance, chose his work randomly, flipping through the pages of his math workbook and stopping at whatever attracted his attention. He insisted on picking the pages himself. If he didn't know how to do a particular problem, he searched until he found the information he needed. Often he persisted; sometimes he didn't. In general, he mastered a problem instantly, because it was usually his decision to learn it. Matthew's perspective, untainted by preconceived notions of who he was or what he was supposed to be doing, was fresh and alive. The order in which he learned the math would have driven developmental and curriculum experts crazy.

When I took him to an educational bookstore to place him in the 'correct' grade level for math, he looked at the first grade book. Then asked for the second, third, fourth, fifth and sixth grade books. And even though he couldn't really read yet, he showed me that each grade only added a skill or two and he was right. Six years to learn fractions, decimals and percents all of a sudden appeared to be a tragic waste of time. So, I bought the whole series, threw out the concept of grade level, relinquished the compulsion to do each book in order page by page from front to back and let Matthew be my guide. He eventually covered all the material, went on to algebra, calculus and trigonometry and at age eleven entered Moorpark College. At eighteen he was admitted to UCLA as a junior in mathematics and graduated with a Bachelors of Science in the same subject. Carlos Castaneda wrote, "The fact of the matter is that many children see.... Most of those who see are considered to be oddballs and every effort is made to correct them." (Quotable Spirit, 32)

3Rs

As time went on it became quite clear that reading, writing, and mathematics were skills and everything else was content. As I looked through the different publishers, I was astonished to learn that children in different schools, districts, counties and states were studying widely varying curriculum at completely different times. It was completely arbitrary. Who made these decisions? (Often administrators in district, county and state offices, even, textbook companies.) There was no consistency. So, it seemed to me that children might as well be exploring their interests. They might as well be trying to find out who they were and what they liked to do by discovering their passions and uncovering their brilliance.

In the beginning, we searched within the standard categories of science, social studies, art and music. But the more we explored, the more those divisions between categories blurred. We ended up studying history through art. Music was astoundingly mathematical. A lot of topics were not available in standard texts or they were so watered down they were uninteresting. So we deserted the textbook publishers and went out into the world to find whatever called us. It was the great hunt. Through bookstores, libraries, museums, magazines and field trips, the world was both our laboratory and our playground.

Then, one day, we took the kids to the Museum of Science and Industry to see a visiting interactive computer exhibit. Stephen took off into the exhibit at lightning speed and disappeared. Shortly afterwards, we saw a group of museum assistants in their official yellow jackets swarm around an exhibit. We approached cautiously and peeked in between their shoulders. There was our son in the middle of the circle. He was playing with an interactive touch screen. But instead of touching the designated buttons on the screen, his fingers were reaching past the image for unseen icons, dragging them down, opening them up and moving into the mechanics of the program just with the touch of his finger. Suddenly, the clown face on the screen vanished and we found ourselves looking at the programming language used to create the illusion. In fact, all the images on all the screens disappeared to display programming language instead. There were no visible icons. No one could figure out how he did it. Even Stephen could not explain what he had done. But the museum staff, much to our surprise, cheered him on—that is, until the director showed up, shut it down and (even though Stephen offered to fix it) kicked us out.

Life was becoming more intuitive by the moment. It was a great feat, attempting to create balance and open new doors, yet leave enough space to allow passion to find its way to the surface. Julia Cameron writes, "We are all conduits for a higher self that would work through us." (211)

Krishnamurti's words rang through my ears. "All that you do makes it impossible for what already is there to express itself." (39)

❧ 23 ❧

Stephen, Just Stephen

Flash forward twenty years. He sleeps in mission control. The only resemblance to a bedroom that I can see is the bed. It is seven o'clock on a Monday morning. I stand in the doorway of his apartment and take in the room. There are books and papers and pieces of electronic equipment everywhere. He says to me, "O.K. Mom. I've learned not to apologize. This is just the way it is. We had a week from h...last week and I haven't recovered yet. I know it's messy right now, but what do you think of the room set up? Do you like the low profile cabinets on the right? I went to bed at one o'clock in the morning last night." His roommate, Jason, drops off a book, "Hacking Exposed," and disappears through the sliding glass door.

I am taking the morning to visit my now grown son, Stephen—twenty-something. He has invited me to a breakfast meeting with his two forty-something partners, Alan and Roger. (After all, I just spent all that time with Erin.) I haven't seen Stephen's apartment since he redecorated. I'm not really sure I can actually see it now. As I look around the room my eyes fall on four running computer monitors and a pile of equipment I cannot identify. There are disks stacked on various spindles and standing freeform. The chrome touch lamp I bought him as a housewarming gift is nicely displayed in front of a can of "Dust Off" and a large Styrofoam cup of coffee with a green lid from the local gas station. A half-empty bottle of Perrier stands nearby. The handwritten sign hastily taped to the wall reads:

Rules

#1

—Go Slow!

—Don't get frustrated—we all don't know everything

—But we eventually will!

—CALM

—Don't interrupt your turn is <u>comming</u>! (sic)

Stephen says he didn't write the sign. But the black sharpie with which it was written lay cap off and drying on a nearby table. The sign is askew and needs tending.

"Matthew was here yesterday using my equipment, so it was sort of moved around and..." Stephen gets up and checks what he refers to as the 'green screen.'

"What's a 'green screen'?" I ask.

"The green screen displays the technical status information for the website we are running," he announces matter-of-factly. Then he gets on the phone. "I have a meeting in a couple of minutes," he says to some unknown source. No hello. Just, "I have a meeting..." He paces while he works. He is still in his bathrobe, programming while he stands, tracking the 'green screen' and talking on his cell. "We have more work than we can handle. If this deal gets set up, I want you back. We took over this business last week and are consulting for the next four weeks. We've got about nine projects going. We spent the last eighteen months building a pipeline...ah uh, ah uh, ah uh.... Got to run. I'll call you back."

Thirty seconds later he is dressed and standing by the door waiting for me. He did not leave my sight. I did not see him get dressed. I do not know how this has happened. We get in the car and in five blocks I find myself back in a coffee shop waiting to be seated.

Alan walks in on his cell, waving the phone in the air at us. "Do you remember 'The Way Back Machine'? Mr. Peabody and Sherman? We found a technology that goes back to people's websites and takes snapshots of prior websites."

Roger's phone rings. He answers. They order breakfast.

"O.K." Alan says, "Now I'm ready to go to the 'to do' list."

"Let me help you," Stephen takes control of the conversation. He addresses each task and outlines how it will get done, what he needs to do, what he will outsource.... "and every engineer who works on that project needs to learn the language. You don't need a database guy; you need a Perl developer. A database guy would be completely inappropriate."

Words like 'balance of power, negotiate, cards, the opposite two weeks ago,' bounce around the table. Roger swaps his pancake for Stephen's toast. They talk about repairing Stephen's tent before they go camping. "Duct tape," Roger quips. Stephen now gets on the phone. Roger leans over to me as he eats the toast up to the crust. "Is this what you anticipated? This is generally how it goes." The waitress drops off the bill and we head back to the apartment, the four of us in three separate cars. Stephen and I arrive first.

"Hold on a minute. I've got to check to see what's on fire."
Stephen heads straight for the open 'green screen.'

"What do you mean, on fire?" I ask, as I can only imagine.

"I'm checking emails to see who is complaining." Stephen designs systems and trouble-shoots the computer operations until the companies who hire him are running smoothly. He does it out of his bedroom.

I take in more of the room. On his bureau sits his p.j.'s, a towel, a department store bag with the merchandise still inside, a dented bottle of Arrowhead water, two unopened cans of Campbell's Cream of Mushroom Soup, two books marked UNIX, one with Roger's name labeled with markers on the side, a screw driver, matte knife, a large opened box stuffed with packing material (it will not close), a black-handled spoon stuck to a blue plate and a book from the UCLA bookstore.

On the floor lay shoes, notebooks, an empty coke bottle, scanner, speaker, 'Fresh Brush' for the toilet tank, dental floss, coupons, stacks of mail and a text marked used, "Computer Organization and Design."

"What's the book behind that one?" I point and ask.

Stephen looks up from the screen, "150 Ways to Date Women!"

"Really?"

"No. Just kidding. It's on CGI programming."

I always fall for the bait.

Stephen reaches for the now three-quarters empty Perrier bottle (uncapped) and takes a few more sips.

Alan and Roger walk in through the sliding glass door from the patio. (Doesn't anyone use the front door?) Alan takes a look around and surveys the damage. "You know what will fix this? Four large bins and finishing a cycle. Can we put some of the books on top of the cabinets?"

Alan pauses and looks at me. He apologizes for the condition of Stephen's room. "We take on really big companies who have problems too big for other companies to tackle. The reason we are successful is because Stephen is not afraid to work the problems through. He is not afraid to fail and pick himself up and start over. He persists until eventually the problem is solved." (I smile to myself—all that self-initiated learning.)

Their talk quickly turns to something about a drive array and a client server. They all talk too fast. Then the chatter ceases. I turn around and Alan and Roger are gone. They have escaped back out again through the patio door. The room is once again silent. The hurricane has come and gone, but I suspect the source is still pacing around the bedroom, talking on his cell.

I survey the room again. There is a large stuffed black office chair, but Stephen is still not in it. The hanging louvers at the window rattle intermittently in the breeze, imitating the sound of a keyboard. Another large flat screen monitor, perhaps a T.V., appears to turn itself on. Stephen explains the two by three foot screen is not a T.V.; it's a computer monitor. It shows pictures of dozens of C.D. albums. Stephen clicks on something titled the 'Buddha-Bar.' All of a sudden, the room is transformed from a pigsty to a monastic sanctuary. Soothing music fills the air. Track lighting sends warm, wonderful light up to the ceiling and bounces back on the workspace. Stephen continues moving around the room, cleaning, stacking and putting things away.

My mind wanders to his childhood and all those baskets of toys. It is how he creates best, in little messes. He always has. I think of all the ways I attempted to get him organized—and failed. I think of all the kids in all the classrooms who are penalized, punished and reprimanded for not conforming to a particular sense of order. I look at my child. What I experience as chaos is the way he creates best. It has facilitated his success in both a real and academic world.

The Perrier bottle is now sitting to the left of the green screen. "I have mastered the art of putting things away," Stephen tells me. "I just have to remember to do it. Do you want a Perrier?" He holds out his hand to show me the now seven-eights empty Perrier bottle.

"Not that one," I reply.

"I didn't mean this one," and he runs out of the room to emerge with two more room-temperature bottles of water.

"Last week, we took over a website. We replaced the technical team for a well-established e-commerce website."

"Why was it so hectic?"

He is now immersed in making me copies of his favorite C.D's. Something Middle Eastern comes spewing out of the speakers.

"Why was it so hectic?" I repeat the question.

"Yes," he answers, either not hearing or not addressing the question. "Because it was the hard work of one man working for eight years by himself and the man left the company so we had to take over his mess. It had a lot of moving parts and there were no passwords. We had to figure out how to fly the airplane we just recaptured while it was still in flight and customers and staff were on board."

He picks up the phone. No hello, he begins, "You know the alerts that Frank prepares. I woke up and there was an alert I have never seen before, seven-thirty and all is well."

Stephen hangs up the phone again and turns toward me. "I had no more than four hours consecutive sleep last week." Then he picks up the conversation we had five conversations ago. "So, we were driving an airplane. The pilot had just jumped and we took over the controls...."

As he speaks, my eyes drift to a red 'Maxtor' box that reads, "What drives you? Speed, power, perfection."

The phone rings. "Stephen speaking." He moves through the room, cleaning up as he talks—the electronically wired version of Mr. Clean. The music is pumping African music now, tribal with an electronic twist. "Goals," he continues, "One, to reduce technical support cost. Two, to improve the ease of use of the system. Three, to generate a revenue stream from people too lazy to do the work properly."

He's back at the green screen, standing there in his shorts. His shirt is missing. When did that happen? I didn't see him take it off.

"Where's your shirt?"

"I hung it up. I don't usually wear a shirt. It's hot and I move around a lot." (The black desk chair is still empty and now a contemporary Hebrew song is coming out of the 'Buddha Bar'.)

He's back on the phone…again no hello. He starts the conversation with, "The last thing, who did he call panicking?" (He's back to rolling up wires and putting them in the appropriate containers as he speaks.) The music switches to Indian reggae.

His phone conversation persists, but his body does not stop moving around the room. He is the grownup version of the toddler who wouldn't sit in "Mommy and Me," only now it is clear how he is utilizing this trait to his advantage. The place is almost perfectly clean. It is hard to believe he cleaned it up so impeccably in such a short period of time. I was thinking, maybe he could come home and apply this hidden skill there.

He switches to speakerphone again and pauses a second with the finally empty Perrier bottle dangling in-between his fingers.

Matthew calls me on my cell phone. "I heard you were spending the day with Stephen. When can you spend time with me?"

I hear Stephen still on his phone, "We are here 24/7 until you're stable. We've taken on a commitment to you and we stand by it. We will support you until you're completely up and running. Can you look at this thing sometime and see if you can tell me why it failed? Let's do it right now. Can we do it right now? I like to keep things off my 'to do' list. O.K?"

The room is quiet again except for the sound of the keyboard, the clacking of the blinds and the faint murmur of Stephen's roommate, Jason, upstairs, strumming away at the guitar.

I wait until I can catch him off the phone again. "Stephen, I need to go home now. It's only noon and I'm exhausted. Do you have a cup of coffee I can take with me?" I ask.

"Actually, mom, let's go to the corner gas station. They make great coffee. Trust me. And while we're at it, let's drive over to the Mexican restaurant. Do you want lunch to go? Jason and I put in an order this morning."

I pack up and go to my car. Stephen hops into the passenger seat. "Come on, mom. Let's go!" I see him at seven and nine and twelve and fourteen years of age, always on his way to the next adventure.

"Yes, for the coffee," I respond. "No, for the Mexican restaurant. I need to get on the freeway before traffic hits." We drive the two blocks to the gas station (I'm thinking we should have walked.) Stephen fills three cups at the mini-market. He explains this is how he and his roommate Jason like it. Can he make it like that for me too? We hop back in the car. I drive around the block.

"Stephen," I ask. "Can I talk to you for just a moment?"

"Sure mom." He hops out of the car. But instead of walking around toward my window, he keeps walking away toward his apartment. (He must have heard me. Didn't he just answer me?)

I roll down the window, "Stephen! Stephen!" All I see is his back disappear beyond the bushes and around the side of the apartment complex. My phone rings. It's Stephen.

"Hi Mom! Gotta run. Let's talk! On the phone? Oops! Got another call. O.K. Mom, how about later? Love ya!"

I pull away from the curb. The phone rings again. "Can you come back? I forgot Jason's coffee." I drive around the block for the second time and pull up in front of the apartment. Stephen bounds out from around the side, leaps toward the car to get the coffee, which I hand him through the open car window.

As he turns, a man appears and hails Stephen.... "Can I talk to you about the server?"

"Hi, Mark! Sure," he says, without skipping a beat. And as they walk back to mission control, I hear Stephen's phone ringing.

Phillip Brooks states that each of us carries within us the ideal life—the one we are supposed to lead—the one we feel in our blood and "will never be still...We feel the thing we ought to be beating through the thing we are." (113)

ঞ 24 ঞ

The Underground

"Once upon a time, the animals decided they must do something heroic to meet the problems of a "New World." So they organized a school. They adopted an activity curriculum consisting of running, climbing, swimming and flying. To make it easier to administer, all animals took all subjects.

The duck was excellent in swimming. Better, in fact, than his instructor, and made excellent grades in flying. But he was very poor in running. Since he was low in running, he had to stay after school and also drop swimming to practice running. This was kept up until his webbed feet were badly worn and he was only average in swimming. But average was acceptable in the school, so nobody worried about that...except the duck.

The rabbit started at the top of the class in running, but had a nervous breakdown because of so much make-up in swimming. So she dropped out.

The squirrel was excellent in climbing until he developed frustrations in the flying class. His teacher made him start from the ground up instead of from the treetop down. He also developed charley horses from over-exertion, and he got a C in climbing and a D in running.

The eagle was a problem child and had to be disciplined severely. In climbing class, he beat all the others to the top of the tree, but insisted on using his own way of getting there.

At the end of the year, an abnormal eel that could swim exceedingly well and also could run, and fly a little, had the highest average and was appointed valedictorian.

The prairie dogs stayed out of school and fought the tax levy because the administration would not add digging and burrowing to the curriculum. They apprenticed their children to the badger and later joined the groundhogs and gophers to start a successful private school of their own."

Anonymous

I remember when it started. It was Jennifer's idea. She was ten. Adam agreed. He was seven. They would rebel. Together they would build a better school than anything they had ever seen or experienced. And as young as they were, they were already experts—having survived both public and private schools.

Concerned with their children's response to education, my cousins, George and Debra Tash, decided to listen to their daughter and open a school of their own. Neither was an educator. They owned a plumbing manufacturing company. Debra had a college degree. George never felt comfortable in school but excelled as an inventor instead. Together they hoped they could protect the natural creativity and spirit of their children and maybe a few others as well.

They remembered their own childhoods and felt that children were pushed into things they weren't ready for and kept from doing what they really needed to do to grow. They took a step back and surveyed our culture as a whole. They saw the American family torn apart. They looked at the increasing economic necessity of having two working parents and heard reports about deficient daycare facilities. They watched single-parent families try to juggle an untenable situation. They witnessed latchkey kids, children who are alone until their parents get home, become commonplace. Putting it all together, they decided to try Jennifer's experiment and offer it to the families of their employees as well.

So, George and Debra searched for a private teacher. It was their vision; they would offer tuition to the school as an employee benefit, right along with health care. It was to be a modified version of homeschooling for the working parent. Everyone would be in the same building together. They would share the same space and work together as a team to raise their children.

But finding a teacher who embodied the spirit of the experiment and would protect the soul of the child was not easy. The salary was good and so were the benefits, but most of the teachers they interviewed appeared to be either lacking in spirit, or invested in power and control OVER the students. They interviewed dozens of teachers for months, but no one understood what they were trying to accomplish. Neither dictatorship nor anarchy, it was going to be a partnership WITH the children. Abraham Maslow writes:

> Contemporary researchers suggest strongly that the organism is more trustworthy, more self-protecting, self-directing, and self-governing than it is usually given credit for (Cannon, 1932; Goldstein 1939; Levy, 1951; Rogers, 1954; and others).... This kind of tendency to growth or self-actualization, in one or another vague form, has been postulated by thinkers as diverse as Aristotle and Bergson, and by many other philosophers. Among psychiatrists, psychoanalysts, and psychologists it has been found necessary by Goldstein, Buhler, Jung, Horney, Fromm, Rogers, and many others. (46)

Then we ran into Brian, Stephen's old Montessori teacher. We hadn't seen him in years. I introduced him to Debra and George, and Brian became headmaster, teacher and co-founder. The school was named the G.T. Water School after the company that sponsored it, G.T. Water Products. It opened in fall, right in the midst of the business office and factory with three children: Jenny, Adam and Martha. It had no pre-canned curriculum. It had no pre-defined structure. It had no mode of assessment. It just followed the hearts of these three children. Carl Rogers writes:

> If I distrust the human being then I MUST cram him with information of my own choosing, lest he go his own mistaken way. But if I trust the capacity of the human individual for developing his own potentiality, then I can provide him with many opportunities and permit him to

> choose his own way and his own direction in
> his learning...students who are in real contact
> with problems which are relevant to them wish
> to learn, want to grow, seek to discover, en-
> deavor to master, desire to create, move toward
> self-discipline. (Freedom to Learn, 114)

When our whole lives are regimented for us, first by school
and then by work, we are hesitant to try new solutions or
create new structures and direction. We do not want to assume responsibility for structuring our own time on a daily
basis. We have been taught to follow orders. We have been
taught not to take risks. We have been taught to be afraid and
we project our fears onto our children.

Not certain what the outcome of this experiment might be,
I homeschooled my children *at home* for the first year while I
continued to watch and wait. But when laughter could be
heard peeling down the hall of the business office and three
relatively mellow, happy children finished the school year apparently undamaged, the rest of the employees took an interest in this new option for their children and so did I. We
would all work together to make it succeed. Margaret Wheatley writes:

> Life takes form from [such] ceaseless motions.
> But the motions of life have direction. Life
> moves toward life. We seek for connection and
> restore the world to wholeness. Our seemingly
> separate lives become meaningful as we dis-
> cover how necessary we are to each other.
> Meaning expands as we join life's cohering
> motions. Meaning deepens as we move into the
> dance.... (A Simpler Way, 88)

At first, I used the school only as a social vehicle for my children while we continued our homeschooling project. We did our work in the morning and then joined the other kids in the afternoon to play. I was somewhat ambivalent about joining the group when they did their work in the park. I questioned the arrangement. I wondered if a park environment would be conducive to 'serious study.' Would they be distracted? Maybe they would play too much, I foolishly pondered. But eventually the breeze beckoned and the trees called and we found ourselves sitting there with the G.T. kids on the grass, happily reading and writing away.

The following year I joined the G.T. Water School full time. I would homeschool my children with the other children in exchange for driving to weekly field trips and pitching in as a member of the team. Everyone would benefit.

The school had now grown to about eighteen children. We were our own, multi-aged, one room schoolhouse (only we had more than one room). The children took their projects and worked right alongside their parents in their offices. The parents joined the kids during their classes. The children were not separated and sorted by any standards—not by grade level, ability or age. Their individual interests drove their curriculum and they went at their own pace. We never tested them unless it was a spelling test for fun. They received no grades. Everyone was relieved. Even the parents of kids who had done well in school enjoyed this new freedom from pressure. And in a way we could never have imagined, we were all about to become free.

❧ 25 ❧

Pray for Chocolate!

The time is now. It is ten-thirteen at night. I am sitting at a sandwich shop the night before Erin's second comprehensive. The sandwich shop is on campus. The management expects students to be sitting here studying. There are neon lights over the service bar: pink, purple, green, red and blue, advertising smoothies, ice cream, coffee and sandwiches. It's a good deal. A foot long sandwich is $1.75. Two kids could split one. The floors are beige and tile. The walls are yellow, green and white. It is a strange array of colors. The tables are café commercial: nice, clean, arranged in neat rows and definitely plastic. Every two minutes a voice behind a loud speaker announces the number of a patron's order. *Number twenty-two.*

Number twenty-eight. You pick up your sandwich when it is ready. The sound is much louder here than it is at Panera. There is nothing soft to absorb the noise and the place holds over a hundred customers, more like a large institutional cafeteria. About every ten minutes another group of kids wanders in.

This is our second move tonight. We started in a little café. We had not studied there before. It was small, dark and crowded. What a contrast! It reminded me of the old hippie, hole-in-the wall, down-and-out café. No two pieces of furniture matched. The high walls, painted in a wide assortment of dark, dark reds, browns, oranges and blues, hosted an over-zealous assortment of amateur paintings and oriental rugs. Small, unique lamps adorned each table, but it was far too dark to see each other let alone read a book. There was no space to breathe and strange incense triggered a coughing spasm for Erin's friend, Stephanie. Erin's eyes started to water. If you crossed your legs, you were likely to hit the person at the table next to you. I couldn't believe someone suggested studying there, neither could the girls. But not wanting to appear too 'stuffy' they had decided to try it. After all, there were other kids who liked it.

I looked at the clientele—a combination of stereotypical college students and kids with flaming hair. I looked at my girls. They had all pushed their hair away from their faces. I don't think they cared about the way they looked in weeks since they started studying for this test. I annoyed the lady to my right as I tried to put my purse under the table. I wondered why she and her friend were there, both middle aged, conservative looking. Maybe the food was good. Then I remembered. I was there, too, sitting in my linen pants and suit blazer. I wondered if they wondered what I was doing there, but I don't think they cared. Stephanie's coughing spasm wouldn't quit. Erin voted to move. All agreed. Now we are at the sandwich place. They are open all night. That is the good news and the bad news.

I sit at a table near the girls, sleepy and praying for chocolate. One, two hours or more pass. I am interrupted by peals of laughter. Erin and Stephanie are turning red in the face. Phebe and Elaine cannot stop laughing. They are hysterical, all of them. I have never seen math be so funny; I just wish I could be let in on the joke. I think they have had it! I know I have. They stop laughing long enough to address a problem. Then they start over. Finally, folding their books, they decide to go home. They will each face the test, in their own way, in the morning. I think about my daughter's schooling.

❧ 26 ❧

The Underground
Part II

"There is only the dance."

T.S. Elliot

Life at the G.T. School was the grand dance. We were a community and it was definitely a cooperative effort. Everyone had something to give. George, the owner, provided the kids with building materials and a little expertise on how to use the tools in the back. Debra, his wife, my cousin, was always ready with an extra van and a plate of freshly baked chocolate chip cookies. Anne worked in sales and taught dance professionally in the evenings. Anne donated a jazzercise class for the parents and any child who had the wherewithal to join us. She had three kids in the program. The controller of the company, Marsha, brought in crafts for all the kids including her two daughters. Dawn worked in advertising, but on the weekend was a mounted ranger, so she offered equestrian related activities to the group. Dawn also had three kids in the program. Everybody brought an expertise in something and the combination was always changing. The trick was to create the dance in a way that paired the steps to the changing beat of the children's needs and still provide a certain amount of predictability and structure.

So we had ritual. First thing in the morning, while their parents were getting ready for their day, Brian gathered up the children and took them on a walk into the hills behind the factory. The older kids carried the little kids on their backs. They reminded me of the Von Trapp family in <u>The Sound of Music</u> off to conquer the Alps, only they'd be back in an hour.

We had predictability. After their walk, we worked on skills—reading, writing, spelling and math…unless of course any particular child was caught up in a project they didn't want to put down…which happened frequently…OR someone decided to do a photo shoot and needed subjects…OR the clay by the potter's wheel looked particularly inviting. Sometimes the park called. Each child had different needs at different times and each day seemed to follow its own rhythm. The kids could count on it.

After lunch, if we were not on a field trip, we spent the afternoon playing in Debra and George's twenty acres of lemon and grapefruit orchard. Children who work at their own pace without interruption get more done than children who work in a homogenous group. Independent children can accomplish in three hours, what takes children in a traditional structure all day. Management issues do not interrupt their time and focus. They do not sit around and wait for directions, wait for other kids to settle down, wait for materials to be passed out and wait for class business to be over. They do not wait. They begin immediately and keep the pace going, uninterrupted. They engage in their work.

Furthermore, children who are asked to sit still, who aren't allowed to move or stand when they are doing their work, require more breaks more often. But when that management time disappears, homeschooled children or those in a self-paced classroom can do all that the traditional structure requires and much more. In fact, they can do more and still have time to spend their afternoons playing and having a childhood.

'Having a childhood' has become a lost concept. It means unstructured time to explore and discover creativity. We have become suspicious of play. We consider anything that cannot be defined or measured a waste of time. If a skill or 'progress' is not readily visible, we dismiss the activity. We fill our children's time with activities, classes and organized sports leaving them little time to breathe. We just keep filling them from the outside in.

But play for a child is creative time. It is inside out time. It is time to dip into the imagination and bring the imaginary to form, to unite psyche and soul, to integrate mind, body, emotions and spirit in a manner indigenous to the growth of the whole child. Fantasy is a component of a child's natural state of being. Why do we think we can do better than nature? If we insisted on regulating how and when our toddlers should talk and walk, we would have a society of damaged, speechless and immobilized children lacking in the skills we take for granted. We would stunt our own growth and threaten our survival as a society. Joseph Chilton Pearce writes:

> Analytical psychologists and behaviorists speak learnedly of fantasy play as wish fulfillment by which the child builds a bulwark between himself and the harsh realities of the world. The child, according to this learned theory, fantasizes to keep from facing the awful truth of human frailty, awareness of his impotence in this

> uncaring universe. Or fantasy play is viewed as
> a kind of psychological safety valve, allowing
> the child to ease the pain of actual existence by
> magical dreams of power over it.
>
> Nothing of the sort is involved. The
> biological plan is vastly more intelligent and
> skillful and the purposes of play and imitation
> are light-years beyond these paltry, facile,
> impotent, and deadly unimaginative academic
> notions. (The Magical Child, 170)

A childhood full of play was the best thing we could give our children. They spent their afternoons playing in that orchard. They made up all kinds of imaginary games full of fantasy and intrigue. They turned the child-size ravine toward the back of the property into a fantasyland. The ravine was maybe fifty feet across and ten feet deep. During the rainy season it was a natural water runoff, but, during the other eleven months of the year, there were little dry islands and places to play cast-a-way. There were big old trees to climb, tree houses to build, pulley systems to create, ropes to string and swing from, and all kinds of ways to rappel down the gentle banks of that ravine. Pearce explains:

> The great rule is: Play on the surface, and the
> work takes place beneath. ...As I have noted,
> growth of intelligence is never a conscious
> process; conceptual changes always take place
> below awareness. Of what is the child aware in
> fantasy play? He is aware of the reality of his
> own play creation, a reality that exists neither in
> the world out there nor in the concrete concepts
> of the child's brain. Play reality, like adult reali-
> ty, is neither world nor brain; it is world plus
> mind-brain. (The Magical Child, 165)

While not all children have an orchard to play in, most children do have room to expand their wings. There are playgrounds to enliven the imagination and parks to put children in touch with what is natural—nature and play.

I chuckle when I see our local middle school's version of physical activity. Children run the track because they have to, not because they want to. Most are about as interested in running that circle as fish are in mountain climbing. Many of the kids run near the instructor and walk the other three-quarters of the way when they are out of earshot.

Our children ran and jumped in the organic course of their play. They grew strong limbs and became skillful climbing those big trees. We never had a 'hyper-activity' problem because each child had an opportunity to work that energy out—they had room to move. And no hyperactivity—no need for medication. They learned about teamwork from the natural course of their play, big kids helping little ones, children sharing ideas in the course of problem solving how to execute their communal plans—plans they negotiated, agreed to and came up with on their own.

They accomplished more in the morning than kids in the regular structure did all day and they still had half the day to play and run and jump and explore and create in the great out-of-doors.

And when they got home, they had time to be a family. We never did homework, although our children were always generating their own projects and exploring everywhere they went. Homework is assigned. Homework is busywork. Homework is irrelevant to the needs of the child in the moment. Homework destroys and paralyzes families. It keeps them from having meaningful family time to share, relax and enjoy each other, time to develop family activities and interests outside the realm of school. Homework destroys relationships as parents battle with children over work that seems overwhelming and extraneous to everyone. We never did that to ourselves. Dr. William Glasser talks about the assignment of excessive, tedious and often irrelevant homework:

> [some]...parents believe that learning is directly correlated with the amount of homework done by a student. The parents' demand for homework even extends to the primary grades, where children cannot understand its use or importance. Often in their attempts to work alone at home, young children make the same mistake over and over, thus learning and reinforcing worse ideas that will be hard to change.... [Furthermore,] excessive homework penalizes the bright, creative student because, by doing it conscientiously, he has little time for other pursuits such as music, dancing, art, theater, science, and crafts. (<u>Schools Without Failure</u>, 73-75)

Families in the traditional structure are torn apart by the homework our public and private schools assign. Our G.T. Water families had the capacity to spend the evening together doing whatever they chose. Children were not scattered and sent to separate rooms to finish their work. Parents were not forced to engage in what might be referred to as the 'great homework battle.' Homework breaks up families. It makes family time a very sad time. Parker Palmer explains:

> If a work does not gladden me in these ways, I need to consider laying it down. When I devote myself to something that does not flow from my identity, that is not integral to my nature, I am most likely deepening the world's hunger rather than helping to alleviate it. (30)

School time was joyous. We had a barn. The kids turned it into a theater. They built a stage with a little structural help from slightly concerned adults. They created their own plays and scenery. They scavenged, built and concocted props. They constructed birds and airplanes that flew across the barn at the appropriate time (all that pulley-experimenting in the ravine was now being applied). They designed sound systems with cassette recorders and old speakers. They figured out they needed 'tech people' and some way to cue everyone.

They ranged in age from four-and-a-half through eighteen and they worked as a team. The younger children made significant contributions. The older children recognized both the limitations and gifts of their younger friends and siblings. The younger kids learned to evaluate and respect the decisions of the older ones. They all learned to structure the creative process so every child had an opportunity to make appropriate and significant contributions. And after they spent months perfecting their play and their technical prowess, they figured out how best to advertise it to the local community. They printed and sold tickets and provided refreshments for the audience during intermission. It was a full-scale project and they produced many such plays over the years. Our children were the happiest when they were creating.

Julia Cameron cites this creative drive as the natural order of life. The universe is creative and so are we. When we are connected to our own creativity, we are connected to what is natural in life. Cameron writes:

> Through my own experience—and that of countless others that I have shared—I have come to believe that creativity is our true nature...at once as normal and as miraculous as the blossoming of a flower at the end of a slender green stem.... (xiii)

And we were becoming more creative by the moment. As the children grew, they needed teachers with expertise we were unable to provide. The cost of the school was picked up by the business, but the parents and staff decided to help. Almost everyone pitched in. The cost was only a few dollars a week per child, but those who still couldn't afford it were given scholarships. We worked out our finances and then we went looking for mentors.

We wanted practical, professional experience. We wanted maturity. We wanted kindness, compassion and camaraderie. So, we directed our attention toward the retired and elderly. Many are energetic, enjoy youthful lives and are highly motivated to share. They not only have the skill and wisdom of a lifetime of experience, but lots of love to give to our children. Bureaucratic requirements keep us as a society from tapping into this abundant resource.

When I worked for the public school system, I was a 'master teacher,' someone who supervised new teachers in training. I had an opportunity to sit in and review a number of teacher training institutions—not to mention my own experience going through the Education Department twice at UCLA. Most of the teacher training I saw had to do with classroom management. It involved getting a concept across to twenty or thirty or more students of varying interests and abilities at the same time. It entailed classroom discipline and how to manage the behaviors of those twenty to thirty students, many of whom would prefer being somewhere else. Our credentialing laws require this training. But people who work with small groups of children—children who want to be doing what they are doing—do not require this skill set. Employing the retired and the elderly would benefit everyone. So, we hired a retired chemical engineer.

He was our own Mr. Wizard. He came with charts and lots of hands on equipment. He made science more than an exercise in rote memorization; he turned it into an exploration in creativity and discovery. There were field trips to tide pools, bird watching and more whale-watching excursions than we could count. Children concocted dozens of experiments based on questions raised during those outings. The world was their laboratory and they constructed their experiments out of string, tin cans, old skateboard wheels, makeshift levers and anything else they could find. They discovered on their own how and where to look up information when they needed it. They learned to take risks and venture educated guesses, the beginning of the scientific process of creating a 'hypothesis.' And if they memorized information, it was out of a need to do something with it. It had a purpose.

As the children became more adept at following their creative paths, it became obvious that, at times, some of them avoided the tedious. So we looked for something that might balance out their experience and help them develop the skill of self-discipline. Then the kids saw the movie 'The Karate Kid.' They loved it! Each was determined to be the next karate champion (who says Hollywood doesn't have an influence?) Karate was the perfect vehicle for learning discipline and the kids themselves had initiated the desire to learn it. So, I pulled out the local phone book and looked for a studio that would send a teacher to our school during school hours at an hourly rate. (Many instructors are available at reasonable rates during school time, because most programs don't begin until after school.)

I started with the A's and worked my way down to the T's when we reached Tom Bloom's Studio. A third degree black belt, Master Michael Richey, would come to our school for an hour at a rate we could afford. We had fifteen kids interested in taking karate. We divided his hourly wage by the number of kids participating. It was so reasonable and most of the children liked it so much, we increased his visits to three times a week.

With all this activity, it was difficult to make time for everything we wanted to do. There was karate several times a week, science one full morning a week, weekly fieldtrips, our play productions, individual projects, the 'three R's' and we still needed enough time to play in the orchard every day. So, we came up with a company solution.

The parents were willing to come to work at seven-thirty in the morning so we could schedule the karate instructor before the business's eight-thirty start time. The children loved school. Unlike many school children who do not look forward to their day, our children were up and raring to go. The company was willing to let the parents start work an hour early. It was a manufacturing plant located in California. A lot of the sales representatives and office workers were dealing with companies on the East Coast. Since there was a three-hour difference, starting earlier actually increased the time the company had to do business with the rest of the country. The management was happy. The parents were happy. They'd rather go home early. It meant more time to get errands done and provided an opportunity to enroll children in after-school sports programs if they were interested. The children were happy. There were no compromises. It was a win-win situation. And we still had time to go on fieldtrips.

Karate became a big success. Six of our children earned first-degree black belts and three of those children ended up second-degree black belts with Instructor's Degrees. Some of the mothers also attained belts right alongside their children.

Our parents were energized. Soon they began to think up classes and find ways to execute them. A used piano showed up after everyone decided music lessons might be a good thing. The piano was donated by a private party in the community and transported by a few of the dads who borrowed a pick-up truck. The rest of the parents came up with the funds for a piano tuner and found a piano teacher. She was a lovely lady who really cared about children, but she was uninspired and so was her teaching. She missed the creative heart of music. It was her profession, but obviously not her passion. After a few months, children who started out so eager to learn, suddenly disappeared when it was their turn at the piano. They bartered and made deals. They attempted to trade out lesson time for playtime. They refused to practice. The only time they touched that piano was when she was there and then only reluctantly.

So, we posted incentive charts—five hours of practice earned a reward. We put a sign-up sheet for piano time hoping that if the children saw each other's names on the list practice would become desirable. We begged, pleaded and nagged. It was a bad idea. Such a tactic rarely entices enthusiasm. We can alter behavior, but we can't demand passion. No passion, no brilliance. I saw the enemy and it was us. So, we unanimously ended the music program or at least with this teacher.

Undaunted we hired a Spanish teacher. This teacher was highly recommended and took the perfect interview. She spoke of the ease with which young children acquire a language by listening to it. She talked at length about the passion of children. She discussed the damage we do to them by constantly forcing them to spend their time focused on what is not involving or intriguing.

Unfortunately, when she entered the classroom, she did not know how to execute her vision. She was rigid, unaware of her effect on her students and closed to suggestion. She was passionless. And every week, we lost a few more children. So we let her go.

In order to succeed, we were not afraid to fail, but finding a good teacher by our definition was tough. We were looking for passion. Many teachers are talented, but deliver their skills without passion, dousing everyone else's in their path. Finding passion is not part of their training and it is usually not part of their personal experience. How could they find in someone else what they had not found in themselves? How would they know how to recognize it?

As a society we do not know how to look for passion and brilliance; it is not operative in our culture. When we see or even suspect these attributes in our children, we do not know how to assist them in their development. There is little in our social structure that accommodates uniqueness, let alone passion. But if we do not actively seek this passion and brilliance, there is little hope we will ever find it. And we rarely find that for which we are not looking. John Gatto writes:

> Over the past twenty-six years, I've used my classes as a laboratory where I could learn a broader range of what human possibility is— and also as a place where I could study what releases and what inhibits human power. During that time, I've come to believe that genius is an exceedingly common human quality, probably natural to most of us. I didn't want to accept that notion—far from it—my own training in two elite universities taught me that intelligence and talent distributed themselves economically over a bell curve and that human destiny, because of those mathematical, seemingly irrefutable, scientific facts, was as rigorously determined as John Calvin contended. The trouble was that the unlikeliest kids kept demonstrating to me at random moments so many of the hallmarks of human excellence—insight, wisdom, justice, resourcefulness, courage, originality— that I became confused. They didn't do this often enough to make my teaching easy, but they did it often enough that I began to wonder, reluctantly, whether it was possible that being in

school itself was what was dumbing them down.... (<u>Dumbing Us Down,</u> xi)

Gatto continues:

> In theoretical, metaphorical terms, the idea I began to explore was this one: that teaching is nothing like the art of painting, where, by the addition of material to a surface, an image is synthetically produced, but more like the art of sculpture, where, by the subtraction of material, an image already locked in the stone is enabled to emerge. It is a crucial distinction. In other words, I dropped the idea that I was an expert, whose job it was to fill the little heads with my expertise, and began to explore how I could remove those obstacles that prevented the inherent genius of children from gathering itself. (<u>Dumbing Us Down,</u> xii-xiii)

Genius requires self-direction and our children were well on their way. First, they decided they wanted to add their own classes and hire their own teachers, so they found a voice teacher. They met as a group, interviewed her and asked her to run both private and small group lessons. They also wanted a choir. But the choir did not work well in a wide age span. The older kids referred to the songs the little kids liked as 'baby songs.' They wanted to sing what they heard on the radio. The little kids couldn't pronounce the big kid's words let alone keep the beat. So they held a group counsel. Each child explained what she or he wanted to do. Then they all worked on the solution. Our saving grace was the holidays. They all wanted to go caroling. The holiday songs held the choir together. They sang at local hospitals, rest homes and schools. They were fine through January, but without another performance to look forward to, most of our kids lost interest. So in spring we ended the voice program, but we were already searching for alternatives. As Margaret Wheatley notes:

> Life is creative. It plays itself into existence, seeking out new relationships, new capacities, new traits. Life is an experiment to discover what's possible. As it tinkers with discovery, it creates more and more possibilities. (A Simpler Way, 10)

And we were not afraid to tinker. While we were at it we looked for interest, involvement, excitement and passionate focus. Wheatley continues:

> Playful tinkering requires consciousness. If we are not mindful, if our attention slips, then we can't notice what's available or discover what's possible. Staying present is the discipline of play. Great focus and concentration are required. We need to stay aware of everything that's happening as it is happening, and to respond with minimal hesitation. (A Simpler Way, 25)

When we are mindful and attentive, we notice the small things that attract a child's attention. We are able to facilitate those fleeting moments of fancy, fueling interest into involvement and excitement into passionate focus. The passion itself will manifest in brilliance. But first we have to be aware enough to be open to the possibilities.

Excited about the opportunities we saw before us, we went looking for another music teacher. By now the school had been running for a few years. "Working Mother Magazine" rated G.T. Water Products in the top ten companies in the

United States and gave it an award each year because of the school. We attracted significant press. Then we attracted significant people—people who were gifted and passionate. We were fortunate to attract Carol Arias as our new music teacher.

Carol is a very gifted composer, dramatist, pianist and teacher. She was delighted to come out during the day when most of her private students were either working or in school. We paid Carol an hourly rate and she, in turn, helped us find creative ways to stretch our dollar. She suggested that our five and six-year-olds initially have fifteen-minute lessons until any child was ready for a full half-hour. She would take the children one at a time, pulling them out of their morning work.

In turn, we explained to the kids who wanted to participate that Carol was only there one day a week. If they wanted to learn to play the piano, they had to stop what they were doing when she was ready for them. All the kids would be affected. It meant that we could not take fieldtrips or go to the park on those days. It had to be a group decision. It could not be about majority rule; everyone's needs had to be worked out. It was a true democracy.

At first, we had mixed consent. The older kids said they didn't know Carol, so they couldn't commit to a program without better information, having learned from their earlier encounter with a piano teacher. They had a point. So we asked Carol if she wouldn't mind coming initially on a trial basis. She agreed and we started over. This time, we had different results.

A graduate of the Julliard School of Music, Carol was Leonard Bernstein's personal protégé. But it was more than Carol's resume that was attractive. Carol knew how to draw the natural musical ability out of each child because she could find it in herself. She created a method for teaching children that developed out of her own passion for music and teaching.

205

Carol began her teaching career working with neurologically impaired and autistic children. Instead of starting with scales (like our first teacher did) or reading music, (so children who were dying to play had a major hurdle to get through first), she taught her students to play by listening. She reasoned, if they can hear the music, they can play it. If they can play it, they can learn to compose music and write it down. If they can write it, they can read it.

Within weeks, we heard beautiful full tones and real music, not just scales, coming out of that piano. By the end of the school year, most of our children played fluently and passionately. We never had to ask anyone to practice; we had to urge them to give up the piano to other waiting children. After a while, I had to put up the old practice sheet. But this time it was not for incentives, it was for making sure that all the children who wanted to practice had the opportunity.

It was brilliance at its finest. The love for exploring and creating, the thirst for passion was so big we couldn't contain it. It grew out of the classroom, down the hall, out the door, covered the town of Moorpark, through the local newspapers and newscasts, and plunk into college. And it wouldn't quit. It was contagious.

Balancing on the Head of a Pin When You Are Not an Angel!

"Seek out that particular mental attribute which makes you feel most deeply and vitally alive, along with which comes the inner voice which says, 'This is the real me,' and when you have found that attitude, follow it."

William James

Stephen was carried by the tide of passion. He was twelve now. He was still not all that interested in reading, even though he had more than mastered the skill. His handwriting was atrocious and his spelling was worse. Had he been in a regular school, he would have exhibited all the behaviors of Attention Deficit with Hyperactivity Disorder (ADHD), Dyslexia (a perceptual reversal of letters and words), and Dysgraphia, (the inability to organize the visual presentation of a paper) and other fine motor coordination skill delays. But he was in love with the computer and the technology that came with it.

Still concerned about balance, we started searching for avenues to broaden his perspective and help round out his experience. We found a children's class in cartooning. He attended one session and came out near tears. They were drawing 'dumb little cartoon people.' We withdrew him from the class. He was restless and we were at a loss. Nothing we tried worked.

Then Dennis found a course in electronics for children offered by Moorpark College, our local community college. It was the day before the class started and we had missed the enrollment deadline. Dennis called the college anyway and got the professor's phone number. We left a message. The professor, Leon Rouge, called us back that evening. He listened intently for twenty minutes and then asked, "May I speak to Stephen?"

"Sure," we replied and put our son on the phone.

They talked for another twenty minutes, at which point Stephen handed the phone back to us. "He wants to speak to you."

Professor Rouge informed us that although we missed the enrollment deadline, he would be happy to have Stephen in the class.

Day One: Stephen emerged happy.

Week One: We had a whole different child on our hands—happy, cheerful and mostly cooperative. That restless quality was starting to dissipate.

Week Two: Stephen picked up a book to read in his spare time.

Week Three: Stephen consented to try an English paper or two.

Week Four: Stephen agreed to work on spelling again.

Week Five: Stephen picked up an interest in mathematics.

Week Six: Stephen began teaching electronics to the other kids in our school. Anthony Robbins comments:

> At a very early age, I developed a belief that we're all here to contribute something unique, that deep within each of us lies a special gift. You see, I truly believe we all have a sleeping giant within us. Each of us has a talent, a gift, our own bit of genius just waiting to be tapped. It might be a talent for art or music. It might be a special way of relating to the ones you love. It might be a genius for selling or innovating or reaching out in your business or your career. I choose to believe that our Creator doesn't play favorites, that we've all been created unique, but with equal opportunities for experiencing life to the fullest.... (22)

About six weeks after we enrolled Stephen in the class an elderly gentleman showed up at our school. He was standing outside the building in the parking lot awaiting our return from a field trip. He introduced himself as Stephen's electronics teacher, Leon Rouge. (We had never seen him before.)

"Are you Mrs. Brown?" he inquired.

"Yes, why?"

"I want to talk to you about your son."

Pictures of blown-up lab equipment, mangled wires and broken equipment parts with my son standing in the middle holding assorted displaced wires and burned fuses, flashed through my mind.

"Did he break something?" I inquired, remembering the church's sound equipment and holding my breath. The man gave me a kind but piercing look, knitted his eyebrows, leaned forward as if he was either about to tell me a secret or search my soul. Then he asked to speak to me privately.

I escorted him to a conference room. The air hung heavy and the office staff disappeared. I watched those eyes watching: present, sentient, clear, sweeping, sensing. I watched those eyes, conscious.

"Your son belongs in college. I want him to take my adult electronics class. He can help teach it if he wants."

Now I had no delusions about my son and my ego was not invested. Stephen was not a scholar. He could never organize his work. He could never find a pencil. Forget a pencil, he could never find two shoes that matched. I thought for a moment. Maybe this man was confused. Maybe he had the wrong 'Brown.' It was not an uncommon name. I attempted to clarify, "Are you referring to *Stephen* Brown?"

He talked for two straight hours, but his eyes danced back and forth in time, always searching, always present, never leaving my gaze.

"So, can he?" Leon asked.

"OK." I answered. Monumental moments often pass understated.

Leon Rouge was an angel sent to intervene. Up to that point, I knew what *not* to do, but that's not the same as knowing what *to* do. Leon led the way. He made his way into our hearts. He was guide and grandfather, father and teacher and friend. His wife, Aileen, invited us for high tea and crumpets, crustless finger sandwiches, cupolas and lemon groves—echoes of a gentler time.

Under the portico of their old ranch house, my children and I learned the art of sipping tea and conversation. We strolled through endless groves of ripening avocados, enticing, romancing the waning rays of the end of the day and welcoming the advancing shadows of moonlight. We read through old leather bound books and sat among antiques that had already acquired the dignity of the ages. We learned that true love was timeless. That there was much more to experience than our feeble years had uncovered. We learned that we could talk from the heart without any words and be perfectly understood. We learned everybody needs a hug and blue eyes (Leon's) can dance at any age.

Leon had Stephen admitted to Moorpark College at the tender age of twelve. This sweet, gentle man bypassed all the rules and regulations by going directly to the Registrar himself. Stephen was the second under-aged child ever admitted to the college at that time. Ten years later, children from all over would come to this quiet little gem of a college in search of their strengths and it was all because of Leon, his compassion, his understanding and his vision.

Stephen adored Leon and loved the class. Within six weeks Leon made Stephen a teaching assistant. By the end of the semester, Leon felt Stephen was ready for college algebra. I still wasn't so sure, but Leon knew two math teachers who structured their classes so that students could go at their own pace and Stephen wanted to try. Osho notes:

> Growth is a rare phenomenon. It is natural, yet rare. When the seed has found its right soil, it grows. It is very natural; growth is natural but to find the right soil—that is the very crux of the matter. (250)

In a few short months, Stephen became an old hand in the electronics lab and a familiar face in the math and science building. Then, one day, as I was walking down the hall to pick him up, a slightly gray haired gentleman once again stopped me. "Excuse, me. Are you Stephen Brown's mother?" (Uh-oh!) "I'm Mr. Wolfe. I'm a computer sciences instructor. Your son, Stephen, was standing by the door. He looked like he couldn't wait to get in, so we welcomed him. Boy, that kid really knows his stuff! Would it be O.K. with you if we let him into the CIS (Computer Information Systems) Department? I have a grandson his age. I know how important it could be."

"Thank you," I said, wondering if he could tell Stephen's age. (They had to see he was young. He was at least two heads shorter than the rest of the kids.) "We'll discuss it as a family and I will let you know."

Stephen enrolled in a computer science class and within a year he was the teaching assistant for the CIS computer lab, working directly under the head of the lab, Guy Campbell. Guy took him under his tutelage and for the next four years worked side by side with Stephen, taking him well past the knowledge base and skill of many professionals. In fact, by the time Stephen was fourteen he was already working professionally as a systems administrator for a division of Warner Bros.

As our children began to develop their passions and discover their brilliance, more and more children from the G.T. Water School entered college at an earlier and earlier age. Our daughter, Erin, then almost age thirteen and David Z. also almost thirteen gained admission, followed by other G.T. students: Adam, age fourteen, our son, Matthew, age eleven, and Candice, age ten. Each child created his or her own path and life story. Each story was different.

Erin developed in a completely different manner than Stephen. Erin spent ages eight to ten almost exclusively wanting to read. Every morning, she plopped herself down on the couch in a horizontal position and read for hours. When we tried to balance her curriculum, she worked with us, but politely let us know we were keeping her from her activity of choice. So mostly we let her read. At age ten, Erin got up off that couch, put her books down and began writing the most beautiful prose we had ever read.

Then one day her interest changed and she decided to do math. She enticed her friend David Z. into doing it with her. They came up with a plan. Most of what they saw in the mathematics texts was repetition. Modeled off Stephen's earlier idea to take his spelling test *before* he studied, so he only had to study what he didn't know, they decided to tackle math in the same manner. First David Z. and Erin reviewed the examples in the beginning of a chapter. Then they took the test. Any time either of them missed a problem they went back into the chapter and did the exercises for that problem. They never went on until they mastered one hundred percent of a chapter, but they never did useless, repetitive work.

Progress was rapid because there was no wasted effort and they helped each other. Before we knew it, they were doing a chapter a day instead of the usual one in two weeks and they were excited about what they were doing—also noisy. Noise comes with excitement, so we gave them a room with a dry erase board all to themselves.

Seizing the teacher's edition, they threw me out because I wasn't fast enough and started doing problems on the board as a team. They were their own teachers. The heated debate and excitement that came streaming out of that back room were contagious. Laughter punctuated their arguments. Passion abounded.

Their enthusiasm attracted the attention of other children, even though those children had not done that level of math. Adam, the owner's son, joined them, picking up the concepts where the others had left off (so much for linear development). Matthew also sat there for hours listening intently. I did not see how he had the math skills to understand what they were doing. I almost wondered if he was sitting there to avoid doing something else. Yet his behavior was thoroughly focused on the topic, so I let him be. After a while, he joined in.

On their own, Erin and David Z. forged their way through eight years of math in three years, working all morning, almost every day, until they went through all of middle school and high school mathematics. They took Moorpark College's mathematics placement exam, tested into college mathematics at age twelve and entered at age thirteen.

Then Candice, age ten, was accepted into the college's art program by the head of the Art Department. Adam, age fourteen, entered in electronics. Matthew was not only accepted at age eleven into electronics, but he had only learned to read with some degree of competence at age ten. He received, however, the second highest grade in the electronics class—second only to an electronics professor from a foreign country who was taking the class to brush up on his English.

Our children never had homework, were never tested, were never sorted into grade levels and never received grades until college. Erin and David Z.'s math tests were only diagnostic. The tests were never scored, recorded or marked with a letter grade. Yet, once in college, most of our students maintained a G.P.A. of 4.0, straight A's. Meanwhile, the G.T. Water School became a magnet for awards.

AWARDS AND FEATURED PRESENTATIONS:

- United States Department of Education, Special Commendation and Press Conference by Secretary of Education Richard W. Riley, 1995
- United Stages Chamber of Commerce Commendation, 1993
- United States Senate, Washington D.C. Personal Letter of Commendation, Senator Pete Wilson, 1989
- League of Women Voters, Letter of Commendation, 1989
- Working Mother Magazine Awards, 1988, 1989, 1990, 1991, 1992, 1993, 1994, 1995

PUBLICATIONS AND BROADCASTS:

- ABC, NBC, CBS, CNN Special Documentary: Head of the Class, 1995
- Prime Time Today Show, NBC, Jan. 1990
- Washington Post, Jan. 1990
- Wall Street Journal, Jan. 1990, Sept.1991
- L.A. Times, Nov. 1987, Sept. 1989, Oct. 1989, Jan. 1990, Aug. 1991, Sept.1, 1991, Sept.4, 1991, Sept.30, 1991, Sept. 22, 1992, Sept.29, 1992, Jan. 10, 1995.
- Chicago Tribune, Jan. 1989
- ESPN, Jan. 1990
- Financial News Network, Jan. 1990
- The League of Women Voters Broadcast, Nov. 1988
- The Donahue Show, Jan. 1990
- The Home Show, 1990
- INC. Magazine, Cover Story, Mar.1991
- Nation's Business, Feb. 1993
- The Reason Foundation Journal, Feb. 1993
- Personnel Journal Magazine, Nov. 1991
- Brigham Young University Documentary: "Schools at Work," 1994
- Moorpark News, Nov. 1987
- Ventura County Star Free Press, Nov. 1987, May 1989, Sept. 1989, Sept. 1992
- The Enterprise, Nov. 1987, Sept. 1991, Dec. 1992
- News Chronicle, Sept. 20, 1989, Sept. 24, 1989, Sept. 1992
- Daily News, Sept. 1989, Aug. 1991, Sept. 1992
- Redbook Magazine Mar., 1991

Then in 1995, we were asked to present a workshop at a United Nations Conference in front of a delegation of international political leaders and businessmen. We were given a full hour—a half-hour to make our presentation and the remaining time to answer questions.

At first Brian, Debra and I were going to do the presentation, bringing the six college students along to view the event. But the kids were so enthusiastic about the presentation they asked to participate. Within a week they put together a movie showing their day at the G.T. Water School and at the college. They borrowed equipment from a professional editing house, figured out how to edit their own material and add a soundtrack.

When it was time to give the presentation, the adults each gave a five-minute talk and turned the rest of the hour over to the kids. These children brought the house down. One by one, they walked up to the podium and opened their hearts to the audience. They spoke with confidence, poise and sincerity. Even more than academic achievement, their ability to converse in a warm, straightforward manner with children and adults alike astounded the people around them. The audience was moved not only by their natural eloquence and grace, but the way they cared for each other; they were a family.

People like the late Dr. Spock took an interest in our little experiment. We met and he asked us to describe in writing what we were doing. This was our response.

Dear Dr. Spock,

G.T. Water Products, a plumbing manufacturer, provides an onsite K-12 school as a benefit for its twenty-eight employees. The sense of joy and strong family atmosphere that permeates the school and office enhances both environments and the benefit is well worth the annual cost to the company. Over ninety percent of families with children take advantage of the school, which was founded eight years ago.

Our parents and students themselves have also initiated many enrichment programs, including science, chemistry, electronics, French, Spanish, drama, music, voice, piano, arts and crafts, photography, and even first aid and CPR. Each student pursues an individual program.

Created with the child, each program is designed to encourage individuality, creativity and self-esteem. The child's genuine spontaneous interest holds sway in any particular moment; the teacher is present to guide and encourage, to provide balance and perspective. The children do very well on standardized, nationally normed tests. Six of our students between the ages of ten and sixteen are presently enrolled in a local college to explore the areas in which they excel. The school is open year round and encourages a broad range of experiences from sports, scouting and 4-H programs to fieldtrips and summer outdoor recreational activities.

The specific benefits are obvious to anyone who spends time with the children. From reporters from the L.A. Times, ABC, NBC and CNN to family and friends, people notice the poise and grace our children exude and are amazed at the breadth and depth of their youthful portfolios. Academics, essential tools that they are, are the least of it. The verb educate means "to draw out," not to "stuff in." As we've learned to trust our children with freedoms and hold them responsible for their choices, they've grown trustworthy and responsible. Our goal is happy, well-rounded children who have the courage to dream and the determination and skills to root those dreams in reality.

As a by-product, their self-confidence and enthusiasm is contagious, overflowing into the offices of their parents and factory as a whole. As our children have succeeded, our parents and co-workers have also become more successful, more innovative and more self-confident. Our employees are more loyal and their morale is higher because they have a mutual sense of community, of family, and of raising our children together. We have fewer absences because both children and parents come to work and school together and all benefit.

We shared a vision to assume direct responsibility for our children's education and we had the will to make it work. The legal paperwork and cost of opening a school were relatively minor. Insurance was minimized because the school was only for employees' children. Government inspectors were generally helpful. When our ideas challenged decades of traditional methods and were met with skepticism, we were patient and let the fruits of our labors speak for themselves. Whenever the size of our company limited us, we used the community, pooling resources with local homeschool groups for greater advantages. We were befriended by a host of local businesses for fieldtrip opportunities. Retired grandparents and friends provided a wealth of resources.

When our parents and students wanted additional teachers, we approached local after-school enrichment sources and offered them employment on their down time during regular school hours. When money was scarce, parents offered co-payments. Families that could not afford the co-payments were given scholarships funded by the monies raised by all the children during candy drives, and dance-a-thons, etc.

With the family breaking down, we've given it a support to lean on. The children are nurtured by everyone. We "do lunch" with our own kids.

When they fall, we're there to comfort them, and when they soar, we're there to applaud. Our program can easily be modified to suit any situation, and we will gladly share our insights. Please call for further information, or better yet, come visit. Our doors are always open.

We spoke afterwards. Dr. Spock was very supportive and asked if he could visit the school. Unfortunately, he passed away before we could meet again.

❧ 28 ❧

Back to the Beach

Plants always grow toward the light; so do children. Even out of the muddiest, most desolate of fields the finest rose blooms. No two flowers are ever identical, yet, like a million buds of hope, they all share the same desire to love and be loved, to fulfill their finest destiny, to blossom.

It is six o'clock in the evening a week and a half after Erin took those horrendous tests. I have spent the day with her again on the island. We have a bond of love, trust and friendship, but I am still 'mom.' She has asked me to work alongside her, as she needs to start studying for the next test in September.

We have just made the forty yards from her apartment to the beach. I have been trying all day to get us here. I envisioned sitting on the sand, working away next to my daughter. The smell of the ocean breeze, the glistening bay water, I always work better connected to nature. I hoped she would too. Meanwhile, it is ten hours later than I anticipated. The day is shot. In my mind, we'd wake up at six o'clock in the morning (having slept late for me), have breakfast and head for the water. Now the sun is setting and we seem to just be beginning.

I carry my laptop. Erin has a far-too-heavy, book-laden backpack and a rambunctious German shorthaired pointer named Max. The dog is on loan from her long-term boy-friend, Derek. I have two sand chairs. She had one. Now I carry it. We plunk down on the sand. We are going to start working. I will continue writing and she will start her studies—finally.

Erin puts her backpack down, nestles her chair into the sand. Max heads full speed ahead for the water, dragging Erin behind him. As I see my daughter disappear into a tempest of splashing foam, she informs me she has, "mastered the art of wasting the day." (I am not sure what to make of this statement since I know she has always been persistent and diligent.) Max is now in the water past where he can stand, paddling around like a strange combination of dog and duck. Erin is in the water up to her hips with her clothes on.

Erin was up way too late the night before. I know. I was up with her, walking Max on the boardwalk at an hour when no one could see if he got into trouble. Erin woke up this morning at the 'crack of nine,' donned her running shoes and the little music gizmo she bought on sale that attaches to her arm, leashed Max and took off to run around the island. I struggled to keep up with her. Then I walked. As she disappeared into the morning mist, she yelled back over her shoulder, "Don't worry mom. I've got the routine down. A short run (an hour) to tire Max out, (it tired me out), a shower, a rest and then exercise the horse. By then it will be time for lunch and a nice afternoon nap. Then walk Max (it will be time again), come back and sit on the patio to recover. Then water the plants. Stare at the wall. Think about studying and then it will be time for dinner. After that, rent a movie, walk Max and it will be time for bed."

It is now an hour later than when we made it to the sand. Erin is still splashing around with Max. It is seven o'clock in the evening. The books lay in the backpack, on the sand, unopened. Max is dripping wet and shivering. Erin runs back to the apartment to dry Max off. I am left sitting here, writing. I have the perfect view of an empty sand chair and an unzipped blue backpack.

I don't think this, "I'll work, you'll work and we'll both get a lot done" thing is happening. Erin informs me this is just our first day together. She needed a day to do nothing.

"What about the week in Florida?" I ask. "What did you do in Florida?"

"Lounged by the boat. Lay on the deck. Slept by the pool. Read two-and-a-half pop paperbacks."

"What would you call that?" I inquired.

"Doing nothing."

"O.K. You came back last Saturday. What did you do Sunday?"

"Nothing."

"What about Monday and Tuesday?"

"Nothing."

"O.K." I said with some resignation, not knowing if I was helpful…or if I should even be helping.

Erin is still passionate about mathematics, perhaps even more so because her level of commitment has been challenged. But Erin's whole being is trying to right itself from the imbalance created during the testing process.

The intensive studying Erin and her friends did all those weeks, to the exclusion of anything else, has burned them out. Erin is thinking about painting her fingernails. Last night she spent two hours painting and repainting her toenails.

Balance. I wish I had insight into balance. I am not sure how to get it, exactly how to define it, but I can see its lack everywhere. I never learned balance. It was not on my curriculum when I was a student in school. And then there was life. I had no role model. I don't think 'balance' was an issue for my mother or her mother, or her mother's mother. I think they were connected to life differently. Or maybe the pace of life was different then. But today, it is a necessity. If we are to deal with the pressures of daily living in our time, we need to be balanced.

Instead, we create a life that is off balance. We allow the demands of an institution, employment, or whatever applies the most pressure to throw us off. School is the worst. We occupy our kid's time all day with school and all night with homework. In between we run to sports or dance or piano or karate lessons or the gym, but we seem to lack the time 'to be.'

The trick is to search for passion without getting run over by that search—to execute that passion in a manner that creates balance inside each day—not three weeks or three months or three years later as we try to recover.

One of the homeschooling moms in the program I facilitate recently suggested we shut our program down one week a month. She thought we should hold no extra classes, no journaling class, no art or music classes, no drama or language classes or fieldtrips. Nothing. So maybe we could all recover from our over-filled style of living. "What shall we call it?" I queried. "We have to package it in a way the district would accept it and the parents would think it was a good idea."

She smiled and took a step forward as if to share a secret, "How about HOME school?" she laughed. "Maybe we could just all stay home!"

❧ PART IV ❧

Catch the Wind
and Soar!

❧ 29 ❧

An Opportunity to Shine

"'Studying the Way' is just a figure of speech.... In fact, the Way is not something which can be studied.... When the fish is caught we pay no more attention to the trap. When body and mind achieve spontaneity, the Way is reached and Mind is understood."

Huang-po

The phone company helped him out because the executives thought that it was such a novel idea that a twelve-year-old kid was going to do this—run twenty-four phone lines into the house and start an online bulletin board business.

Stephen had no clue where he left off and where the world began. He experienced no separation. He had little notion of limitation. Effort was not struggle. With enough effort over enough time, he could do anything. He was already in college. He was plugged into the universe as he perceived it: open, limitless and transcendent.

R.Griffin speaks of an education that "seeks to revere the wholeness of the learner as a unique member of the universe." A holistic education incorporates not only mind and body, but also spirit—"that life spark, that sense of consciousness, our individual persona that defines us as humans." (Wilson, 43)

Stephen has always had an entrepreneurial spirit—a spirit that was nurtured early in life as he had the time and freedom to tinker his way into experiments and projects, fiddle around the barn with his cousin Adam, and rummage through the garage with his friend David B. While he was at it, he started his first business. Stephen explains:

> A bulletin board system is a computer or set of computers that you dial up to using a modem. It's a teleconferencing environment. So if you have six people all dialed in they can chat and talk on the computer. There were a number of multi-line bulletin systems in the area. David B. and I ended up making friendships with the system administrators. We helped out in some cases and co-sys-opped in others, which meant helping with the set up and administration of the systems. After a while, I decided to put up my own bulletin board system.
>
> There was a relatively new software system out called Major BBS and I wanted to write my own programs with it, but I needed to get phone lines set up for it. My parents told me I had a two hundred dollar limit. So I stayed within my budget and arranged for twenty-four phone lines to be put into the house and managed to get a trench dug.

The phone company was usually cooperative. They said, "You know what, you don't have to sign up all your phone lines right now, but here, let's put a telecommunications trunk into your home." So there's this huge box that supports thirty-two lines on the side of our house, and I think we only ended up running four or five lines into the house while we were testing. But it was great. It was pretty heavy duty. So, I got all the physical equipment into the house for under my budget. Then I found out I had to invest seven hundred dollars more to get all the software I needed. It halted the project, but not for long.

This is what happened: Erin needed to sell Girl Scout Cookies and Matthew was helping her. So Matthew dragged me away from my computer and said, "Come on, you're going to go with us." And we went around the neighborhood selling Girl Scout cookies, when we met a new neighbor who had recently moved in. She opened the door and I noticed a large number of computer boxes in her living room. I turned around and asked, "Oh, are those yours?"

And she said, "Oh, these are my husband's."

"Really," I said. "What line of work is your husband in?"

And she said, "Well, he runs an online bulletin board system."

So, I made an appointment with her husband, Steve, to talk to him. I showed him the system I was building and he said that he had bought the same software, but hadn't had the time to set it up because he hadn't been able to learn the system yet. Then I said, "Well, I know the system!

I'll help you set it up!" And he said, "Great!" And that was a lot of fun!

He was just starting the business and didn't really have technical help, so I enlisted help from my friends and we set up his bulletin board. And we backed it up. Our deal was basically, I would help him around the office for free in exchange for books, experience and conferences. So we ended up traveling around the country going to bulletin board, game developers and telecommunication conferences and later Internet conferences. Over time bulletin boards were replaced with the Internet.

Stephen's educational career did not remain either within the bounds of academia or small entrepreneurial ventures. He stepped out at an early age, under the age of fourteen, into a larger world—one whose standards and rules would have been foreign to him had he gone through a traditional school structure. In the business world, interactions are not restricted because of age level or subject matter. People are not all doing the same thing at the same time, and direction is often internally dictated to fit the needs of the situation; it was more like the upbringing he had being homeschooled through the G.T. Water School.

In the business world, Stephen often had to figure out what role he could play or how to identify a problem and correct it. No one was testing his work, but if it wasn't going smoothly, it was up to him to recognize and fix it. As a result of his schooling, he was familiar and comfortable in a business environment.

So, when he was at the age most people treat as incompetent, he was invited to work at Warner Bros. Studios. This is how he describes his experience in an interview:

Given I'd been doing all this computer innovation, my grandfather asked if I wanted to see what my father's cousin was doing. He knew that this cousin was working on a computer project involving one of the studios. So we went to meet my cousin, Alan, for the first time and we got a tour of the facilities. I thought it was all very, very interesting. But when Alan and Grandpa got involved in a lengthy conversation, I walked off and started talking to a number of the engineers and artists.

I started asking questions about what they were doing. At first they gave me over-simplified answers. When I asked, "What type of computers are these?" they answered, "fast ones." And then I said, "No, no, no, seriously, what type of computers are these?" Then they started going into details and I started delving into more details and asking about the operating system and what tools and packages they use. I knew some 3D rendering programs already. And they were obviously not prepared for me to ask questions with that level of detail. I ended up getting into more detail than even they knew. And that apparently got back to Alan because Alan contacted me several days later and said, "I'd like to meet with you. Could you please sit down with me?" And I said, "absolutely."

I had breakfast with him and he began the conversation with, "Well, apparently you made quite the impression on my engineers! I was very impressed, as were they, as to the level of competency you exhibited. How would you like to become an intern at Warner Bros.? They want to have you around." So, I said, "Terrific!

That would be...I have to ask my mother. Hold on." And we approved it and it was lots of fun. And they set me up with a computer.

Initially, however, not much was asked of me. They basically left me to sink or swim. But they did say, "Do whatever you can; figure out some way to be useful." So I did and I got involved in the production process at Warner Bros. I did things that I could do easily, which was system administration—P.C. side. I even did some McIntosh administration. For the most part, I had the opportunity to teach myself UNIX and I got involved with the Silicon Graphics workstation.

I remember my first desk job at Warner Bros. The first time I actually got my own desk. It was in the machine room, which meant it was in the freezer. I had to bundle up to go to work because I was working in there. They had a whole bunch of audio-video equipment and I was working with the Director of Network Engineering to put together a Probell router—which was an automatic AV switch which allowed you to dynamically route video from any one source to multiple video sources. I was instrumental in getting that set up.

I spent a good amount of time at Warner Bros. helping with administration and set up. In fact, Alan started to spin off a product called Cinebase and I was invited to go to the trade shows with him. I helped set up the booths and demo the product. I didn't think about it, but apparently it was a big novelty that they had a fifteen-year-old kid talk your ear off about the quality of the product.

While I was at Warner Bros., I learned a lot of interesting things. I gained friendships and worked on a number of interesting movies through supporting the engineering projects: The Little Princess, Batman Forever, Space Jam. They had a whole floor devoted to Space Jam. And I ended up knowing quite a number of people down there. In fact, the editor would call me up and say, "Stephen, we've got a new batch of films I'm going to review. Do you want to come down and join me?" And I would go down and watch the new production shots. And it was really funny for me because it was an animated film with live action. So, they would show Michael Jordan doing the live action and they just penciled in the 'extra activity.' So, it would be Michael Jordan interacting with a bunch of sketches, which I thought was terribly amusing.

One night, one of the databases went down for Space Jam. It kept them from being able to log the day's shots. It was going to set their production behind. They called me in. Mom drove. I found the problem and helped them debug it. I was there all night. I cat-napped on the floor. I did that a couple times. I also helped get the mail server up for Cinebase and that took all night because it was new product, a new version of Exchange.

So, I was young, but I was a glorified support agent, which was great. The fact that I could actually do something useful and evolve my coding skills even further was terrific.

As Cinebase grew, I was assigned a program to write. The bad news is they ended up actually using it in Cinebase as a utility. I remember having no information about how it was supposed to work or what it was supposed to do. I spent hours and hours and hours tearing apart the documentation for the Silicon Graphics station to figure out what this particular file format was, and what the documentation of the file format was, so I could figure out how to read the format.

More than anything, though, I loved the artistic side of it. I loved watching the artists work! I loved the fact that Alan gave me access to the rendering equipment and said, "When the artists aren't using it, feel free to build anything you like!" I had access to over seven million dollars worth of production equipment. It was a lot of fun! That was when I started focusing all my activities at Warner Bros. And then soon after that I decided I wanted to go to UCLA to expand my knowledge base.

While addressing a group of students in a school gym, Joseph Campbell talked about the human spirit as a luminescence that is both what we are and what comes through us in the here and now—our operative essence. He looked up at the industrial lights overhead and remarked how much we were like light bulbs; a light bulb is made up of tangible parts, filament and glass, but that does not explain what a light bulb is. A light bulb is more than the sum of its parts. It is the light that comes through the bulb that makes the bulb complete in function and form. When he looks at people, Campbell explained, he looks for who they are—for the quality of light that comes through them, their individual pattern of luminescence, their radiance.

When we look at our children, we must look past the outward trappings. We must look past the personalities, the self-concepts, the experience we have created for them that tells them who they are and who they are not. We must look past all these storylines and past the damage we have done to them through limiting, testing and judging them, through not trusting or even listening to their internal sense of direction. We must look past it all and help them uncover their true radiance. Then we must give them the opportunity to shine.

The Team

"Perhaps the greatest social service that can be rendered by anybody to this country and to mankind is to bring up a family."

George Bernard Shaw

Our family is a team. It is what keeps us whole. From the time the kids were little, Dennis, my husband, their father, has been telling us all, "We are here for each other." His particular perspective, support and encouragement has guided us, empowered us and made us the unit we are today. He firmly believes:

> Our children are a celebration of life. They source awe and wonder at ordinary things. Children bring us back to our best, our feelings of joy at discovery, and delight at the world unveiling. As parents, our best gift to our children

is sharing these experiences in genuine pleasure. Our children will internalize this pleasure
and become the adults who are attractive to others, happy in themselves, and armed with the resources to succeed in this world.

Parenting Magazine published an article that, according to
Dennis, "put parents on notice." The article said that praising
children is fine, but overdoing it has its perils. It cited a family counselor in Austin, Texas who said, "Praise can under-
mine kids self-confidence and self-esteem. It can make kids
dependent on other people's opinions instead of trusting
themselves."

The article warns, "Kids easily learn the behaviors that get
praised and then repeat those actions strictly for the payoff.
They can become people-pleasers who look to others for
clues about how to act, rather than being independent, self-
motivated thinkers and doers." Dennis writes in response:

> This article about praise shines a light on a
> murky area of parent-child interactions. There is
> something faintly unsavory about managing and
> quantifying the praises we do or do not deliver.
> Counseling parents to worry about praising too
> much, praising for the wrong reasons, or using
> the wrong words for praise reinforces unstated
> but powerful assumptions about the parenting
> experience. I have observed that as parents have
> become busier with their own lives and issues,
> the time and energy they spend on their children
> has been reduced. We know of few families
> where all members manage to sit down together
> for dinner each night. In this context, counsel-
> ing parents not to over-praise their children
> sends a dangerous message.

I believe that children internalize their parents' messages over time. With intensity varying over the months and years, children hear in their heads the messages parents have delivered. They act out their lives to an internal audience composed of parents who applaud them, boo them, or ignore them. The children tend to enact scripts their parents write.

There are several "hard" scenarios, which the article does not address. Consider the child who discovers something which is not original. The child begins to manifest delight at his accomplishment. The parents are often in a quandary over this issue. They do not wish to set standards of accomplishment which are too low. The parenting article explicitly cautions against this danger. The article is dangerous. Parents who try to follow its prescriptions become parsimonious in their praise, guarded in their reactions. The children of these well-intentioned parents detect this penury and their delight is reduced.

We should share in our children's delight at every opportunity. First, it is fun. It is terrific for us and we shouldn't miss it. Inexpensive thrills are hard to find. Second, the children will find their delight reinforced, and they will tend to internalize the capacity to produce it. They will tend to make more of it as the years go by. The ability to produce joy is a skill that is invaluable in later life. People who can find and make their own delight will probably be happier and more socially successful than those who cannot.

Consider a second common scenario: a child is proud of an achievement that is not very good by adult standards. I remember the first time Matthew wrote a letter to someone. He worked on it all day on my word processor, writing, typing, deleting, erasing and moving text around. In the end, he had a half page of child-ish misspellings. He was proud. He showed it to me. I was ready to start helping him make it better, thinking about how to format a letter and help him correct his spelling mistakes when I stopped cold. It hit me. "This is wonderful," I said. "I'm sure Sean will love to receive it." I managed to put aside my adult editorial criteria and touch Matthew's delight at his accomplishment.

Since then, Matthew has become a dedicated letter-writer. He's written many letters to his friends and even wrote to Bill Gates when his book came out. In retrospect, it is clear to me that this would not have happened if I'd sat down at that point to help Matthew with his spelling and his grammar. He'd have had his delight tempered and his sense of accomplishment reduced. As it was, his skills have improved and his letters are terrific. And above all he delights in writing them.

Dennis continues to explain:

We must be vigilant, on guard to protect the big picture. We must ask ourselves, "What is the highest value, the most important interaction for this moment?"

One day, Matthew declared that sand was the central element of the universe. He carefully explained that the beach was made of sand, sand supported the ocean, sand was part of the cement, the glass and the concrete we lived on. Trees grew in the ground and got their nutrition from the sand, he said. I listened to this explanation with growing impatience. Matthew went on and on, an orgy of discovery, excited and sure. I could hardly wait to straighten him out. Then I remembered about the letter writing.

That's wonderful, Matthew," I said smoothly, appreciating his experience of feeling able to interconnect knowledge and experience—of coming to an epiphany. He can always look up the facts later. What were important were his joy of discovery and his process of thinking things through. The content, in this case, was not important. To this day, Matthew continues to astound us with his insights into the world and its processes.

Dennis concludes:

Give the children success. Engineer situations where all children can win. If the job of our schools is to educate and grow our children into successful adults, then we need to implement policies where they can achieve and sustain that crucial success. Most children are wonderful, genius is widespread, and the most productive thing we can do is enable them and then get out of the way.

∽ 31 ∾

Passion is Not a Mistress

"Follow your bliss."

Joseph Campbell

Passion is not a mistress that can be kept. It knows no boundaries, no containment. It does not discriminate between the young and old. It flaunts itself in confidence. It rejects prejudice and fear. It cannot be silenced. It cannot be stopped. It just cannot.

By the time Stephen was sixteen, he had outgrown both the G.T. Water School and Moorpark College. He applied to the

University of California at Los Angeles as a junior with a dual major in computer sciences and computer engineering.

> To Whom It May Concern:
>
> I am impassioned with the possibilities of the unknown, believing that the frontiers of exploration are open to all who do not hinder themselves by convention or fear. My life is an active testimony to my beliefs. Age has never been a limiting factor. I am now sixteen years old. I am applying for transfer as a junior to the School of Science and Engineering, but my college career blanches compared to my global entanglement with the technological future.
>
> Stephen Brown

His application was rejected because he was short four classes. Per his counselor's suggestion, he wrote a letter of petition for reconsideration:

> Director Undergraduate Admissions and Relations with Schools, University of California, Los Angeles
>
> Dear Director,
>
> I hereby petition the Admissions Office for reconsideration of my application for advanced placement to the UCLA School of Engineering for the fall semester as a Special Considerations Student. This reconsideration request is based on my conversation with a UCLA counselor in April. She cited a number of important factors

that were overlooked by the Admissions Committee and in her opinion need to be presented. She directed me to write this letter:

1. At age twelve, I was admitted to college, skipping junior high and high school. I am sixteen now.

2. When I was twelve, my family had conversations with UCLA about entering UCLA in their Gifted Students' Program for Computer Sciences. Instead, I entered Moorpark College because of the geographical distances involved in attending UCLA.

3. For over four years, I have sustained a nearly perfect GPA, all A's except two B's.

4. Over the ensuing years, my family and I have had ongoing conversations with UCLA, and at every point along the way, we were assured we were on track and I would be admitted.

5. Last fall, counselors at both UCLA and Moorpark College looked at my record and told us that we had "no problem" and all our necessary coursework was completed to enter the School of Engineering.

I now understand that four classes are missing. I was incorrectly counseled and I will need to take those classes in order to complete my sophomore year with a junior standing. The counselor recommended that I write this letter given we have relied on information provided for us many times over the years by UCLA.

Per her recommendation, the following points also need to be considered:

1. At a recent conference on new technologies, I was selected to present the capabilities of new Silicon Graphics based software to such companies as TRW, Pac Bell, Industrial Light & Magic, NASA and Sony. On the basis of the quality of my presentation, I was invited to Japan to speak on High Speed Video Transfer Technologies for a conference sponsored by Photron Corporation.

2. Because of my technical capabilities, I have been selected by the Computer Animation Department of Warner Bros. to work with their engineering staff. I have been there for a year and a half—since I was fourteen! I was one of a three-man team with sole responsibility for the design and implementation of their high-speed video distribution system. This involved my design, creation of wiring diagrams, equipment layout and integration with existing systems through touch-screen systems, programming and even building a custom E-Prom to handle hardware translation. When the team presented its recommendations to Warner Bros. senior executives, I was selected by the team to make the presentation.

3. I have been working with hardware and developing software for the Silicon Graphics platform. In terms of raw technical prowess, I have been programming since I was four. Many of the platforms I have worked with and debugged at Warner Bros. are also in use at UCLA. The number of people with my depth of experience with this technology is very small and I will be an asset to the university. My experience is current, practical and leading edge.

4. I have been in the field long enough to realize that a large portion of trade knowledge is useless without a firm academic grounding. For the past year and a half, I have been working with low-level Silicon Graphics code, which requires an understanding of three-dimensional mathematics beyond my documented academic record. I am already working with concepts of linear algebra and vector calculus in a practical context, although I have not had the classes yet.

More specifically, I am already working with such concepts as NERBS, B-Splines, "Blobbies" and other mathematical and computer based entities, but I need to comprehend the full underlying mathematics. The following companies are counting on me to develop this understanding and apply it to their real-world and theoretical applications. I can provide letters from executives at Warner Bros., Silicon Graphics, FORE Systems, E Systems and Pacific Bell supporting this claim.

I believe these factors justify my request for reconsideration. In the event that more information is needed, I would like to meet with the Dean of the School of Engineering to review what it will take to gain admission in the fall.

Very truly yours,
Stephen R. S. Brown

Dr. Carl Rogers spoke of the necessity to trust our inner channels of guidance and be who we are. Our stories have a better outcome when we do. Rogers explains:

Toward Trust of Self—Still another way of describing this pattern which I see in each client is
to say that increasingly he trusts and values the
process which is himself...Watching my clients,
I have come to a much better understanding of
creative people. El Greco, for example, must
have realized as he looked at some of his early
work, that 'good artists do not paint like that.'
But somehow he trusted his own experiencing
of life, the process of himself, sufficiently that
he could go on expressing his own unique perceptions. It was as though he could say, 'good
artists do not paint like this, but I paint like
this.' Or to move to another field, Ernest Hem-
mingway was surely aware that 'good writers
do not write like this.' But fortunately he moved
toward being Hemingway, being himself, rather
than toward someone else's conception of a
good writer. Einstein seems to have been unusually oblivious to the fact that good physicists
did not think his kind of thoughts. Rather than
drawing back because of his inadequate academic preparation in physics, he simply moved
toward being Einstein, toward thinking his own
thoughts, toward being as truly and deeply himself as he could. This is not a phenomenon that
occurs only in the artist or the genius. Time and
again in my clients, I have seen simple people
become significant and creative in their own
spheres, as they have developed more trust of
the processes going on within themselves, and
have dared to feel their own feelings, live by
values which they discover within, and express
themselves in their own unique ways. (On Becoming A Person, 175)

Boxes and boxes and boxes and boxes...

A box for what I know
and a box for what I know not.

A box for what I have been
and a box for what I have turned off.

A box for what I believe
and a box for what I refuse to see,

That infinite box
that yet
might be,

Of limitless thought,
Through which
I find
me.
Stephen age 16

Marianne Williamson writes:

You are a child of God. You were created in a blinding flash of creativity, a primal thought when God extended Himself in love. Everything you've added on since is useless. (29)

She then proceeds to explain:

When Michelangelo was asked how he created a piece of sculpture, he answered that the statue already existed within the marble. God Himself had created the Pieta, David, and Moses. Michelangelo's job, as he saw it, was to get rid of the excess marble that surrounded God's creation. So it is with you. The perfect you isn't something you need to create, because God already created it.... (29)

Letter from UCLA, May 25:

University of California at Los Angeles
School of Engineering and Applied Science
Computer Science—Engineering

Dear Stephen,

Congratulations! We have reconsidered your application and are pleased to offer you admission to UCLA for the Fall Quarter.

Our admissions officers and faculty reviewed more than 33,000 applications for admission. The School of Engineering & Applied Science admitted only 2,000 students this year. We believe that the students selected will contribute intelligence, imagination, and energy to the University and the Los Angeles community. You are one of those students and deserve to be proud of your achievements.

Joining UCLA's academic community will connect you with students and faculty who will challenge you to grow personally and intellectually. You will share in UCLA's reputation as an international leader in research and development. Distinguished faculty, nationally recognized academic departments, and opportunities for special study programs, in addition to numerous social and cultural activities, combine to provide a stimulating environment in which to pursue your education.

Please review the enclosed Admission Contract to insure that you will meet the provisions of our offer of admission. Your admission materials also contain information regarding enrollment and university housing. Read the enclosed materials carefully and note deadlines for the return of critical documents. Again, congratulations on your accomplishments. Should you have any questions, please contact us. We look forward to welcoming you to the UCLA community.

Every child is born brilliant. Every birth is miraculous. We come into this world not as empty vessels, but as full human beings with our divinely given gifts intact. As a seed is directed by nature to grow into a tree, our motivation to explore and create is directed by the need to manifest these gifts.

Within the first two years of life, a baby exhibits incomparable motivation and brilliance. The act of organizing information into meaning, of understanding relationships, of assimilating a culture, even of talking or reproducing sound into language takes an intelligence and an internal drive we can only begin to imagine. How much greater, then, are our individual talents, passions, and brilliance!

Stephen started to manifest his passion and brilliance at an early age. Erin and Matthew followed suit. But so did David Z. and Adam and Candice and a million other children. My children are not gifted in the sense of better than or even different from other children. All children are born with a passion that will guide them to their brilliance; it's just that most children are denied the opportunity to find it. Rudolf Steiner reminds us:

You will remember, that we need not devise educational programs, but rather that we need to perceive how human beings grow and then surround them with the food they need. (189)

As a seed contains the pattern for the whole tree, our being is encoded with the unlimited pattern of our brilliance. The desire to express this brilliance within the format of love is the fullest and highest expression of our being.

~ 32 ~

Holding Back the Tide: In His Own Words

"So each of us must seek, so each one of us must dance through life...[until] we arrive at that stage of Nirvana, that absolute oneness with Life."

J. Krishnamurti

Stephen recounts his journey:

I couldn't wait. I actually wanted to go to UCLA much earlier, but every time I said I wanted to go, my parents said, "Stephen, you've got plenty of time, just wait." But I went and talked to the counselor myself. She said, "Here's the classes you need to take to get accepted to UCLA. And here is the bare minimum of classes you need to get accepted to UCLA." And I had half of them and said, "O.K. I'm ready! Take me!" And they did. That's pretty much how it went.

But I got turned down the first time I applied so I went in and appealed. I said, "Look. I'm fifteen years old. Look at my record. Look at what I've done so far. Look at the systems I've designed. Look at my interaction with Warner Bros. Did you actually read my bio?" (They had not read my bio.) They hadn't read my resume or my entrance essay at all. They just saw that I hadn't completed the required classes. Then they basically said, "You know what...never mind, we'll let you in. Just take the classes here!" And so I did and I did well in them.

In fact, one of the classes I had to take before transferring was my physics lab. I ended up not taking the lab until four or five years later. But I did get it done. It was actually during my last quarter at UCLA as an undergraduate that I took that class.

For a while it was difficult for me at UCLA because I really had no place to fit in. I didn't even know where all the lounges were. But I was introduced to Damien at work and we became friends.

Damien was a UCLA student, but he had a small game development company. So I went to participate. They couldn't pay me a lot, but they ended up paying enough so I could get my car insurance so I could actually drive there, except I didn't have a car. I barely had my learner's permit. It was a great experience. I am still friends with them today.

I hit it off with Damien and we scheduled some classes together. He helped me get started at UCLA and introduced me to the lounge and the foosball table. I ended up spending many years at that lounge. I actually had a base of operations and a place to work from.

Then I got involved with CSUA, the Computer Science Undergrad Association. It sounded far more impressive on the web page than it actually was because the organization of that place varied dramatically from year to year. I ran for vice-president and was actually elected. I had a circle of friends and some of them I liked more than others, but they were all my friends. And I took my classes and that was fun. I ran into people and teachers I knew from Moorpark College.

Some of the teachers from Moorpark were now teaching at UCLA part time. I had a great relationship with the professors, but I did not hit it off well with the chair of the Computer Science Department. Now I just think he was busy and that could have been in my head, but I think I came off as being unfocused because I was so interested in so many different things rather than just following the curriculum.

I remember the first time I met with my counselor. She made some sort of statement that I couldn't work at Warner Bros. and get credit for that at UCLA. And I asked her if there was anyone higher up I could talk to? And that didn't really appeal to her because she said, "No! I'm the Law!" And that was it. And we didn't hit it off really well, especially since I wasn't particularly diligent about meeting my filing deadlines or when I was going to take classes or not take classes. I got in trouble on more than one occasion. Now we are good friends, but for a while there she was the Gestapo. Somehow it turned as we came to know each other better. So, it was great. She gave me a big hug when I graduated and said, "You finally made it." And I've been responsible for several years.

At UCLA I actually got to develop friendships with people nearer my age because I was older. It was great! I had some great friendships. I lived on campus. Had some interesting experiences with roommates and fellow engineers as well as other students. And I really hit it off with a number of people, developing what I believe will be lifelong friendships. And all the while I was working part time at Warner Bros.

But getting to Warner Bros. was sometimes a challenge. I was still young and only had my learner's permit, so I took the bus. There was a bus that picked up at the edge of campus and dropped off in Sherman Oaks, across the street from Warner Bros. It got to the point that the bus driver knew me so well because I always went at the same time, that I would go to sleep and he would send someone to wake me up when we got near the destination. On several occasions I had forgotten my fares or didn't have change so he would just let me on board and say, "Oh, never mind. Just come on board, Stephen." And I'd pay next time. Or he'd pay. The bus driver became a friend as well.

So, as I saw my graduation looming near, I had a year left and had to make a decision about what I wanted to do for graduate school. There were two active areas in computer sciences that intrigued me. One was computer graphics and one was computer architecture. Database systems actually interested me as well, but not so much from an implementation standpoint. The graphics department wasn't very mature at UCLA. There were one, maybe two professors, who did anything with computer graphics. The Computer Department was focused on computer architecture, which is how computers are built. I wasn't primarily interested in fault tolerance or numerical computing. I really wasn't interested in devising faster ways for computers to add. I figured they were fast enough and did not need my help. So I talked to the Engineering Honors Society.

The gentleman from the Honors Society made the suggestion that if I were interested in graphics and hardware, I should go talk to Carl in the Electrical Engineering Department. He did some unusual projects with MPEG and image compression and things that I would find interesting.

I was very encouraged by this and went to the Engineering Department looking for him. Well, his office was closed. But next to his office was a gentleman and I walked in and asked him about research opportunities. I said, "I'm sorry. I was looking for Carl, but here's my background. Here's what I've done. Here's what I'm looking for. Here are my goals. I am looking for research opportunities. I'd like to do this. Do you think Carl would be interested in talking to me?"

And the man introduced himself as Dr. Bill Maggione-Smith and said, "You know what? Two things. Yes, I think he would be interested in talking to you, but so would I. I'd like to offer you a managed research course with me. Let's do something!"

I listened to some of the projects that he was working on and one of the projects was profiling the open GL Pipeline with a graduate student of his. I thought that sounded like a lovely idea. So I signed up and started working with Bill. And Bill was very grateful to have someone, in his words, "who could code their way out of a paper bag," because he didn't feel that any of his graduate students could.

And I went around helping his graduate students with their projects. I ended up getting a paper published because of my work with another colleague on Branch Projection Systems. I built a whole simulation environment and helped him profile a number of research ideas using the simulator that I built.

I ended up becoming friends with Bill as well. I mean, he wasn't just my professor. We were doing independent studies together, but I talked to him about some of the business things I was doing on the side. I had my ideas about vertical market systems and he brought up this business opportunity that I kind of shirked off and then started listening to in more detail.

One of the owners of this business had been coach of the UCLA Bruins football team. He needed engineers so he went to the Dean of the Engineering School at UCLA who put him in touch with the Chairman of the Electrical Engineering Department. The chairman contacted Bill Maggione-Smith, a professor in the department. And Bill came to me.

We formed a company. It was the three of us, Bill Maggione-Smith, the Chairman of the Electrical Engineering Department and me—plus five engineers. I spent four years working with them. I dropped my involvement with the Warner Brother's and Cinebase crew to do this full time. It delayed my graduation by two years.

Now, I have recently gone back to graduate school. I am in the Electrical Engineering Department. Bill's my professor and I'm looking forward to having the time to do research with him. And I'm going to enjoy my time and enjoy the beach and my friends, and try to focus a bit on me and making me into the person that I want to be or letting myself become the person that I was meant to be.

It is an interesting time. I believe there's a lot of change in the world. I think that we've done so much to destabilize our environment, both physically and spiritually. That's going to have repercussions and I don't know what those repercussions will be. I don't know why people are so linear or so close-minded, but it may be that ignorance is bliss. I see some of us evolving and some of us not. I hope that I am one of the ones who evolve. I find that the world is far shallower and devoid of life than it needs to be. But on the other hand, there are pockets of pure brilliance and beauty that are worth discovering if we know how to look.

The Last Chance Tests
and
Corn Flakes

*"We have to assume that the distance
between the edge is half delta one."*
Erin Brown

I can't believe we are back at Panera. I can't believe *I* am back here again. Erin has passed her comprehensives on the masters, but not yet the Ph.D. level. It is three months since the first set of tests. THEN they were here all summer …studying for the next chance, the next opportunity to realize their dreams. Erin and her friends pore over another two zillion reams of mathematics. I bet if they put all their math problems in a line, characters end to end, they could wrap their work around the world.

"They should give us a half a point just for seeing where to begin on this problem," I hear one of them say. (They should give us our own table—permanently, I thought.)

"Wait a minute. Wait a minute. Wrong order," one of them says.

Phebe replies, "I think we're going to be O.K." Stephanie nods.

The jazz music is upbeat.

Erin is excited. There is a good chance they will do really well. This test is a cattle call. There will be entering students along with the second year grads who still need to pass on the Ph.D. level (including my daughter).

Stephanie pipes in, "I think that will boost your confidence, when you see all those first-year grad students there. They don't know anything. I remember when I walked in. All these kids thinking they have to pass this test. They write these tests so you can't pass, especially that first set. Half of the room was second-years still trying to pass that first test. You talk to a handful of people…" Phebe and Stephanie stop and take a good look at Erin. I am sitting at a table behind her and only see the back of her head, but I can feel the look on her face. That look must have stopped Phebe and Stephanie too. They tell her, she looks *calm*. I *know* what she probably looks like is *contemplative*.

Phebe speaks, "Half of me says I can do this. The other half says *ugh!*" Erin does not respond.

Stephanie works at lightening things up. She starts talking about the word Panera. "I don't think it really means *bread*. I think it's a play on the word, like *bread store*."

A phone rings. It is mine. It is far too loud and interrupts their conversation. It's Matthew. "Hey Mom! So I walk into Evon's office and tell him I want a design internship two times a week. I walk in unannounced, no appointment, nothing. And he says O.K.! Is that cool! O.K. mom. Got to run. Give Erin my love." They go back to solving the math.

Erin has a sore throat. The 'last chance' tests are tomorrow and the day after. The table is littered with Ricola Nature's Protection Vitamin C, a supplemental drop with elderberry

and other natural systems. The package is purple. In white letters at the bottom is written "helps support immune system." I
think we need all the HELP and support we can get. There is
a spray bottle of Silver Spray ultimate colloidal silver. There
are the crusts of left over French baguettes. There is a zip-
lock baggie full of colorful, multi-colored foil-wrapped mini-
ature candies.

"What's that?" I ask.

"Confetti candy from Trader Joes."

"What's it for?"

"Mom...it's *candy!*"

"Oh."

Erin gives me that 'enough talking look.' She does a practice test over. She times each problem. "Are you doing
O.K.?" she asks me out of concern in case the look she gave
me was too severe. But she does not stop, not even to pose the
question. Her hand continues to write. Her hand moves quickly. The table shakes. It looks something like this:

Let R be a principal ideal domain. Let B be a torsion R-
module and let p be a prime in R. Prove that if pb = 0 for
some nonzero element b in B then the annihilator of B is
contained in the ideal generated by p.

Consider Rb, the submodule of B generated by b. Then
the annihilator of Rb is the set of all r in R such that
srb=0 for all rb in RB. Note that sr is an element in R.
Since Rb is contained in B, we know that the annihilator
of B is contained in the annihilator of Rb. To see that the
annihilator of Rb is contained in the ideal generated by
p, recall that the annihilator of Rb is contained in R,
which is a principal ideal domain. So, the annihilator of
Rb must be equal to an ideal generated by a single element in R. Call this element y. Since pb=0, and p is in
the ideal generated by y, the ideal generated by p must
be contained in the ideal generated by y. Thus y divides
p, so yx=p for some x in R. Since p is a prime...

It is a book of writing…all mathematics…all hers. There is no way to tell where one problem leaves off and the next begins. It is pages and pages and pages of writing.

I look around Panera. I feel flat. I have no insight, no words of encouragement except, "It is all going to be O.K." I feel directionless. I do not know how to help. Nothing is going through my head accept this one image. I see myself trying to carry corn flakes out of the market without a box. I ponder the image. I try to come up with the right words of advice and encouragement, but, alas, no box.

I love my daughter.

❧ 34 ❧

Our Daughter

Putting my flashlight in my mouth and reaching forward, I pulled my body, head first, into the abyss. In the midst of the Negev desert, marked only by a boulder on the side of the mountain, I found the passageway to the ancient holy altar.

The deep dark tunnel wound downhill like Jung's metaphor for a journey into the subconscious. Lying flat, my stomach pressing against the unforgiving rock, I felt minutes turn into eternities. Intermittent waves of panic washed over my confidence. I wanted to break out of the rock. I stopped crawling and lay there for a few seconds, envisioning with envy Michelangelo's "Prisoners" escaping their marble.

All my senses begged me to keep moving, but my mind told me not to flee. I turned off the light and remained motionless. I had never experienced such darkness, such stillness, yet I never felt so free. Feeling as if I filled up the whole mountain, I lost the sensation of confinement. I could not judge where the mountain ended and I began. I was so large and so small at the same time. I triumphed. I turned on my light and kept moving.

This is Erin's college admission essay to UCLA. It is a true story. All of it. Erin writes about an adventure she had when she was seventeen and spent the summer in Israel. She continues:

Challenge promotes growth. Receiving a scholarship to study Hebrew and biblical history in Israel, I rafted down the Jordan River, climbed the face of Masada at sunrise, rappelled down lofty cliffs, and survived in the desert with only a small sleeping bag and backpack for a pillow.

I helped excavate a 2,000 year-old tomb at Tel Maresha and spent a physically and emotionally demanding week in field and weaponry training with the Israeli Army.

The summer before, I had fallen in love with the art of Europe. I saw beauty everywhere from the austerity of Stonehenge to the treasures of the Louvre, Musee d'Orsay, the Uffizi of Florence and the National Gallery of London. Challenge and beauty now merged in my experience of the desert, while scope and diversity opened my eyes to the immeasurable ingenuity and capacity of the human spirit—mine included.

When I was eight years old, I fell in love with horses, trading my labor for free riding time at a local ranch. I was too short to bridle a horse at that age, but I am inventive. I hung from the horse's neck, and with a maneuver that belongs in Cirque de Soleil, within thirty seconds the horse had a bit in its mouth and a bridle on its head. I learned to ride from an Apache Indian named Bess, whose authoritative voice was enough to make anyone stop dead in their tracks. With fierce determination she taught me to ride like the wind. I never needed a saddle.

Now I work with the many-time-over world champion and former Olympic Judge, James Frazier. Together we take a revolutionary approach to training my three-year-old horse. Eliminating the necessity for tack or riding equipment, we built a language based solely on hand and voice commands and body movements. I have learned there is always an alternative solution.

I excelled in academics. By thirteen years old I had completed my high school studies and tested into Moorpark College. I maintained full time status, making the Dean's Honor List every year with an overall G.P.A. of 4.0. I have taken every math course the college offers. I enjoy working with people and am frequently asked to head study groups or tutor. [I am told]...my energy, enthusiasm, breadth of perspective and sense of adventure are contagious.

> I look forward to bringing these attributes to UCLA and using them to explore topics in a depth not available at Moorpark College; there is so much more that entices me.

When we see children as 'students,' we confine our perceptions of who they are to a particular set of behaviors and performances. We create a caricature. But children are living beings. They have whole lives of their own which most school systems disregard and even discourage. They are busy thinking, feeling, sensing and living, regardless of what we ask them to do or what we ask them to be. They are busy creating and recreating their own life stories, their own personalities, which they will incorporate into their particular sense of identity. They will carry these stories forward with them throughout time. This is Erin's story:

Erin entered Moorpark College at thirteen. Unlike her brothers, she started with a full load; it was something she wanted to do. It became quickly obvious she was gifted in art, as well as math. She was admitted to the Art Department at the invitation of the Head of the Art Department Frank Sardisco. She worked directly under his tutelage in the areas of drawing, life drawing and painting every semester for five years. At fourteen, she was the teaching assistant for the college's Computer Information Systems Lab. At fifteen, she was employed by the college to tutor mathematics and English for Moorpark College's tutoring center. By sixteen, she made the Moorpark College Girl's Soccer Team, competing in the Intercollegiate Division. At the end of the season, she was given the Academic All Conference Athletic/Academic Award for outstanding achievement in both the academic and sports arena by the Western State Conference. At seventeen, she was nominated by the faculty out of 12,000 students and the sole recipient of the Outstanding Student in Mathematics

Award and Scholarship, awarded in front of faculty, staff and student body.

While pursuing an academic life at the college, Erin continued her karate training, achieving both First and Second Degree Black Belt designations, participating in a world-class demonstration team and joining the Olympic Ladder in Judo. She won second place in an international Judo competition in her division. Still finding time to be a child, she raised her horse, played in the orchard, spent summers windsurfing, kayaking and sailing. She never had a grade or homework in her life until college. Then she took over one hundred units at that college and maintained a perfect straight A average. Erin explains how her path evolved:

> Stephen was taking an adult electronics class in college. He did that for a while and he really liked it. He had a lot of fun. So I wanted to try to do that too. So, I asked my mom, "What can I do?" And she said, "Maybe try math and English. You could take those entrance exams and get in."
>
> I really wanted to go to college. So, my friend David Z. and I spent many, many hours all day—many, many, days—doing math on the dry erase board, going through all the advanced mathematics books we could find. David Z. and I did this for two years, most mornings, all morning and it was great fun. We'd do it on a big white board and we'd get so excited! We'd yell and scream and laugh and correct each other and erase and rewrite and just worked with each other!
>
> It was our choice. It was something we wanted to do and for the most part the adults got out of our way. Every now and then it would be

'suggested' that we do some reading as well, or study a little bit more about government or writing, science or spelling, put a little balance into our lives. (I spent a long time trying to spell 'immediately.' That word—I just couldn't get it right for a while, but that's O.K.).

Then David Z. and I took the math placement exam and we both got in. We went to college. We were twelve when we took the placement test and had just turned thirteen about two months after the semester started.

So my first semester I took math, electronics and art. Stephen always stopped and talked to the art teacher, Frank Sardisco, so he built up a friendship with him. I did a lot of drawing on my own. I'd always draw cartoon characters and so my brother asked if I could be in his class and he let me in. Candice, also from G.T. Water, went into the art class with me. She was ten.

I liked going there so much I stuck around and was there for five years (laughter). I always took a math class and I always took an art class every semester. And then the other class I'd usually take was a computer science or programming class. I was a lab assistant at the computer lab that my brother had been a computer assistant at before me. Stephen paved the way. And then Stephen went to UCLA and I was still going to Moorpark. I stayed at Moorpark until I was seventeen. Then I applied to UCLA.

But I loved Moorpark. I loved it! I started tutoring math and English in the tutoring center. It was drop-by tutoring and anybody could come in and then we would help them. Life at Moor-park was terrific. I got to meet a lot of people because I tutored there and I was actually a pretty good tutor. A lot of the teachers recommended me to their students, and so that was really cool! Friends told me that I got recommended from teachers I never had!

Then, my last year there, I was taking linear algebra, the hardest math course. It was after two regular algebra classes, trigonometry, three calculus classes and differential equations. Then came linear algebra. This was a whole different level of algebra. I was having a really hard time with it because all of a sudden it wasn't math anymore; it was very abstract. Then it clicked in one giant cube and all of a sudden I understood the whole thing and was really proficient in it. So I helped tutor the class that I was in, and because of my rapid advancement the teacher was kind enough to nominate me for a scholarship, which I got. It was a math scholarship, which they hadn't given out for a long time. So that was really cool! The dean presented it to me in front of the faculty and student body in a big ceremony. And then I applied to UCLA.

And when Erin asked her professors for letters of recommendation, they were delighted to reply.

A professor of mathematics wrote:

An instructor, in the course of her career, gets a chance to encounter many academically gifted students who also show a high degree of task commitment and diligence. But, rarely, can one see such a fine balance of academic potentials, curiosity, love of knowledge, total commitment, and maturity as I saw in Miss Brown....

Another mathematics professor wrote:

As indicated by her transcripts, Ms. Brown is an outstanding student, and her knowledge of how to be successful in an academic environment will allow her to attain each of the degrees to which she aspires. What is particularly impressive in this context is her ability to grasp abstract concepts and to apply such theory in both theoretical and practical situations across a broad range of subject areas.

I am continually impressed by Ms. Brown's communication skills, both written and oral, in both the English and mathematical languages....

And Erin is a warm, friendly person with a smile and a kind word for everyone with whom she comes in contact. Demonstrating a level of maturity far beyond her years, she cares deeply about the people around her, and works hard to make her environment a better place for all. Her service to Moorpark College is just one example of her caring.

The Head of the Art Department, Mr. Frank Sardisco wrote:

Erin has been a student of mine for nine semesters.... In thirty-four years of teaching art, I have found her to be one of the most outstanding students I have ever had. This is especially significant since Erin is not an art major. She continually demonstrates an outstanding intellectual capacity to learn complex concepts in art. She also possesses the disciplined work habits to allow her to succeed in any project she starts.... I expect great things from her in whatever field she decides to specialize in.

Her English professor wrote:

Erin Brown is without doubt one of the most outstanding students I have had the pleasure of teaching in my ten years as a college English instructor. I would rank her in the top one percent of students at our institution and consider her an excellent candidate for academic awards.

I first met Erin in the Fall of 1998; she was desperate to add an English 1B class, and although my class was already full, I sensed that this was a determined, bright, articulate young woman who would only enhance my literature and composition course. I turned out to be right. Thank goodness I said yes to adding her! Otherwise the class would have missed out on Erin's insightful comments and questions, her high standards for her work, and her joyous company....

Probably the thing I'll never forget about Erin was the amazing creative project she did for the class. One of the assignments was a creative interpretation of a novel. Erin, a gifted artist, painted a six-foot by four-foot painting that was truly breathtaking. It pictured a woman tied to a post, leaning away, trying to be free; this was a very thoughtful interpretation of the main character in the novel, <u>Like Water for</u>

<u>Chocolate</u>, which we were studying. The students were all completely blown away, as I was, by Erin's talent, thinking skills, and her humility about this project. She was proud of it, but Erin is not the kind of person to show off. She knows she is multi-talented—after all, how many of us get A's in English, want to major in math, are accomplished painters and practiced martial artists?

Erin is a real 'Renaissance' person: intellectual, healthy, positive minded, artistic, well read, focused. It is rare to meet such a young person with so many of the qualities we expect to see in someone with more years to accumulate knowledge and expertise.... I continue to see Erin around campus this semester, and although she is busy with school and her extra-curricular activities, she always has time to say 'hi' and share what is going on with her. It is such a pleasure to talk to Erin; she has a beautiful smile that comes from within and she radiates a self-confidence and a comfortability with herself rare in women her age.

Thanks to an environment that protected Erin's authenticity and integrity, she has emerged uniquely Erin. She has learned to bring all that she is to each situation. Erin's perception is integrated. Warren Bennis says, "The key to understanding is learning—from one's own life and experience...." (3) Erin does not isolate and compartmentalize information the way school children are taught to do. Jerome Bruner reminds us:

...the boundaries that separated such fields as psychology, anthropology, linguistics, and phi-

losophy were matters of administrative convenience rather than of intellectual substance. (xvi)

Erin's understanding of the world around her is not limited
in that way. Instead she synthesizes information, expanding it
and integrating it within her own experience to create new
forms and understanding. She sees the math she loves as integrated into the life around her. She sees it operative in movement, the movement of her karate, the flow of her art. Erin
writes:

> The relationship of mathematics to movement
> holds my fascination. It is never far from my
> mind. Karate is one vehicle in which I exercise
> and nurture this fascination. I earned a second-
> degree black belt in Tang Su Do under the guid-
> ance of two world-renowned martial artists,
> Master Tom Bloom and Sensei Cecil Peoples.
> While I train, I think about mass, the reluctance
> of an object to move. I ponder inertia, the reluc-
> tance of an object to rotate about a single point,
> or hinge. I relate these concepts to karate in per-
> haps the most obscure ways. The concept of in-
> ertia and all its properties apply to a move
> called a 540, the rotation of an object, or a leg
> around a point, or a hip.
>
> I have sat watching piece after piece of chalk
> being thrown across the room until everyone in
> my math class has seen the parabolic line the
> chalk creates before it lands.
>
> I, too, create parabolic lines. Working on
> ways to calculate the maximum height, depen-
> dent on certain conditions, of a projectile, I
> wonder what my maximum height would be if
> all conditions were optimized during a jump-

kick. I understand that the maximum force applied to an object is dependent upon the angle in which the force is applied. I think of sparring and how I constantly move to acquire an angle that will best suit the technique I want to use. I study the moment of a lamina (abnormal shape) in 3-d space, finding the center of gravity of an object of non-uniform density. The whole object can be balanced on the tip of a pin at this point.

I once saw a photograph of a man balancing on one arm while the rest of his body is parallel to the ground. Some of my karate forms require such precise balancing skills. I know how to work out the center of gravity of an object on paper, but I can't say how many times I wish I knew where it was during a handstand competition.

An advertisement often runs through my mind. A woman is jumping backwards through the air, her whole body focuses on her toes. A man also in mid-air stretches his arms and legs. Their toes touch at the very tips. They are both sculpted and beautiful. Their whole essence conveys precision. The photo is in black and white, and although it is a still frame, it is easy to witness the motion the camera omits. In white letters at the bottom of the page, the ad says, "precision" and presents a picture of a watch; but I reflect on the people. They are unbound by the laws of physics, but powered by the veiled equations of movement. I study mapping motion and force; how to break them down into vectors, single lines with arrows indicating magnitude, length, and direction of force. It is a way to map tornadoes, whirlpools, or forces that are applied to objects. But I would love to map the dancers from the precision ad.

I am captivated by the connection of mathematics to our daily existence. Through my travels, I realize what an enchanted world we live in, and I have come to understand that mathematics is the language of process and structure for that world. I want to know more about that language. Imagine if I were fluent. I sense the music of the great dance of creation, but I am still in the dark, without a flashlight, searching for the dancers. I find myself trying to stick pins into the shadows they have left behind, hoping for a glimpse of the reality that fuels the world in which I live.

Jersild writes:

...to encourage the process of self-discovery, we must raise the question of personal significance in connection with everything we seek to learn and everything that is taught from the nursery school through postgraduate years. What does it mean? What difference does it make? What is there in the lessons we teach, the exercises we assign, the books we read, the experiences we enter into, and in all of our undertakings, that can help us to find ourselves and, through us, help others in their search? (136)

Erin is a gifted artist. She has figured out how to combine her two passions, art and mathematics, as she interned at one of Hollywood's leading special effects house. She has created models for them and rotoscoped special effects images—pictures of horses in water, rivers, mountainous landscapes and more. Twenty-two of her frames went into the final print of <u>Lord of the Rings</u>, an unprecedented achievement at that time for an intern. They are using the computer code she wrote for them to track lighting vectors in computer-generated images. The world famous Art Center College offered her admission to the college, an honor only a very few get, but Erin chose a Ph.D. program in mathematics instead.

Nothing stops children who are whole and intact. They are confident and poised, unpretentious and open. They interact, communicate and engage clearly with all. Warren Bennis refers to these qualities as being those of a natural leader. He says, the process of becoming a leader is:

> ...much the same as the process of becoming an integrated human being. For the leader, as for any integrated person, life itself is the career... each of them amounts to more than the sum, because they have made more of their experiences. These are originals, not copies. (4)

35

The Sun God

"May Shamash [the sun god] give you your heart's desire, may he let you see with your eyes the thing accomplished which your lips have spoken; may he open a path for you where it is blocked, and a road for your feet to tread. May he open the mountains for your crossing, and may the night time bring you the blessings of night, and Lugulbanada, your guardian god, stand beside you for victory."

Epic of Gilgamesh

Connection to spirit is more than just a search for self. It is a connection to Chi, to the flow of life's energy. It is much greater than any concept or belief system in our contemporary paradigm. It is grander than unlocking the mysteries within. It is bigger than exploring the wonders without. It connects and intertwines what we have previously thought as separate, unifying and weaving our complete experience, body, emotion, mind, spirit and soul, through the fiber of this world. It opens up doors of opportunity without explanation. It creates pathways of experience and magic. It is no less than divine.

The path to self not only reveals the breadth of majesty that is ours, and the passion through which we find brilliance, it connects us to experiences that otherwise would have not been accessible to a less-than-receptive smaller self. When we are bigger, our experience of life becomes exponential as well. We do big things. We have big experiences. Life plucks us out of the living room and puts us on paths of mystery and wonder.

The world called out. It reached into the hearts of my children and took them abroad. It showed them the 'human experience' through the eyes of those living in other cultures and in other places.

At sixteen, after Matthew had taught at the college computer science lab, tutored math and astronomy at the college tutoring center, started an online sports magazine with three other adults that came to boast a staff of over a hundred through the U.S. and Canada, earned first and second degree black belts in Tang Soo Do and was on the Olympic ladder for Judo, he fell in love with the art of dance.

Within six months, Matthew was dancing with a professional company. Six months after that he was invited to train with the male members of the Berlin Ballet Opera in Germany. His position at the bar was between the two principal dancers of their production, 'Anastasia.' Then he was invited to train with and be evaluated by the Hamburg Ballet Academy. A year later he was living in Monaco and training full time at Le Academie de Danse Classique, Princess Grace.

It was tough to get into the Academy. About a hundred young people ages eight to twenty-something were accepted representing a total of thirty-two nations. Only two students were from the United States. The other two English-speaking students were from Canada and Ireland. Instruction was in French and Italian. There were translators all over the place, everywhere except from the English speaking countries, and none of these four students spoke any language other than English—Matthew included. But they worked it out.

The Italian-speaking children whispered to our English-speaking children. The French and any other students who spoke English helped them. And they all helped each other.

The training was grueling. It began at eight o'clock in the morning and continued until five o'clock in the evening. It often included two to three hours of class lecture in addition. Students were told that if they could not understand something, staff would work with them until they did—but once they did, there was NO excuse for going backwards. By the end of the first week, twenty percent of the dancers were either sent home or quit. Matthew was not one of them.

Matthew and the remaining students aided, practiced, coached, tended, hugged and took care of each other. They were a team. Speaking Japanese, Chinese, Bulgarian, Spanish, Italian, French, German, Swedish, Polish, Russian and a number of other languages coming from countries we had never heard of, they laughed, cried and supported each other through the ongoing weeks. They gave rise to new hope for the human spirit and peace in our world in their time.

While Matthew was in Monaco, our little family spread across the globe; we had three children living on three different continents at the same time. Erin had been in Italy and was now back home going to graduate school in mathematics. Matthew was in school in Monaco. And Stephen was in Asia.

We put Stephen on a plane to Asia a month after the tragedy of September 11th He was headed for China to lead a team of programmers for a company in Hong Kong. Last year he was again asked to work for this company, this time building the computer architecture for their programmers in Singapore.

He left a year ago May for Singapore. Erin and I joined him for that summer, taking breaks to travel with him by backpack through parts of China, Hong Kong and the third world countries of Malaysia and Thailand. We saw the wonders of the great center at Kuala Lumpur, a city lit to the sky, and the poverty of Bangkok, Thailand with children bathing in and drinking sewer water. We took a two-day trip from Singapore to the island of Redong, a paradise so far out in the Pacific it is barely on the map. It took two days, two taxis, two airplanes (landing in an airport so small they turned the lights on just for our family), a bus, a boat and a tractor to get there. But we now understand Eden.

At Redong, the water was as blue and as clear as turquoise food coloring. The fish had no fear of man, iridescent, rainbowed, patterned and in shapes and colors we thought only Disney could invent. There is a greater Creator. It was earth as it was created, as it could be, as it should be...everywhere.

Then, last Christmas, it was Matthew's turn to visit Stephen in Singapore. Stephen's gift to Matthew was a weekend in Phi Phi, Thailand and a date to go scuba diving there. Their Aunt Judi was with them as well.

Stephen, having negotiated through the jungles of Malaysia, was a superb travel planner. He left no detail unattended...except this time. For some reason, Stephen neglected to make reservations in Thailand. They would wing it. Then they left a day late. Stephen's friend from Italy convinced the boys to stay in Singapore and celebrate Christmas Eve with her so Matthew could meet her younger sister.

A day later than they planned, they arrived in Ao Nang, Thailand. Their clocks were an hour off. They did not know it. They got on the wrong boat, at the wrong time and it saved their lives.

This is the email Matthew sent to his family and friends four days later:

The night before the tsunami, my aunt, my brother, and I stayed in a very nice hotel in Ao Nang. We walked along the water and ate a luxurious dinner.

The following morning, due to a time change mix up, we awoke at six o'clock in the morning instead of seven. We walked up and down the beautiful beaches; I even experienced my first wild coconut cracking. At seven-thirty we ate breakfast at the hotel and by eight we were on a "shuttle" to Ao Nang Harbor. We were going to take a ferry to Phi Phi Dan and spend our vacation on the beach, snorkeling, scuba diving, and hiking.

The shuttle was similar to a pickup truck with handmade walls and a ceiling in the back. I kept thinking, "Where are the chickens?"

When we arrived at Ao Nang Harbor, the boat was large and sturdy looking. We went onboard and went straight to the sundeck. It was a beautiful trip. The water was clear, the sun was hot, and the wind was refreshing. Different tourists had interactions with my family. There were a few German couples, some Swedish tourists, a French man, a few British couples, plus a couple of Americans.

For the most part people spoke English and not Thai. The ferry was part of a tour as well as a transportation device. Some people came from Phi Phi Dan and got on the boat to return home. Some people were on a one-way route like we were, going to Phi Phi Dan, Phi Phi Lay or Phuket.

Our boat stopped and picked up another German couple on their way to Phuket. We found out later just how lucky those two people were. As we approached Phi Phi Dan, I was excited to see the shore from a great distance, but I noticed that there were a lot of boats waiting in a line. This happened a little before eleven o'clock in the morning. I thought we were waiting for some sort of landing clearance.

After about an hour of looking at the shore and not landing, people started to ask the staff what was going on. I think only two staff members spoke English and then only a very little English with a very strong accent. The general consensus among my family and a number of our newfound tourist friends was that we were either waiting for a 'whale underwater,' or a 'wave.' The best we could think of, as the sea was calm and the sky was clear, was that we were waiting for the tide to be high enough to land. Some people thought this was poor planning.

The sun was very hot. I felt like I was roasting so I found an air-conditioned section of the boat and complimentary cookies and soft drinks down below. I took a quick nap, not knowing that I would spend the next seven hours there.

As time went by more people found my special air-conditioned room as well. More people talked and more rumors spread. At one point, a similar looking boat pulled beside us and docked by latching on to our ship. At this point, the rumors included an earthquake in Phuket. We heard that somewhere between twenty-three people and one thousand people were dead. Most people didn't believe this rumor.

Then a Thai man from the other boat, dressed in island clothes with his shirt unbuttoned and mud all over his clothes, frantically ran down to the lower room. His Thai friends jumped up in surprise; there was some exchange of information.

At that point, I was confused and hungry for information, as were the other tourists on the boat. I asked what happened. He looked at me, still disoriented, and made a gesture with his hands. I later understood that gesture to mean, "Wiped out, flat, gone." A friend of his lifted up the man's shirt revealing a four-inch cut.

The rumor that a big wave was coming or that the underwater current was too strong seemed to be the best answer we could get at that moment. Some of us thought the other boat was attached to our boat for stability; others thought we were to get on to that boat because perhaps our boat was having problems or maybe that boat had a shallower bottom and would be easier to dock.

When that boat left, we thought maybe it had been there to transfer supplies to us. We thought perhaps we would be here even longer than the couple of hours we had already spent just sitting there in the water. Some people were saying that something bad happened to that ship. Some of the crew members were missing. Most people started to think that something serious was in fact happening, but we were not sure what. The faces on the captain and his crew seemed a bit worried.

Despite the wait, a large number of people were still expecting to arrive at Phi Phi Dan. A rumor that we might be going back to Ao Nang disappointed many tourists and the people who were trying to get back to the island.

It wasn't until the next incident that anyone onboard could actually feel something terrible was happening. By then, most of the boats on the water seemed to be facing the same direction and clumping together behind a large mountain on Co Phi Phi.

A long-tail boat, with some considerable speed, docked to our boat. Onboard was a Thai man with numerous cuts and scratches up and down his body. He was passed out in a daze. His feet were wrapped in old, dirty bandages. A couple of the guys carried him onboard and down the stairs. He lay across all four seats. A crowd of people followed him to see what was happening. A friend of his sat near by in a beat-up life vest. He too had open cuts and scratches.

At this point I noticed a few life vests that were removed from the seats below. Someone was worried. Seeing this man and waiting for many hours invoked the non-English speaking tourists to seek information. A German couple turned to me and said they didn't speak much English, could someone tell them what was going on? The same for a French man traveling by himself. My brother went to find some of our new German friends as I tried to explain what we knew in French to the man from France.

By now, we were sure there was an earthquake somewhere, either in one spot or multiple spots. We heard that there were massive tidal waves. We heard that the place where we picked up the German couple was pretty messed up. More specifically that all the long-tail boats were washed away, as well as the little shops on the beach.

A larger boat came by and docked by lashing onto us. This boat confirmed the terror. There were people onboard wearing life vests. I saw one man walking around holding a rag to his head. He had blood dripping from his forehead, chest and legs. I asked a woman on the other boat if she knew what was going on. She confirmed our thoughts and added that the passengers that they had onboard were in fact from Phi Phi Dan; until then, we did not think Phi Phi Dan was affected. More tourists were asking for more information. I helped spread the news.

Meanwhile, downstairs, one of the German couples had an emergency kit and treated the man with the feet injuries. They thought that perhaps his foot was broken. They used antiseptics and clean bandages to sterilize his wounds to avoid infections. I thought this was very noble of them.

The current news was that there was an earthquake that caused tidal waves. We did not know the scale of the damage. We were told that we were going to wait behind the mountain for another half hour; we were waiting for another wave to pass. Then we would return to Ao Nang. The ferry said they would help with any cancellations on Phi Phi Dan that people had.

For my family this was not too bad. We had no reservations and all of our stuff was with us; we packed very lightly. But for other people, they had nothing but their swimming clothes on, perhaps a small handbag, and a book (which they had probably finished in all this time). The German couple from Raleigh beach had their passports back at their resort, which was reported as gone.

On our way back we saw the sea littered with debris. I saw tree branches, coconuts, wood pieces and even long-tail boats snapped in half. We found out that Ao Nang Harbor was hit too. So we arrived at Krabi Harbor—one large dock with a narrow pathway. Later I would see this harbor on the news carrying injured people and many, many, tourists.

There were already boats offloading many tourists with a lot more luggage then our boat had. I also noticed life jackets clasped to the railings; this boat had some problems. We pulled up along side of the boat. When it was our turn we loaded onto their boat and then onto the dock.

My family and another American from Maine stuck together through a crowd of anxious people. It was crazy. All the little "handmade" busses converted from pickup trucks were out in the parking lot. Whenever an empty transportation vehicle pulled near, it would be rushed with people and baggage. It would have no time to park. People flooded the parking lot and street.

My party didn't know exactly where these busses were going, but we managed to find a small one and get in. After my body was numbed from the waist down from being crammed in the back of this converted pickup, we heard something about how they were taking us to a school.

When we got to the school, we found out that the truck was actually an ambulance and the school was at the end of his jurisdiction. After a few moments, he got clearance and continued to drive us to Ao Nang. He didn't take us to the beach. He stopped about two blocks from the beach. He refused our tip. The town was active. Lots of traffic. Lots of police. Lots of ambulances.

We found a place to check the Internet. For the first time we confirmed the news: earthquake, tidal wave, and death count. All the places we had been and were planning on going were affected. At that point, spending seven hours instead of the scheduled hour and a half on an air-conditioned ferry, eating cookies and drinking soft drinks, seemed like a luxurious harbor cruise.

We were able to write one email to our family saying we were fine and press 'send' seconds before the power went out.

We conversed with a British family who was on the beach in Ao Nang when a wave hit. They said that the water came all the way up to where we were standing. I did not see the hotel we stayed at the night before, but given the distance and height that we were at, I could guess that our hotel was probably completely covered by the wave.

My family and I decided to cut the vacation short. We found a taxi and headed straight to the airport. On the way we saw the Indian Embassy completely filled with people. We saw two different hospitals with no standing space and many helicopters. At the airport, all flights to Phuket were understandably cancelled. There were many flights to Bangkok and only one flight to Singapore, our destination. So we ended up getting a hotel in Krabi Town and waited for the only flight out at six in the morning the following day.

It was chaos at the airport. There were no lines; everyone was crowding around, waiting to get to the ticket counter. There were less than ten windows for check-in and tickets. There were a large number of people waiting standby. People inched their way to the counter. People were there, limping, in bandages, with cuts, scratches, bruises and torn bathing suits. A lot of people were in their bathing suits.

I managed to talk to a number of people who were trying to fly to Bangkok, who were hit hard. An American couple had only one bag with no passport. They managed to find their flight booking confirmation in a zip lock on the beach after the wave cleared. The man was limping and his shorts were ripped so that his boxers were hanging out and the women, in her bikini and shorts, had massive scratches on her back. Sand was everywhere. They said that the wave came and flooded everything. Then it quickly pulled back into the sea and slammed everyone and everything back into island. Apparently they were holding on to a bungalow for dear life.

Another man explained how he was snorkeling at the time. Everyone in his party had made it. I heard about a woman who was scuba diving at the time. She was thrown onto some rocks. She lived, but her companions were missing.

We made it into one of the two gates. The airport officials came by with bottled water, orange juice, some bread snacks and even offered sandals to those who needed them—all complimentary.

My brother, aunt and I are now back in Singapore reading about all that has happened. We were very lucky. It turned out that we were literally in the right place at the right time. We were a hundred yards away from the tidal wave, protected by a limestone cove. The wave missed us. But if we had been a half hour later, we would have been on the boat that was tossed by a wave in Ao Nang, or an hour earlier, we would have been docking at Phi Phi dan right as the wave hit.

I am extremely grateful for my survival. The more I read about what happened the more grateful I am.

I have to say, I am very impressed with the officials who helped us in Thailand, on the boat, in the harbor, and in the airport. With all that had happened and all the tourists they had to deal with, they were still friendly and patient. I never saw any one of them appear angry or annoyed or even frustrated.

From my point of view, there were plenty of opportunities for a native to take advantage financially of the situation. This did not happen. The taxi drivers were very friendly, patient and honest. Despite the lack of communication on the ferry, the crew apparently did a wonderful job. They kept us alive and out of harm's way. And I am very grateful for their help and their spirit. My prayers are with the thousands of people less fortunate then myself and my family.

With much love and gratitude,
Matthew

Grateful. My children are grateful. Matthew is grateful for the divine intervention that protected them from the tidal wave. Stephen is grateful for, as he explained to us on the phone, the many things that seemed to have 'gone wrong' that led him to the right spot at the right time. Erin is grateful to have her brothers and aunt back home. And Dennis and I are grateful for the divine guidance that has allowed our children to connect to a universe mysterious, unpredictable and yet magnificent in its glory.

Being alive entails more than just breathing. Brother David Steindl-Rast says that we all have moments in which we experience a heightened awareness framed by a deep and moving sense of gratitude. That gratitude springs directly from our hearts. Brother David writes:

> Those moments of deep gratefulness are, in fact, our moments of true prayerfulness, moments in which our heart is wide awake... prayer and thanks spring from the same root, from the heart. It is to those peak experiences of the heart that we must go back if we want to learn to live gratefully. (85)

And it is to those moments of gratitude we must go to feel truly alive. It is to those peak experiences we must go to live fully.

36

The Vision

"To see a world in a grain of sand
And a heaven in a wild flower,
Hold infinity in the palm of your hand
And eternity in an hour."

William Blake

I am sitting on the beach on a cool, misty morning in the middle of September looking across the bay at the Newport Peninsula. The sand is wet from the morning tide. The air is clear. The sun is peaking through the fog. The familiar sounds of the gulls, seals and early morning fishing boats echo through the dawn. I am not alone.

Matthew is back from Le Academie de Danse Classique, Princess Grace in Monaco, back from his journeys through Europe, and the adventures he and Stephen had in Asia. He has also received his degree in Mathematics/Applied Science, Management and Accounting—Specialization in Computing from UCLA. Now he is working on a book, a screenplay and is setting up a business with his father. In the middle of all this, he was hired as script-supervisor for a short film. There is no end to his talent.

Erin is sleeping in her apartment one hundred and ten feet from where I write. She is living here, on my favorite island, not far from the university. She passed her comprehensives on both the masters and the Ph.D. level. So did her friends, Stephanie, Elaine, Josh and Phebe. Congratulations team! Now Erin sleeps in. Congratulations my daughter! You deserve a rest. She still lives in her darling little apartment above the flower shop. How perfect! She has created her own cornucopia of flowers as she tends her exuberant terrace garden. An abundance of careening blossoms greets each visitor who steps off the ferry. It would be nice if we had such a welcome everywhere.

Stephen is back from Singapore. He lives thirty minutes up the coast from Erin. He, too, is finishing his graduate degree and working on his business. At the end of this year, he might go back to Singapore for a while. He misses his friends there.

The book is almost done. It has had a long birth, scribbled on the backs of envelopes and scrap paper, in parking lots and karate tournaments, dance studios, train stations and airports across three continents over a period of fifteen years. I hope it has a long life. I hope it will help. There is so much more to learn, but we have already come such a long way.

We have both circumvented and worked our way through learning institutions that tried to sort and weed our children out. We have bypassed an industrial education, re-entered on the college level and triumphed despite all odds. We took along anyone who wanted to go with us. We created non-judgmental, non-competitive learning communities and environments, where adults and children alike were not afraid to take risks and explore, to open their hearts and minds to new information and experiences. We have emerged intact and passionate, living a life full of possibilities.

I, too, now have a passion. I have learned much from the nest. It sings to me like a reoccurring dream. In my mind, it has already taken form—a *river* school. It echoes:

> I found love. It caressed my soul with the rapture of warm summer breezes. It lured my spirit with promises made on moonlight whispers of unseen beauties and sensations of peace beyond all remembrance. It sang to me from the depths of the aged wisdom of old knurled trees and beckoned arise, arise, awake and meet your destiny. Dance with me for the full-faced moon and sing to the stars as they fly by. Youthen and arise. Fly across the water and through the golden dipped-seas. Sing to me in voices angelic and sweet. Move to me, rhythmic and lyrical, burdenless and light. Learn.
>
> Sparkle with the eyes of sages. Timeless. Speak to me of approaching spring and blossoms past winter's cold. Teach me that I am not alone. Show me that I am all that I am. Just be. Quiet, timeless, enduring. Show me. Effortless, but steadfast. Show me. Lead me and follow. Teach.

It is the place in our hearts for which we long. *The River School* calls us home. I envision the waters of a river flowing across our country, bringing a renewing wellspring of psychological, intellectual, physical and spiritual health to our fertile lands, our villages, our cities. It empowers our families, strengthens our communities and nurtures balanced individuals capable of the full range of human potential. It creates environments in which children have the physical, emotional, mental and spiritual freedom to grow into creative, energetic, balanced, compassionate human beings.

Why a *river* school? The river is an enigma. It is never the same water twice. The current, the flow, the physical molecules move on, changing from second to second. The river is never rigid in form. It knows how to shift its course facilitating adaptive change and creative transformation. So does the school. As Margaret Wheatley writes:

> What is it that streams can teach about organizations: I am attracted to the diversity I see, to these swirling combinations of mud, silt, grass, water, rocks. This stream has an impressive ability to adapt, to shift the configurations, to let the power balance move, to create new structures. But driving this adaptability, making it all happen, I think, is the water's need to flow. Water answers to gravity, to downhill, to the call of ocean. The forms change, but the mission remains clear. Structures emerge, but only as temporary solutions that facilitate rather than interfere.... Streams have more than one response to rocks; otherwise, there'd be no Grand Canyon. Or else Grand Canyons everywhere. The Colorado realized that there were ways to get ahead other than by staying broad and expansive. (Leadership and the New Science, 15-16)

And like the river, the school will dedicate itself to finding the passion and brilliance, tranquility and light that exists in every child, in every one of us.

At the G.T. Water School and the other homeschooling groups I have been involved with, I have seen it work. I have already experienced small groups of children, engaged as they were in play, exploring texts, creating projects, helping each other in their individual and group efforts. I heard laughter and song—the joy of passion. I saw children moving back and forth between groups, five to eight-year-olds conversing with nine to twelve-year-olds. I saw older teens helping each other, nurturing the little ones and multi-age groupings united not by skill level, but by camaraderie and the need for relationship. I saw parents homeschooling and creating classes, uniting with teachers whose hearts are in their skills, using the best of our resources, building the best of our relationships, finding passion and brilliance at every turn.

But to achieve this kind of success we cannot keep industrializing the growth of our children. We cannot continue the destructive testing, the prodding, the behavioral wars to fit human-shaped children into mechanized slots. Haven't we had enough?

It is time. Now is the time to build environments that facilitate the best of our humanity. Now is the time to validate our desire to explore and create, to recognize our longing, to nurture our passion and brilliance, to find our way home. Only then will each of us know who we are and why we are here.

Dr. James Hillman has created a model of growth that I find useful. Instead of viewing our children and ourselves as 'growing up,' Hillman suggests that we view ourselves as a greater self trying to arrive in its grandeur and complexity. He explains:

> Organic images of growth follow the favorite symbol for human life, the tree, but I am turning that tree upside down. My model of growth has its roots in heaven and imagines a gradual descent downward toward human affairs. (43)

When we view ourselves in this manner, Picasso's statement, "I don't develop. I am," makes perfect sense. We free ourselves to re-member, put back together, who we are, fueled by passion and directed toward our individual and innate brilliance.

When my children were little, I saw the old soul in their eyes. I reminded myself that the child who just dumped spaghetti all over his head in the high chair was the same life force that traveled from his Creator through unfathomable dimensions to get here. Children are spirits on a trip. Unencumbered by the conventions of culture and society, their bodies, their senses, the pure physics of the earth are all new and marvelous toys for them. In the absence of convention and fear, they are limitless. Like the angels, they play. And when they threw an emotional fit on the floor, I reminded myself that working within the format of the physical was new to them— that the emotions experienced through their bodies are overwhelming. I conjectured what it felt like to be in the womb. Was there comfort and peace? Were all their needs met? What a shock birth must have been! I tried not to confuse 'emotionally immature' with 'lack of soul, direction or intelligence.' I tried to remember that all spirit is brilliant because it is not disconnected from Source. Children are born whole— they are their greater selves, all empirical evidence to the contrary. They are, certainly, much more than 'the sum of their parts.' I did not try to 'train' them.

When Stephen became of school age, my perception became a problem. I saw no way to act on it. It did not exist within the confines of contemporary thought or practice. For all I knew, I was the only one who perceived this anomaly. So at first I was not strong enough or brave enough to act on it. I was afraid. I did not yet trust my own intuition. What if I were wrong? Was I willing to bet the lives of my children on my subjective perception? Ultimately, I was and I did.

Now, over fifteen years later, after seeing the success of this perspective, I feel pulled to creating a bigger envelope—a learning community—one that holds this consciousness for all who would like to participate. We need never make the journey alone again.

If we shift focus and drop our old expectations and thought patterns, we can find not only passion and brilliance, but also the compassion and inner peace that living this greater identity brings. I saw it happen. And when there is peace within, there is peace without. We can create environments that facilitate a kinder, healthier and more fulfilling world for us all—a world of joy and exuberance.

I saw my children as babies. I remember their births as if it was just yesterday. The commanding dancer in Monaco is the infant I swaddled and nursed. The two are one. So is the sage he already is and will become. It took an effort to find my children amongst the toys, sleepovers, piano lessons, art projects, scout outings, soccer practices, karate tournaments, science experiments, c.d.'s and sophisticated electronics. I had to look for their passions and brilliance. It was not always readily obvious, but we usually don't find what we're not looking for.

The search for passion and brilliance is a creative exploration that begins between parent and child. A nurturing relationship reliably creates the child's sense of self and his ongoing relationship to the world. The effectiveness of this relationship perpetuates a sense of well-being and empowerment.

As we breathe, we learn. The goal is to continue this nurturing relationship so that WHAT we are learning contributes to the effective well-being and empowerment of our children and society. When our children experience a sense of well being, they are open to the higher values of compassion and cooperation. Acting with a sense of empowerment, they can take the initiative to explore and create positive forms and re-lationships that benefit our world.

The process is simple. An interplay of mutual exploration and creation between teacher and student, parent and child nurtures this sense of empowerment. The adult provides the base and support that nurtures this process. The interaction between them is catalytic, dynamic and spiraling in nature. It directs the exploratory process out of the needs, desires, tal-ents and passions of both participants. It leads to the sponta-neous creation of new opportunities and discoveries.

When we change the structure within which we interact, we strengthen these relationships, igniting interest into pas-ion and accomplishment into brilliance. I have seen it work over and over and over again.

We could expand on the concept and create a community based on this model of exploration and creation. We could share the vision. Student experience could be integrated into the active life of the community through mentors, just like Stephen did at Warner Bros. Skilled professionals interested in passing on their passion and talent could help mentor our students. Both parties would benefit, the child gaining respect and experience from the adult world, and the adult recovering the excitement and awe of the child immersed in exploration.

Parker Palmer moves this concept forward. He talks about creating a community of learners. He explains that our educa-tional system ignores our relationship with the 'great things' that might call us together in a 'community of truth,'—teach-ers and students alike.

By 'great things,' he means the subjects themselves, not the textbooks or modes we have employed to study them, not the theories we have already constructed, but the magic and awe that attracts "a circle of seekers." (107)

Today we offer both student and teacher a dead curriculum. It numbs the souls of teacher and student alike. We give them dead history and outdated science. We replace mathematics with calculation or give them mathematics without the ability to solve problems. We make reading a chore because we decide what they should read and tell them it is interesting instead of allowing them to explore their interests. We flatten teachers' passions in that way too—what excites the adult can rarely be passed to the children because it is not on the curriculum.

We ply our children with 'facts' and rob them of the opportunity to discover something new. We tell them that finding new things is an adult's job. We have stopped raising inventors, trailblazers, and explorers. When this community of pioneers disappears we will have a slave mentality—sheep that follow the leader. We disable our ability to survive as a civilization, because systems that don't grow die. Life is either creating or atrophying. It never stays the same. If we were to be presented with a dramatic change in the nature or quality of life on this planet, we would need our trailblazers, inventors and explorers back—immediately. After generations of— as John Gatto has stated—'dumbing us down,' our future would look bleak.

In Palmer's 'community of truth,' however, the subject calls to us and enters into an interactive relationship or communion with us. As I watched my children grow, I saw Erin called to art and numbers from the age of two. Matthew has been exploring the physical realm since he was a baby. Stephen was called to taking things apart for as long as I can remember. They were called to their talents by the things themselves because these things answered the call of their souls.

Palmer explains that knowing of any kind is relational. It is fueled by a desire to enter a living relationship with what we know:

> Why does a historian study the 'dead' past? To reveal how much of it lives in us today. Why does a biologist study the 'mute' world of na-

ture? To allow us to hear its voice speaking of how entwined we are in life's ecology. Why does a literary scholar study the world of 'fiction'? To show us that the facts can never be understood except in communion with the imagination.... Knowing is a human way to seek relationship and, in the process, to have encounters and exchanges that will inevitably alter us. At its deepest reaches, knowing is always communal. (54)

Some subject talks to each of us, speaks to our heart about who we are and the greater issues of the universe. It is transcendent—the grand dance. It is "the numinous energy at the heart of reality.... The Idea of the Holy—the mysterium tremendum" (Palmer, 111)—the sacred, the holy that transforms and transcends. Palmer writes:

...Openness to transcendence is what distinguishes the community of truth from both absolutism and relativism. In this community, the process of truth-knowing and truth-telling is neither dictatorial nor anarchic. Instead, it is a complex eternal dance of intimacy and distance, of speaking and listening, of knowing and not knowing, that makes collaborators and co-conspirators of the knowers and the known. (106)

To my children:

I have loved being
your mother, your student,
your teacher,
your friend.

With you,
I have discovered
my own passion and brilliance.

Through you,
I have re-membered
identity and integrity.

For you,
I have
encircled the sun.

And found
my way home.

Through this interactive process, passion and brilliance is revealed. Through this process we explore the infinite possibilities of universal relationships. Music and mathematics, physics and philosophy, ad infinitum, come together. Through this process, we nurture effective, dynamic and compassionate human beings who explore and recreate the unlimited range of human passion and brilliance.

Thank you
Stephen, Erin and Matthew,

I love you.
Mom

Our learning institutions are faltering and need to be restructured not because they lack socially or academically redeeming qualities, but because they no longer fit our needs.

Our families need to be strengthened not because they are fundamentally weak, but because we do not give them the time or the opportunity to demonstrate strength.

And our communities are not cohesive for lack of desire, but for lack of support.

We need to see things differently.
We need to reconnect our world.

What we seek is what we find:

If we look for genius, we find it.
If we look for trust, suspicion evaporates.
If we foster self-discipline, punitive threat dissipates.
If we preserve self-initiative, internal direction prospers.
If we nurture moral intelligence, callous indifference flees.
If we allow laughter,
we gain joyful motivation and revelation.
If we recognize awe, wonder, gratitude, we strengthen faith.
If we identify balance, we continue in growth toward it.
If we aim for perspective, we counter tunnel vision.
If we build mutual respect, teamwork blossoms.
If we offer community, isolation vanishes.
If we touch families, they strengthen.

If we guide, we learn.
If we love, we grow.

We can do this,
If we do this together.

❧ Postscript ❧

Across the country, in little groups, in unexpected circumstances and indeterminate places, children are tripping over their own brilliance. I see passion forming out of the corner of my eye, when I turn my back, when I leave a room, when the wind whispers, "don't miss this one…don't run over this child, don't leave this child behind. She is beautiful, he is magnificent…gather them up, protect them, allow them all to shine!"

Resa Steindel Brown

❧ About the Author ❧

Resa Steindel Brown's expertise is in building educational processes and environments that enable children to find their passion and develop their individual and innate brilliance. She has been involved in alternative education since 1970 and homeschooling since 1987. She homeschooled her own three children from kindergarten to college.

Resa is credentialed by the State of California through the University of California at Los Angeles. She maintains Elementary, Secondary and Community College credentials in multiple subject areas. She has been teaching for thirty-five years from kindergarten through the university level. She has a specialized credential in reading and teaches special education and mathematics remediation. Resa received her Bachelor of Arts in Theater Arts and Master of Fine Arts from UCLA in Art and Theater Arts with full minors in English and psychology.

Resa is unique in that she successfully implements educational systems and philosophies that experts have been talking about for years.

Anshen, Ruth Nanda. Introduction. *Beyond the Chains of Illusion*. By Eric Fromm. New York, N.Y.: Simon and Schuster, 1962. xiii.

Ayers, William, and Gloria Ladson-Billings. *To Teach, the Journey of a Teacher*. New York, N.Y.: Teachers College, 1993, 2001. 16, 19.

Bennis, Warren. *On Becoming A Leader*. Reading, Massachusetts: Addison Wesley, 1994. 3, 4.

Borysenko Ph.D, Joan. *Guilt is the Teacher, Love is the lesson*. New York, N.Y.: Warner Books, 1990. 213.

Bruner, Jerome. *Acts of Meaning*. Cambridge, Massachusetts: Harvard University Press, 1990. xvi.

Cadwell, Louise Boyd. *Bringing Reggio Emilia Home: An Innovative Approach to Early Childhood Education*. New York, N.Y.: Teacher's College Press, 1997. 63.

Cameron, Julia. *The Artist's Way: A Spiritual Path to Higher Creativity*. New York, N.Y.: A Zachary P. Tarcher/Putnam Book, 1992. xiii, 3, 211.

Capra, Fritjof. *The Turning Point: Science, Society, and the Rising Culture*. New York, N.Y.: Bantam Books, 1988. 44.

Castaneda, Carlos. *The Teachings of Don Juan; A Yaqui Way of Knowledge*. New York, N.Y.: Pocket Books, 1985. 17, 20, 21.

Covey, Stephen R. *First Things First*. New York, N.Y.: Simon and Schuster, 1994. 180.

---. *The Seven Habits of Highly Effective Families*. New York, N.Y.: Golden Books, 1997. 99.

Dalai Lama, Tenzin Gyatso. *The Opening of the Wisdom-Eye*. Wheaton, Illinois: Quest Books, 1996. iii, 28.

Dewey, John. *The School and Society; The child and the Curriculum*. London, England: University of Chicago Press, 1902. 60-61.

Ferguson, Marilyn. *The Aquarian Conspiracy: Personal and Social Transformation In Our Time*. New York: Zachary P. Tarcher/Putnam, 1987. 9, 31, 45, 46, 287-288.

Fields, Rick. *Chop Wood, Carry Water: A Guide to Finding Spiritual Fulfillment in Everyday Life*. New York, N.Y.: Zachary P. Tarcher/Putnam, 1984. 260.

Freke, Timothy. *The Sacred Scriptures*. Wheaten, Illinois: Theosophical Publishing House, 1998. 92.

Fromm, Eric. *The Art of Loving*. New York, N.Y.: Perrenial Library, 1956. 8.

Gatto, John Taylor. *Dumbing Us Down: The Hidden Curriculum of Compulsory Schooling*. Philadelphia, Pennsylvania. New Society Publishers, 1992. xi-xiii.

Bibliography

---. *The Underground History of American Education.* New York, N.Y.: The Oxford Village Press, 2001. 284.

Ginsburg, Herbert, and Sylvia Opper. *Piaget's Theory of Intellectual Development: An Introduction.* Englewood Cliffs, New Jersey: Prentice Hall, 1969. 7.

Glasser M.D., William. *Choice Theory.* New York, N.Y.: Harper Collins, 1998. 44-45.

---. *Schools Without Failure.* New York, N.Y.: Harper and Row, 1969. 28, 29, 73-75, 144.

---. *The Quality School Teacher.* New York, N.Y.: Harper/Perennial, 1993. 19.

Grof, Christina. *The Thirst for Wholeness: Attachment, Addiction, and the Spiritual Path.* San Francisco: Harper, 1993. 22-23, 27, 51.

Hillman, James. *The Soul's Code: In Search of Character and Calling.* New York: Random House, 1996. 3, 4-5, 7, 8, 9, 14, 43.

Houston, Jean. *The Possible Human: A Course in Enhancing Your Physical, Mental, and Creative Abilities.* New York, N.Y.: Zachary P. Tarcher/Putnam, 1982. 200.

Jersild, Arthur T. *When Teachers Face Themselves.* New York, N.Y.: Teachers College Press, 1955. 33, 34, 125-128, 136.

Kessler, Rachael. *The Soul of Education: Helping Students Find Connection, Compassion and Character at School.* Alexandria, VA: Association for Supervision and Curriculum Development, 2000. Introduction.

Krishnamurti, Jiddu. *Education and the Significance of Life.* San Francisco: Harper Collins, 1981. 9, 39.

Lorie, Peter, and Manuela Dunn-Mascetti. *Quotable Spirit:* New York, N.Y.: Hungry Minds, 1996.

    Assagioli, Roberto. *Psychosynthesis: A Manual of Principles and Techniques.* 250.

    Blake, William. *Auguries of Innocence.* 67.

    Brooks, Phillips. *(1835-1893) Perennials.* 113.

    Campbell, Joseph: Motto: *Follow your bliss.* 249.

    Castaneda, Carlos. *The Fire Within.* 32.

    Epic of Gilgamesh. 243.

    Huang-po, *The Zen Teaching of Huang-po.* 129.

    Krishnamurti, U.G. *Conversations with a Man Called U.G.* 39.

    Osho. *(1931-1990) Discourses.* 250.

May, Rollo. *Love And Will.* New York, N.Y.: W.W. Norton and Co., 1969. 28.

Maslow, Abraham. *Motivation and Personality.* New York, N.Y.: Harper Collins, 1970. 46.

Montessori, Maria. *The Absorbent Mind.* New York: Henry Holt & Company, 1995. 8, 19, 293.

---. *The Secret of Childhood.* New York: Ballantine Books, 1966. 31-32.

Moore, Thomas. *The Education of the Heart.* New York, NY: HarperCollins, 1996. 1.

---. *The Re-Enchantment of Everyday Life.* New York, N.Y.: HarperCollins, 1996. Introduction.

Oakes, Jeannie, and Martin Lipton. *Teaching to Change the World.* Boston, McGraw-Hill College, 1999. 252.

Ornish M.D., Dean. *Love and Survival: The Scientific Basis for the Healing Power of Intimacy.* New York, N.Y.: Harper Collins, 1997. 2-4.

Palmer, Parker. *The Courage to Teach: Exploring the Inner Landscape of a Teacher's Life.* San Francisco: Jossey-Bass Publishers, 1988. 2, 25, 30-31, 54, 106-107, 111.

Pearce, Joseph Chilton. *The Biology of Transcendence.* Rochester, Vermont: Park Street Press, 2002. 113, 121, 128, 141, 257, 261.

---. *The Magical Child.* New York, New York: Bantam Books, 1989. 165, 168, 169, 170.

Richards, Mary Caroline. *Toward Wholeness: Rudolf Steiner Education in America.* Hanover, New Hampshire: University Press of England, 1980. 5, 189.

Riesman, David. *The Lonely Crowd.* New Haven, Connecticut: Yale University Press, 1961. 58.

Robbins, Anthony. *Awaken the Giant Within.* New York, N.Y.: Simon and Schuster, 1991. 22.

Rogers Ph.D., Carl. *Freedom to Learn.* Columbus, Ohio: Merrill Publishing, 1969. 5, 101, 114, 228.

---. *On Becoming A Person.* Boston: Houghton Mifflin, 1961. 154, 166, 174, 175.

Steindl-Rast, Brother David. *Gratefulness and the Heart of Prayer: An Approach to Life in Fullness.* New York: Paulist Press, 1984. 85, 191.

Steiner, Claude M. *Scripts People Live: Transactional Analysis of Life Scripts.* Chicago, Illinois: Grove Press, 1990. 1, 3.

Toffler, Alvin. *The Third Wave.* 1st Edition, New York, N.Y.: William Morrow and Co., 1980. 44, 45-46.

Vaughan Ph.D., Frances, and Roger Walsh, M.D., Ph.D., *Gifts From a Course in Miracles.* New York: Zachary P. Tarcher/Putnam, 1986, 1995. 73.

Wheatley, Margaret. *A Simpler Way.* San Francisco. Berret-Koehler Publishers, 1996. 10, 25, 88, 89, 90, 103.

---. *Leadership and the New Science: Learning about Organization from an Orderly Universe.* San Francisco, California: Berrett-Koehler, 1994. 15-16.

Bibliography

Williamson, Marianne. *A Return to Love.* New York, N.Y.: Harper Collins, 1992. 29.

Wilson, Leslie Owen. *Every Child Whole Child: Classroom Activities for Unleashing Natural Abilities.* Tucson, Arizona: Zephyr Press, 1994. 19-20, 41, 43.

A

academic excellence, 123, 124
academics, 33, 263
ADHD, 91, 132, 208
agenda, 11, 12, 14, 17, 91, 138, 155
answers, 4, 7, 17, 24, 31, 64, 89, 121, 142, 153, 154, 175, 178, 230, 292
anxiety, 23, 24, 52, 68, 91, 119, 149
Assagioli, 54
assignments, 68, 71, 76, 77, 139, 269
authentic, 4, 49, 72
authenticity, 5, 18, 48, 49, 50, 270
Ayers, 73, 79

B

Bennis, 270, 274
Berne, 125
Blake, 289
Bombeck, 88, 93, 115
Borysenko, 63
brilliance, 7-10, 13, 17, 38, 44, 73, 91, 111, 128, 145, 150, 158, 160, 171, 256, 276, 292-296
Brother Steindl-Rast, 45
Bruner, 60, 271

C

Cadwell, 142
calling, 4, 7, 13, 18, 19, 49, 106, 157, 160
Cameron, 58, 172, 197
Campbell, 176, 212, 233, 240
Capra, 119
Carpenter, 6
Castaneda, 51, 52, 53, 81, 170
change, 20, 24, 31, 33, 53, 59, 70, 87, 108, 124, 134, 152, 167, 196, 253, 256, 279, 292, 296,

child development, 22, 75, 117
childhood, 3, 5, 69, 76, 156, 158, 160, 177, 193, 194
classroom, 30, 31, 32, 55, 68, 70, 71, 74, 77, 120, 122, 123, 128, 138, 193, 198, 201, 206
college, 15, 34, 37, 61, 76, 91, 123, 128, 184, 189, 206-217, 227, 241, 242, 262-269, 274, 276
compassion, 66, 78, 100, 122, 138, 139, 144-147, 198, 211
competition, 31, 38, 92, 265, 272
compliance, 44, 79, 92, 138, 139, 140, 144, 145, 146
confidence, 16, 34, 69, 91, 216, 217, 236, 240, 258, 261, 270
conflict, 20, 99, 100, 144
confusion, 16, 18, 25, 27, 56, 110
connection, 4, 19, 58, 62, 70, 107, 145, 146, 186, 273, 275
conscience, 51, 139, 140, 144
consciousness, 6, 10, 11, 22, 23, 53, 54, 59, 100, 101, 204, 227
cooperation, 38, 78, 295
Course in Miracles, 107, 146
Covey, 86, 139
creativity, 16, 19, 58, 70, 80, 165, 184, 193, 197, 199, 217, 246
culture, 21, 59, 94, 184, 202, 248
curriculum, 3, 21, 43, 59, 74, 79, 80, 91, 92, 124, 137, 143, 152, 162, 170, 182, 183, 185, 187, 212, 223, 252, 296

D

Dalai Lama, 54, 146
destiny, 7, 15, 27, 152, 156, 158, 202, 220, 291
Dewey, 17
dreams, 3, 5, 7, 58, 74, 113, 194, 217, 257
dysfunction, 12

Give the Gift of *The Call to Brilliance* to
Your Family, Friends and Colleagues

☐ I would like ____ copies of *The Call to Brilliance*. I have included a check for $21.95 ($17.95 plus $4.00 for shipping and handling) per each copy. Do not send cash. Please make a check out to: fredric press.

☐ I am interested in having Resa Steindel Brown speak or give a seminar to my school, event, or organization. Please send me information.

☐ I would like to submit a review or endorsement of *The Call to Brilliance*.

Name_____ Title_____

Organization_____

Address_____

City/State/Zip_____

Phone_____

E-mail_____

Please mail this form to:

fredric press
1336 moorpark road, #332
thousand oaks, ca 91360

Or visit our websites!
www.fredricpress.com
www.thecalltobrilliance.com